Frommer's

P O R T A B L E

Washington, D.C.

Macmillan • USA

MACMILLAN TRAVEL

A Simon & Schuster Macmillan Company
1633 Broadway
New York, NY 10019

Find us online at **http://www.mgr.com/travel** or
on America Online at Keyword: **Frommer's**.

ISBN 0-02-861551-4
ISSN: CIP data available from the Library of Congress upon
request.

Editor: Kelly Regan
Production Editor: Beth Mayland
Digital Cartography: Ortelius Design and John Decamillis
Design by Michele Laseau
Maps copyright © by Simon & Schuster

SPECIAL SALES

Bulk purchases (10+ copies) of Frommer's and selected
Macmillan travel guides are available to corporations, organizations, mail-order catalogs, institutions, and charities at special
discounts, and can be customized to suit individual needs. For
more information write to Special Sales, Macmillan General
Reference, 1633 Broadway, New York, NY 10019.

Manufactured in the United States of America

Contents

1   Planning a Trip to Washington, D.C.   1

1 Visitor Information & Money   1

★ *What Things Cost in Washington*   2

2 When to Go   3

★ *Washington Calendar of Events*   3

3 Tips for Travelers with Special Needs   8

4 Getting There   11

2   Getting to Know Washington, D.C.   15

1 Orientation   15

2 Getting Around   20

★ *The Metro Way*   26

★ *Fast Facts: Washington, D.C.*   27

3   Accommodations   29

1 Best Bets   31

2 Downtown   32

3 Near the White House   38

★ *Family-Friendly Hotels*   39

4 Foggy Bottom/Georgetown   40

5 Dupont Circle   45

6 North Washington/Adams-Morgan   51

7 Capitol Hill/Mall   54

4   Dining   56

1 Best Bets   57

2 Restaurants by Cuisine   59

3 Downtown/Capitol Hill   60

4 Near the White House/K Street Restaurant Row   65

5 Foggy Bottom/Georgetown   67

★ *Family-Friendly Restaurants*   71

    6 Dupont Circle   72

    7 Adams-Morgan   77

    8 At Sightseeing Attractions   80

5   **What to See & Do in Washington, D.C.**   **85**

    1 The Three Major Houses of Government   85

    2 The Presidential Memorials   90

    3 The Smithsonian Museums   95

    4 Other Top Attractions   106

    5 More Attractions   116

    6 Outside the District   121

    7 Parks & Gardens   125

    8 Especially for Kids   129

    9 Organized Tours   130

  10 Active Sports   131

  11 Spectator Sports   134

6   **Washington Scandals: A Walking Tour**   **136**

    ★ *G. Gorden Liddy & the Watergate Follies*   140

7   **Shopping**   **155**

    1 Shopping A to Z   155

8   **Washington, D.C., After Dark**   **164**

    1 Theater   164

    2 Other Performing Arts   167

    3 The Club & Music Scene   169

    ★ *Today's Headlines, Tomorrow's Punchlines*   170

    4 The Bar Scene   174

    5 More Entertainment   175

Index   **178**

List of Maps

Washington, D.C.,
  at a Glance   18

Taxicab Zones   24

Georgetown & Downtown
  Accommodations   34

Adams-Morgan & Dupont
  Circle Accommodations   47

Georgetown & Downtown
  Dining   62

Adams-Morgan & Dupont
  Circle Dining   75

Capitol Hill   89

Washington, D.C.,
  Attractions   92

Arlington National
  Cemetery   122

Walking Tour—
  Washington Scandals   137

Washington, D.C.,
  Shopping   156

AN INVITATION TO THE READER

In researching this book, we discovered many wonderful places—hotels, restaurants, shops, and more. We're sure you'll find others. Please tell us about them, so we can share the information with your fellow travelers in upcoming editions. If you were disappointed with a recommendation, we'd love to know that, too. Please write to:

Frommer's Portable Washington, D.C.
Macmillan Travel
1633 Broadway
New York, NY 10019

AN ADDITIONAL NOTE

Please be advised that travel information is subject to change at any time, and this is especially true of prices. We therefore suggest that you write or call ahead for confirmation when making your travel plans. The authors, editors, and publisher cannot be held responsible for the experiences of readers while traveling. Your safety is important to us, however, so we encourage you to stay alert and be aware of your surroundings. Keep a close eye on cameras, purses, and wallets, all favorite targets of thieves and pickpockets.

WHAT THE SYMBOLS MEAN
✪ Frommer's Favorites

Hotels, restaurants, attractions, and entertainment you should not miss.

✪ Super-Special Values

Hotels and restaurants that offer great value for your money.

The following abbreviations are used for credit cards:

AE	American Express	JCB	Japan Credit Bank
CB	Carte Blanche	MC	MasterCard
DC	Diners Club	EU	Eurocard
DISC	Discover	V	Visa

Planning a Trip to Washington, D.C.

A lot of what you'll want to see and do in the capital can be arranged after you arrive, but some things should be planned in advance, while you're still home.

1 Visitor Information & Money

Before you leave, contact the **Washington, D.C., Convention and Visitors Association,** 1212 New York Ave. NW, Washington, DC 20005 (☎ **202/789-7000**), and ask them to send you a free copy of the *Washington, D.C., Visitors Guide,* which details hotels, restaurants, sights, shops, and more. They'll also be happy to answer specific questions.

Also call the **D.C. Committee to Promote Washington** (☎ **800/422-8644**), and request a free copy of *Discover Washington, D.C.* It lists low weekend rates at dozens of Washington hotels.

SPECIAL TICKETS FOR VIP CONGRESSIONAL TOURS

Based on ticket availability, senators and/or representatives can provide their constituents with tickets for VIP tours of several major attractions. Thousands of people write in, so make your request as far in advance as possible—even six months ahead is not too early—specifying the dates you plan to visit and the number of tickets you need. Their allotment of tickets for each sight is limited, so there's no guarantee you'll secure them.

Address requests to representatives as follows: name of your congressperson, U.S. House of Representatives, Washington, DC 20515; or name of your senator, U.S. Senate, Washington, DC 20510. Don't forget to include the exact dates of your Washington trip. When you write, also request tourist information and literature. *Note:* Before writing, you might try calling a senator or congressperson's local office; in some states you can obtain passes by phone.

What Things Cost in Washington	U.S. $
Taxi from National Airport to downtown	10.00–12.00
Bus from National Airport to downtown (14.00 round-trip)	8.00
Local telephone call	.25
Double at the Jefferson Hotel (very expensive)	245.00–265.00
Double at the Radisson Barceló Hotel (expensive)	155.00–180.00
Double at the Channel Inn (moderate)	110.00–125.00
Double at the Days Inn Downtown (inexpensive)	89.00–109.00
Three-course dinner at the Willard Room (very expensive)	55.00
Three-course dinner at Petitto's (expensive)	35.00
Three-course dinner at Jaleo (moderate)	18.00–22.00
Three-course dinner at Scholl's Cafeteria (inexpensive)	7.00–8.00
Bottle of beer (at a restaurant)	3.00
Coca-Cola (at a restaurant)	1.50
Cup of coffee (at a restaurant)	1.25
Roll of ASA 100 Kodacolor film, 36 exposures	4.50
Admission to all Smithsonian museums	Free
Theater ticket at the National	25.00–65.00

THE CAPITOL   There are special, more comprehensive tours of the Capitol departing at intervals between 8 and 8:45am, Monday to Friday, for those with tickets.

THE WHITE HOUSE   Tuesday through Saturday between 8 and 8:45am the doors of the White House are open for special VIP tours to those with tickets. Write far in advance, because each senator receives only 15 tickets a week to distribute, and each representative only 10. These early tours ensure your entrance during the busy tourist season. The VIP tours are also more extensive than those held later; guides provide explanatory commentary as you go.

THE FBI   The line for this very popular tour can be extremely long. One way to beat the system is to ask a senator or representative to make a reservation for you for a scheduled time.

BUREAU OF ENGRAVING & PRINTING Guided VIP tours are offered weekdays at 8am, except on holidays.

THE KENNEDY CENTER VIP tours departing Monday through Saturday at 9:30am and 9:45am enable you to avoid a long wait with the crowds who did not take the trouble to write to a senator or representative.

2 When to Go

THE CLIMATE

If you have a choice, I'd recommend visiting D.C. in the fall. The weather is lovely, Washington's scenery is awash in fall foliage colors, and the tourists have thinned out. If you hate crowds and want to get the most out of the sights, go in winter. It's not that cold, there are no long lines, and hotel prices are lower.

Spring weather is delightful, and of course there are those cherry blossoms. Along with autumn, it's the nicest time to enjoy D.C.'s outdoor attractions. But keep in mind the city is crowded with millions of tourists. The throngs remain in hot, humid summer. Though there's occasional relief, those 90° days do arrive with frustrating frequency. The advantage: This is the season to enjoy numerous outdoor events—free concerts, festivals, parades, and more.

WASHINGTON CALENDAR OF EVENTS

Listed below are some of the major annual events. When in town, check the *Washington Post,* especially the Friday "Weekend" section. The Smithsonian Information Center, 1000 Jefferson Dr. SW (☎ **202/357-2700**), is another good source.

January
- **Martin Luther King Jr.'s Birthday.** Events include speeches by prominent civil rights leaders and politicians; readings; dance, theater, and choral performances; prayer vigils; a wreath-laying ceremony at the Lincoln Memorial; and concerts. Many events take place at the Martin Luther King Memorial Library, 901 G St. NW (☎ **202/727-1186**). Call 202/789-7000 for further details. Third Monday in January.

February
- **Chinese New Year Celebration.** A friendship archway, topped by 300 painted dragons and lighted at night, marks Chinatown's entrance at 7th and H streets NW. The celebration begins the day of the Chinese New Year and continues for 10 or more days, with

traditional firecrackers, dragon dancers, and colorful street parades. Some area restaurants offer special menus. For details, call **202/789-7000.** Late January or early to mid-February.

March

• **Spring Antiques Show,** D.C. Armory, 2001 E. Capitol St. Features close to 200 dealers from the United States, Canada, and Europe. Admission (about $5 for all three days) is charged. Call **301/738-1966** for details. Usually Friday through Sunday the first weekend in March.

✪ **Smithsonian Kite Festival.** A delightful event if the weather cooperates—an occasion for a trip in itself. Throngs of kite enthusiasts fly their unique creations and compete for ribbons and prizes.

Where: On the Washington Monument grounds. **When:** A Saturday in mid- or late March. **How:** If you want to compete, just show up with your kite and register between 10am and noon. Call **202/357-2700** or 202/357-3030 for details.

✪ **Cherry Blossom Events.** Washington's best-known annual event: the blossoming of the famous Japanese cherry trees. Festivities include a major parade (marking the end of the festival) with princesses, floats, and celebrity guests, not to mention bands, clowns, fashion shows, concerts, a Japanese lantern-lighting ceremony, a ball, and a marathon race. There are also special ranger-guided tours departing from the Jefferson Memorial.

Where: The trees bloom by the Tidal Basin in Potomac Park. Related events take place all around town. **When:** Late March or early April (national news programs monitor the budding). **How:** For parade information—or tickets for grandstand seating ($12 per person)—call the D.C. Downtown Jaycees (☎ **202/728-1135**). For other cherry-blossom events, check the *Washington Post* or call **202/789-7038** or 202/547-1500.

April

Cherry blossom events continue (see above).

✪ **White House Easter Egg Roll.** The biggie for little kids. In past years, entertainment has included clog dancers, clowns, storytellers, Easter bunnies, Ukrainian egg-decorating exhibitions, puppet and magic shows, military drill teams, an egg-rolling contest, and a hunt for 1,000 or so hidden wooden eggs, many of them signed by celebrities (Tom Hanks and Barbra Streisand, for example), astronauts, or the president. *Note:* Attendance is limited to children ages three to six.

Where: The White House South Lawn and the Ellipse; enter at the southeast gate on East Executive Avenue. **When:** Easter Monday between 10am and 2pm; arrive early. **How:** Hourly timed tickets are issued at the National Parks Service Ellipse Visitors Pavilion just behind the White House at 15th and E streets NW beginning at 7am. Call **202/208-1631** for details.

✪ **Taste of the Nation.** This fund-raiser (which takes place in more than 100 cities throughout the nation every April) is among my favorite events. In Washington, about 90 major restaurants and wineries participate annually, and 100% of the profits go, rather aptly, to feed the hungry. Each of the participants sets up a tasting booth and offers some of its finest fare. For the price of admission, you can do the circuit, sampling everything from bouillabaisse to Beaujolais.

Where: Union Station. **When:** Mid-April. **How:** Tickets are $65 if purchased in advance, $75 at the door. To obtain them call **800/955-TASTE.**

- **Justice Douglas Reunion Hike,** C&O Canal. If you love hiking, don't miss this event. In 1954, Supreme Court Justice William O. Douglas, bless him, walked the entire 184^1/$_2$-mile towpath in protest against a plan to build a scenic parkway along the canal. The annual hike in honor of this event covers about 12 miles, on a different section each year. A buffet banquet wraps up the day's activities, and there's a bus to take you back to town. For details and tickets (there's a charge for the bus and buffet), contact the C&O Canal Association, P.O. Box 366, Glen Echo, MD 20812 (☎ **301/983-0825** for reservations). Usually the last Saturday in April.

May

- **Georgetown Garden Tour.** View the remarkable private gardens of one of the city's loveliest neighborhoods. Admission (about $18) includes light refreshments. Some years there are related events such as a flower show at a historic home. Call **202/333-6896** for details. Early to mid-May.

- **Memorial Day.** At 11am, a wreath-laying ceremony takes place at the Tomb of the Unknowns in Arlington National Cemetery, followed by military band music, a service, and an address by a high-ranking government official (sometimes the president); call **202/685-2851** for details. There's also a ceremony at 1pm at the Vietnam Veterans Memorial—wreath-laying, speakers, and the playing of taps; call **202/619-7222** for details. On the Sunday before Memorial Day, the National Symphony Orchestra performs a free concert at 8pm on the West Lawn of the Capitol; call **202/619-7222** for details.

June

✪ **Smithsonian Festival of American Folklife.** A major event with traditional American music, crafts, foods, games, concerts, and exhibits. Past performances have ranged from Appalachian fiddling to Native American dancing, and demonstrations from quilting to coal mining. All events are free.

Where: Most events take place outdoors on the Mall. **When:** For 5 to 10 days, always including July 4th. **How:** Call **202/357-2700,** or check the listings in the *Washington Post* for details.

July

✪ **Independence Day.** There's no better place to be on the Fourth of July than Washington, D.C. The festivities include a massive National Independence Day Parade down Constitution Avenue, complete with lavish floats, princesses, marching groups, and military bands. There are also celebrity entertainers and concerts. A morning program in front of the National Archives includes military demonstrations, period music, and a reading of the Declaration of Independence. In the evening the National Symphony Orchestra plays on the west steps of the Capitol with guest artists (for example, Leontyne Price). And big-name entertainment also precedes the fabulous fireworks display behind the Washington Monument. *Note:* You can also attend an 11am free organ recital at Washington's National Cathedral.

Where: Most events take place on the Washington Monument grounds. **When:** July 4th, all day. **How:** Just show up. Check the *Washington Post* or call **202/789-7000** for details.

August

• **Tchaikovsky's 1812 Overture,** Sylvan Theatre on the Washington Monument grounds. The U.S. Army Band gives a free performance of this famous work, complete with roaring cannons. For details, call **703/696-3399.**

September

• **Washington National Cathedral's Open House.** Celebrates the anniversary of the laying of the foundation stone in 1907. Events include demonstrations of stone carving and other crafts utilized in building the cathedral; carillon and organ demonstrations; and performances by dancers, choirs, strolling musicians, jugglers, and puppeteers. This is the only time visitors are allowed to ascend to the top of the central tower to see the bells; it's a tremendous climb, but you'll be rewarded with a spectacular view. For details, call **202/537-6200.** A Saturday in late September or early October.

- **Annual Kennedy Center Open House Arts Festival.** A day-long festival of the performing arts in late September or early October, featuring local and national artists on all of the Kennedy Center stages and outdoors. Admission free; no tickets required. Call **202/467-4600** for details.

October

- **Taste of D.C. Festival,** Pennsylvania Avenue between 9th and 14th Streets. Dozens of Washington's restaurants offer international food-tasting opportunities, along with live entertainment, dancing, storytellers, and games. Admission is free; purchase tickets for tastings. Call **202/724-5430** for details. Three days including Columbus Day weekend.
- **White House Fall Garden Tours.** For two days visitors have an opportunity to see the famed Rose Garden and South Lawn. Admission is free. A military band provides music. For details, call **202/456-2200.** Mid-October.
- **Marine Corps Marathon.** More than 16,000 runners compete in this 26.2-mile race (the fourth-largest marathon in the United States). It begins at the Marine Corps Memorial (the Iwo Jima statue) and passes major monuments. Call **800/RUN-USMC** or 703/784-2720 for details. Anyone can enter; register up to a week ahead. Fourth Sunday in October.

November

- **Veterans Day.** The nation's war dead are honored with a wreath-laying ceremony at 11am at the Tomb of the Unknowns in Arlington National Cemetery followed by a memorial service. The president of the United States or a very high-ranking government personage officiates. Military music is provided by a military band. Call **202/685-2851** for information. At the Vietnam Veterans Memorial (☎ **202/619-7222**), observances include speakers, a wreath-laying, a color guard, and the playing of taps. November 11.

December

- **St. Nicholas Festival,** at the Washington National Cathedral. An evening for families that includes a visit from St. Nicholas, dancers, choral groups, crafts, caroling, bell ringing, and much more. Call **202/537-6200** for more information, or to inquire about other Christmas concerts, pageants, services, and children's activities. Early in December.

- **Christmas Pageant of Peace/National Tree Lighting,** at the northern end of the Ellipse. On a selected Wednesday or Thursday in early December at 5pm, the president lights the national Christmas tree to the accompaniment of orchestral and choral music. The lighting inaugurates the three-week Pageant of Peace, a tremendous holiday celebration with seasonal music, caroling, a Nativity scene, 50 state trees, and a burning Yule log. Call **202/ 619-7222** for details.

- **White House Candlelight Tours.** On three evenings after Christmas from 5 to 7pm, visitors can see the president's Christmas holiday decorations by candlelight. String music enhances the tours. Lines are long; arrive early. Call **202/456-2200** for dates and details.

3 Tips for Travelers with Special Needs

FOR TRAVELERS WITH DISABILITIES

Two helpful travel organizations, **Accessible Journeys** (☎ 800/ TINGLES or 610/521-0339) and **Flying Wheels Travel** (☎ 800/ 535-6790 or 507/451-5005), offer tours, cruises, and custom vacations worldwide for people with physical disabilities; Accessible Journeys can also provide nurse/companions for travelers. **The Guided Tour Inc.** (☎ 800/783-5841 or 215/782-1370) offers tours for people with physical or mental disabilities, the visually impaired, and the elderly.

Mobility International USA, P.O. Box 10767, Eugene, OR 97440 (☎ 503/343-1284), provides accessibility and resource information to its members. Membership ($25 a year) includes a quarterly newsletter called *Over the Rainbow.*

There's no charge for help via telephone (accessibility information and more) from the **Travel Information Service, MossRehab Hospital** (☎ 215/456-9600; TDD number is 202/456-9602). Another organization, the **Society for the Advancement of Travel for the Handicapped** (SATH), 347 Fifth Ave., Suite 610, New York, NY 10016 (☎ 212/447-7284), charges $5 for sending requested information.

Visually impaired travelers can obtain large-print and braille atlases of the Washington area (though they're slightly out of date) from **Washington Ear,** 35 University Blvd., E. Silver Spring, MD 2090l (☎ **301/681-6636**).

SIGHTSEEING ATTRACTIONS   Washington, D.C., is one of the most accessible cities in the world for the disabled. The **White House** has a special entrance on Pennsylvania Avenue for visitors arriving in wheelchairs who, by the way, do not need tickets. For details, call **202/456-2322.**

All **Smithsonian museum buildings** are accessible to wheelchair visitors. A comprehensive free publication called *Smithsonian Access* lists all services available to visitors with disabilities, including parking, building access, and more. To obtain a copy, contact the Smithsonian Institution, SI Building, Rm. 153, MRC 010, Washington, DC 20560 (☎ **202/357-2700** or TTY 202/357-1729). You can also use the TTY number to obtain information on all Smithsonian museums and events.

The **Lincoln, Jefferson, and Vietnam Memorials** and the **Washington Monument** are also equipped to accommodate disabled visitors and keep wheelchairs on the premises. There's limited disabled parking on the south side of the Lincoln Memorial.

Call your senator or representative to arrange wheelchair-accessible tours of the **Capitol;** he or she can also arrange special tours for the blind or deaf. If you need further information on these tours call **202/224-4048.**

GETTING AROUND TOWN   Each **Metro** station is equipped with an elevator (complete with braille number plates) to train platforms, and rail cars are fully accessible. Conductors make station and on-board announcements of train destinations and stops. More than half of the District's Metrobuses have wheelchair lifts and kneel at the curb (this number will increase as time goes on). The TDD number for Metro information is **202/638-3780.** For other questions about Metro services for travelers with disabilities, call **202/637-7000.**

Regular **Tourmobile** trams are accessible to physically impaired visitors. The company also operates special vans for immobile travelers, complete with wheelchair lifts. For information, call **202/554-5100.**

FOR SENIORS

Bring some form of photo ID that includes your birth date since many city attractions, theaters, transportation facilities, hotels, and restaurants grant special senior discounts.

Contact the **D.C. Office on Aging,** 441 4th St. NW (☎ **202/ 724-5626**) to request its free directory, *Golden Washingtonian Club Gold Mine.* It lists numerous establishments offering 10% to 20% discounts to seniors on goods and services.

Elderhostel, a national organization that offers low-cost educational programs for people over 55 (your spouse can be any age, but a companion must be at least 50), sponsors frequent week-long residential programs in Washington. Some of these focus on government and American history, others on art, literature, and other subjects. Cost averages about $355 per person, including meals, room, and classes. For information, call **410/830-3437** or contact Elderhostel headquarters at 75 Federal St., Boston, MA 02110 (☎ **617/426-7788**).

Saga International Holidays, 222 Berkeley St., Boston, MA 02116 (☎ **800/343-0273**), offers tours in the United States and abroad designed for travelers over 50. In Washington, D.C., their five-night, six-day Smithsonian Odyssey Tours program offers a behind-the-scenes look at several of the major museums and other D.C. institutions. For this specific program call 800/258-5885. Prices are moderate.

Amtrak (☎ **800/USA-RAIL**) offers a 15% discount off the lowest available coach fare (with certain travel restrictions) to people 62 or over.

Greyhound also offers discounted fares for senior citizens. Call your local Greyhound office for details.

FOR SINGLE TRAVELERS

Of major interest to single travelers is the opportunity to meet others. There is, of course, the bar scene (see chapter 8). Another good way to meet people is to go on a hike, river-rafting trip, or other such excursion, many of which are listed in the *Washington Post* Friday "Weekend" section.

Another tip: Choose a bed-and-breakfast facility or a hotel with concierge-level accommodations; it's easy to meet people over coffee and muffins in the communal dining room.

FOR GAYS & LESBIANS

The complete source for the gay and lesbian community is *The Washington Blade,* a comprehensive weekly newspaper distributed free at about 700 locations in the District. Every issue provides an extensive events calendar and a list of hundreds of resources, such as crisis centers, health facilities, religious organizations, social clubs, and student activities. Gay restaurants and clubs are, of course, also listed and advertised. You can subscribe to the *Blade* for $45 a year, or call the *Blade* office at **202/797-7000** for places to pick up a copy around town. One final source: Washington's gay bookstore, **Lambda Rising,** 1625 Connecticut Ave. NW (☎ **202/ 462-6969**), also informally serves as an information center for the gay community.

4 Getting There

BY PLANE

Washington is served by three major airports: **Washington National Airport,** just across the Potomac in Virginia and a 15-minute drive from downtown; **Dulles International Airport,** about 45 minutes from downtown, also in Virginia; and **Baltimore-Washington International Airport,** between Baltimore and Washington, about 45 minutes from downtown.

Most visitors come in via National, which is served by **American** (☎ 800/433-7300); **America West** (☎ 800/235-9292); **Continental** (☎ 800/525-0280); **Delta** (☎ 800/221-1212); **Northwest** (☎ 800/225-2525); **TWA** (☎ 800/221-2000); **United** (☎ 800/ 241-6522); and **USAir** (☎ 800/428-4322). All of these domestic airlines also fly into BWI, as do **Southwest Airlines** (☎ 800/ 435-9792) and the following international carriers: **Air Jamaica** (☎ 800/241-6522); **British Airways** (☎ 800/241-6522); **El Al** (☎ 800/241-6522); and **Icelandair** (☎ 800/241-6522). The major foreign airlines that are served by Dulles Airport include: **Air Canada** (☎ 800/776-3000); **Air France** (☎ 800/237-2747); **All Nippon Airways** (☎ 800/235-9262); **British Airways** (☎ 800/ 247-9297); **KLM** (☎ 800/374-7747); **Lufthansa** (☎ 800/ 645-3880); **Saudi Arabian Airlines** (☎ 800/472-8342); **Swissair** (☎ 800/221-4750); and **Virgin Atlantic** (☎ 800/862-8621). Also offering flights into Dulles are **Delta** and **United**.

BEST-FOR-THE-BUDGET FARES   When evaluating airfares, take into account the bus and/or taxi fares to and from departure and arrival airports. The taxi and bus fares listed below will help you make these computations.

As we go to press, airline prices are being restructured, so quoting specific fares here would be meaningless. Always remember, however, that it pays to book flights as far in advance as possible, since advance-purchase fares are often substantially lower. Also, when you call, also inquire about special fares for seniors, children, and students, as well as money-saving packages that include such essentials as hotel accommodations, car rentals, and tours with your airfare.

SHUTTLES TO & FROM NEW YORK The **Delta Shuttle** (☎ 800/221-1212), which flies between New York's LaGuardia Airport and Washington's National Airport, departs New York every hour on the half hour Monday to Friday, 6:30am to 8:30pm. Weekdays the first flight leaves Washington at 6:45am, with flights every hour on the half hour after that until 9:30pm. Frequent service is also offered on Saturday and Sunday. **USAir** (☎ **800/ 428-4322**) also has hourly departures from LaGuardia Airport and National Airport weekdays between 7am and 9pm, with almost as many flights on Saturday and Sunday.

FLIGHTS TO & FROM BOSTON Both **Delta (Business Express)** and **USAir** offer frequent service weekdays between Boston and Washington; the least expensive tickets must be purchased in advance and entail certain restrictions.

FLIGHTS TO & FROM CHICAGO **Southwest Airlines** (☎ **800/435-9792**) offers hourly service between Chicago's Midway Airport and Washington's BWI Airport weekdays between 7am and 8pm; round-trip fares vary, depending upon availability.

GETTING DOWNTOWN FROM THE AIRPORT Washington National Airport is right on the Blue and Yellow **Metro** lines, from which you can reach just about any point in town. A courtesy van will take you from the airport terminal to the Metro station.

The **Washington Flyer** (☎ 703/685-1400) operates buses between the centrally located Airport Terminal Building at 1517 K St. NW and both Dulles and National Airports. Fares to/from Dulles are $16 one way, $26 round-trip; to/from National, $8 one way, $14 round-trip. Children six and under ride free. There are departures in each direction about every 30 minutes. At the K Street Terminal Building you can board a free loop shuttle that goes to eight Washington hotels: the Sheraton Washington, Omni Shoreham, Washington Hilton, Mayflower, Washington Renaissance, Grand Hyatt, J. W. Marriott, and Harrington. The Harrington alone requires an advance reservation, since it's not on the loop unless someone requests it.

The **Airport Connection II** (☎ **800/284-6066** or 301/ 441-2345) runs buses between the Airport Terminal Building at 1517 K St. NW and Baltimore-Washington International Airport, with departures about every hour or two in each direction (call for exact times); reservations must be made at least 24 hours in advance. The fare is $19 one way, $30 round-trip, free for children five and under. You can also get van service from the BWI airport direct to your hotel or any other D.C. destination. Price is $30 for one person, $37 for two, $44 for three, $49 for four. Once again, reservations are required.

Taxi fares come to about $9 between National Airport and the White House, $42 to $45 between the White House and Dulles or BWI. (From National, take a D.C. cab rather than a Virginia cab—it's cheaper.)

Note: There have been price-gouging incidents in which tourists going from the airports into town have been overcharged by taxi drivers. If you think you're being ripped off, make sure to write down the company name and number of the cab (they're on the door), get an accurate receipt for the fare, and, if possible, the license plate number of the cab and the driver's name. Call **202/331-1671** to report any problems.

BY TRAIN

Amtrak trains arrive at historic **Union Station,** 50 Massachusetts Ave. NE, a turn-of-the-century beaux arts masterpiece that was magnificently restored in the late 1980s. Offering a three-level marketplace of shops and restaurants, this stunning depot is conveniently located and connects with Metro service. There are always lots of taxis available there. For rail reservations, contact Amtrak (☎ **800/ USA-RAIL**). (For more on Union Station, see chapters 7 and 8.)

Like the airlines, Amtrak offers several discounted fares; although not all are based on advance purchase, you have more discount options by reserving early. The discount fares can be used only on certain days and hours of the day; be sure to find out exactly what restrictions apply. I also suggest that you inquire about money-saving packages that include hotel accommodations, car rentals, tours, etc., with your train fare. Call **800/321-8684** for details.

Metroliner service—which costs a little more but provides faster transit and roomier, more comfortable seating—is available between New York and Washington, D.C., and points in between. *Note:* Metroliner fares are substantially reduced on weekends.

The most luxurious way to travel is **First Class Club Service,** available on all Metroliners and some other trains as well. For an additional fee, passengers enjoy roomier, more upscale seating in a private car; complimentary meals and beverage service; and

Metropolitan Lounges (in New York, Chicago, Philadelphia, and Washington) where travelers can wait for trains in a comfortable, living-room–like setting while enjoying free snacks and coffee.

BY BUS

Greyhound buses connect almost the entire United States with Washington, D.C. They arrive at a terminal at 1005 1st St. NE at L Street (☎ **800/231-2222**). The closest Metro stop is Union Station, four blocks away. The bus terminal area is not what you'd call a showplace neighborhood, so if you arrive at night, it's best to take a taxi.

The fare structure on buses is not necessarily based on distance traveled. The good news is that when you call Greyhound to make a reservation, the company will always offer you the lowest fare options. Call in advance and know your travel dates, since some discount fares require advance purchase.

BY CAR

Major highways approach Washington, D.C., from all parts of the country. The District is 240 miles from New York City, 40 miles from Baltimore, and 600 miles from Chicago and Atlanta.

If you're driving from New York or other points north, you'll probably take I-95 south to U.S. 50 west, which becomes New York Avenue in D.C. This avenue will be on your map, so you can easily figure out how to reach your hotel. If you start elsewhere, your best bet, if you're a member of AAA, is to call for exact directions. Otherwise, the Convention and Visitors Association (☎ **202/789-7000**) can help you find the way; have a map in front of you when you call.

Getting to Know
Washington, D.C.

Washington is one of America's most delightful cities—a fitting showplace for the nation's capital. It's a city designed for strolling, offering both natural beauty and stunning architecture. Finding your way around is quick and easy.

1 Orientation

VISITOR INFORMATION

There are two excellent tourist information centers in town, and though each focuses on a specific attraction, they can also provide information about all other Washington sights.

The **Smithsonian Information Center,** 1000 Jefferson Dr. SW (☎ **202/357-2700**), is open daily 9:30am to 5:30pm.

The **White House Visitor Center,** Pennsylvania Avenue between 14th and 15th streets NW (☎ **202/208-1631** or 202/456-7041 for recorded information), is open daily 7:30am to 4pm. Try to visit both facilities when you're in town to garner information and see interesting on-site exhibits.

The **Travelers Aid Society** is a nationwide network of voluntary nonprofit social service agencies providing help to travelers in difficulty. This might include anything from crisis counseling to straightening out ticket mix-ups, not to mention reuniting families accidentally separated while traveling.

In Washington, Travelers Aid has a central office in the Capitol Hill area at 512 C St. NE (☎ **202/546-3120**), where professional social workers are available to provide assistance. It's open only on weekdays 9am to 4pm for walk-ins; you can call up to 5pm.

There are also Travelers Aid desks at Washington National Airport (open Sunday to Friday 9am to 9pm, Saturday 9am to 6pm ☎ **703/419-3972**); on the lower concourse at the west end of Dulles International Airport (open Monday to Friday 10am to 9pm, Saturday and Sunday 10am to 6pm ☎ **703/661-8636**);

and at Union Station (open Monday to Saturday 9:30am to 5:30pm, Sunday 12:30 to 5:30pm ☎ **202/546-3120,** ext. 25); TDD (telecommunications device for the deaf) is provided at all the above-mentioned locations except the main office on C Street.

CITY LAYOUT

Pierre Charles L'Enfant designed Washington's great sweeping avenues crossed by numbered and lettered streets. At key intersections, he placed spacious circles. Although the circles are enhanced with monuments, statuary, and fountains, L'Enfant also intended them to serve as strategic command posts to ward off invaders or marauding mobs. After what had happened in Paris during the French Revolution—and remember, that was current history at the time—his design views were quite practical.

Finding an Address   Once you understand the city's layout, it's easy to find your way around. You'll find it helpful to have a map handy when reading this.

The city is divided into four basic quadrants: **northwest, northeast, southwest,** and **southeast.** If you look at your map, you'll see that some addresses—for instance, the corner of G and 7th streets—appear in four different places. There's one in each quadrant. Hence you must observe the quadrant designation (NW, NE, SW, or SE) when looking for an address.

The **Capitol** dome is the center of the District of Columbia, the dividing point for the four quadrants. Each of the four corners of the District of Columbia is exactly the same distance from the dome. The White House and most government buildings and important monuments are west of the Capitol (in the northwest and southwest quadrants); so are important hotels and tourist facilities.

Numbered streets run north-south, beginning on either side of the Capitol with East 1st Street and West 1st Street. **Lettered streets** run east-west.

Avenues, named for U.S. states, run at angles across the grid pattern and often intersect at traffic circles. For example, New Hampshire, Connecticut, and Massachusetts avenues intersect at Dupont Circle.

With this in mind, you can easily find an address. On **lettered streets,** the address tells you exactly where to go. For instance, 1776 K St. NW is between 17th and 18th streets (the first two digits of 1776 tell you that) in the northwest quadrant (NW). *Note:* I Street is often written Eye Street to prevent confusion with 1st Street.

To find an address on **numbered streets** you'll probably have to use your fingers. For instance, 623 8th St. SE is between F and G streets (the sixth and seventh letters of the alphabet; the first digit of 623 tells you that) in the southeast quadrant (SE). One thing to remember though: There's no J Street (skipping the letter *J* was meant as a slap in the face to the unpopular Chief Justice John Jay). So when counting, remember that K becomes the 10th letter, L the 11th, and so on.

As you go farther out, beyond Washington's original layout, the letter alphabetical system ends and a new one begins: two-syllable names in alphabetical order—Adams, Bryant, Channing, and so forth. When the two-syllable alphabet is used up, the system begins anew with three-syllable names: Albemarle, Brandywine, Chesapeake, and so on.

NEIGHBORHOODS IN BRIEF

The Mall   This lovely tree-lined stretch of open space between Constitution and Independence Avenues, extending for 2¹/₂ miles from the Capitol to the Lincoln Memorial, is the hub of tourist attractions. It includes most of the Smithsonian Institution museums and many other nearby visitor attractions.

Downtown   The area roughly between 7th and 22nd Streets NW going east to west, and P Street and Pennsylvania Avenue going north to south, downtown is a mix of Federal Triangle's government office buildings, K Street and Connecticut Avenue restaurants and shopping, and F Street department stores. Too large an area to have a consistent character, it includes lovely Lafayette Park, Washington's tiny porno district, its ever expanding Chinatown, and a half dozen or so sightseeing attractions.

Capitol Hill   Everyone's heard of "the Hill," the area crowned by the Capitol. When people speak of Capitol Hill, they refer to a large section of town, extending from the western side of the Capitol to RFK Memorial Stadium going east, bounded by H Street NE and the Southwest Freeway north and south. It contains not only the chief symbol of the nation's capital, but the Supreme Court building, the Library of Congress, the Folger Shakespeare Library, Union Station, and the U.S. Botanic Garden. Much of it is a quiet residential neighborhood of tree-lined streets and Victorian homes. There are many restaurants in the vicinity.

Foggy Bottom   The area west of the White House to the edge of Georgetown, Foggy Bottom was Washington's early industrial

Washington, D.C., at a Glance

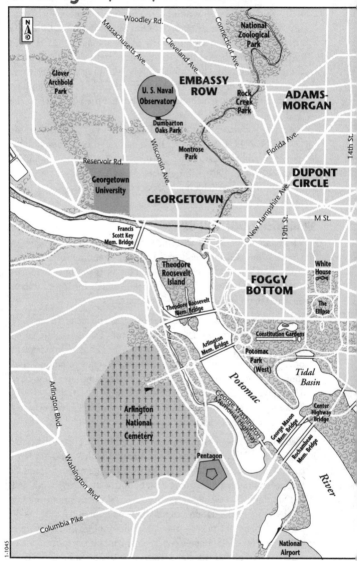

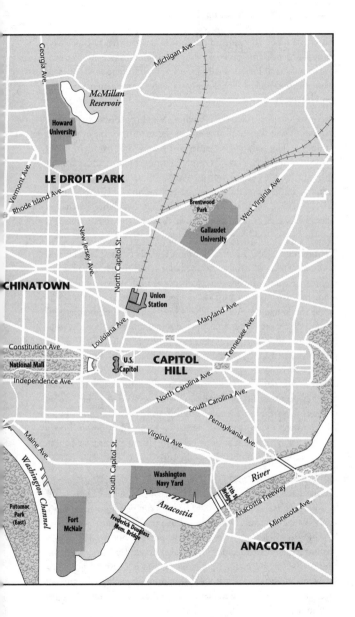

center. Its name comes from the foul fumes emitted in those days by a coal depot and gasworks, but its original name, Funkstown (for owner Jacob Funk), is perhaps even worse. There's nothing foul about the area today. The Kennedy Center and George Washington University are located here.

Dupont Circle   Generally, when Washingtonians speak of Dupont Circle they don't mean just the park, they mean the area around it. The park itself, named for Rear Adm. Samuel Francis Dupont of the U.S. Navy, is centered around D.C.'s most famous fountain, at the intersection of Connecticut and Massachusetts avenues, and is a popular rendezvous spot. Dupont Circle is one of the liveliest sections in town, rivaled only by Georgetown and Adams-Morgan for nightspots, movie theaters, and restaurants. It is also the hub of D.C.'s gay community.

Georgetown   This historic community dates from colonial times. It was a thriving tobacco port long before the District of Columbia was formed, and one of its attractions, the Old Stone House, dates from pre-Revolutionary days. Georgetown action centers on M Street and Wisconsin Avenue NW, where you'll find numerous boutiques (see chapter 7 for details), chic restaurants, and popular pubs (lots of nightlife here). But do get off the main drags and see the quiet tree-lined streets of restored colonial row houses and check out the C&O Canal.

Adams-Morgan   This increasingly trendy multiethnic neighborhood is popular for its restaurants serving myriad international cuisines. Try to plan at least one meal up here; it's a good opportunity to see an authentic, untouristy area of Washington. Friday and Saturday nights it's a hot nightlife district. Adams-Morgan centers around Columbia Road and 18th Street NW.

2 Getting Around

Washington is one of the easiest U.S. cities in which to get around. Only New York rivals its comprehensive transportation system, but Washington's clean, efficient subways put the Big Apple's underground nightmare to shame. There's also a complex bus system with routes covering all major D.C. arteries, and it's easy to hail a taxi anywhere at any time. Finally, Washington—especially the areas of interest to tourists—is pretty compact, and often the best way to get from one place to another is on foot.

BY METRO

Metrorail stations are immaculate, cool, and attractive. Cars are air-conditioned and fitted with upholstered seats; tracks are rubber-cushioned so the ride is quiet; service is frequent enough so you usually get a seat; and the system is so simply designed that a 10-year-old can understand it.

Metrorail's 74 stations and 89 miles of track (83 stations and 103 miles of track is the eventual goal) include locations at or near almost every sightseeing attraction and extend to suburban Maryland and northern Virginia. If you're in Washington even for a few days, you'll probably have occasion to use the system, but if not, I suggest you create one—perhaps dinner at a Union Station or Dupont Circle restaurant. The Metro is a sightseeing attraction in its own right.

There are five lines in operation—**Red, Blue, Orange, Yellow, and Green**—with extensions planned for the future. The lines connect at several points, making transfers easy. **Metro stations** are indicated by discreet brown columns bearing the station's name and topped by the letter *M*. Below the *M* is a colored stripe or stripes indicating the line or lines it serves. When entering a Metro station for the first time, go to the kiosk and ask the station manager for a free "Metro System Pocket Guide" (available in six languages). It contains a map of the system, explains how it works, and lists the closest Metro stops to points of interest. The station manager can also answer questions about routing or purchase of fare cards.

To enter or exit a Metro station you need a computerized **fare card,** available at vending machines near the entrance. The minimum fare to enter the system is $1.10, which pays for rides to and from any point within 7 miles of boarding during nonrush hours; during rush hours (Monday to Friday from 5:30 to 9:30am and 3 to 8pm), $1.10 only takes you 3 miles. The machines take nickels, dimes, quarters, and bills from $1 to $20; they can return up to $4.95 in change (coins only). If you plan to take several Metrorail trips during your stay, put more value on the fare card to avoid having to purchase a new card each time you ride. There's a 10% discount on all fare cards of $20 or more. Up to two children under five can ride free with a paying passenger.

When you insert your card in the entrance gate, the time and location are recorded on its magnetic tape and your card is returned. Don't forget to snatch it up, and keep it handy; you have to reinsert it in the exit gate at your destination, where the fare will automatically be deducted. The card will be returned if there's any value left on it. If you arrive at a destination and your fare card doesn't have enough value, add what's necessary at the Addfare machines near the exit gate.

If you're planning to continue your travel via Metrobus, pick up a **transfer** *at the station where you enter the system* (not your destination station) from the transfer machine on the mezzanine. It's good for a discount on bus fares in D.C. and Virginia. There are no bus-to-subway transfers.

Metrorail operates Monday to Friday from 6am to 10:30pm, weekends and holidays from 8am to 10:30pm. Call **202/637-7000** for information on Metro routes.

BY BUS

While a 10-year-old can understand the Metrorail system, the Metrobus system is considerably more complex. The 15,800 stops on the 1,489-square-mile route (it operates on all major D.C. arteries as well as in the Virginia and Maryland suburbs) are indicated by red, white, and blue signs. However, the signs tell you only what buses pull into a given stop, not where they go. For **routing information,** call **202/637-7000.** Calls are taken Monday to Friday from 6am to 11:30pm, weekends and holidays from 8am to 11:30pm.

If you travel the same route frequently and would like a free map and time schedule, ask the bus driver or call **202/637-7000.** Information about parking in Metrobus fringe lots is also available from this number.

Base fare in the District is $1.10; bus transfers cost 10¢. There are additional charges for travel into the Maryland and Virginia suburbs. Bus drivers are not equipped to make change, so be sure to *carry exact change or tokens.* The latter are available at 375 ticket outlets (call **202/637-7000** for locations and hours of operation). If you'll be in Washington for a while and plan to use the buses a lot, consider a two-week pass, also available at ticket outlets.

Most buses operate daily almost around the clock. Service is quite frequent on weekdays, especially during peak hours. On weekends and late at night, service is less frequent. Up to two children under five ride free with a paying passenger on Metrobus, and there are reduced fares for senior citizens (☎ **202/962-7000**) and people with disabilities (☎ **202/962-1245**).

BY CAR

Within the District, a car is a luxury since public transportation is so comprehensive. Having a car can even be an inconvenience, especially during spring and summer, when traffic jams are frequent, parking spaces almost nonexistent, and parking lots ruinously expensive. But there's a great deal to see in the D.C. vicinity, and for most attractions in Virginia and Maryland you will want a car.

All the major car-rental companies are represented here. Here are some handy phone numbers: **Budget** (☎ 800/527-0700), **Hertz** (☎ 800/654-3131), **Thrifty** (☎ 800/367-2277), **Avis** (☎ 800/331-1212), and **Alamo** (☎ 800/327-9633).

BY TAXI

District cabs operate on a zone system. If you take a trip from one point to another within the same zone, you pay just $4, regardless of the distance traveled. So it would cost you $4 to travel a few blocks from the U.S. Botanic Garden to the Museum of American History, but the same $4 could take you from the Botanic Garden all the way to Dupont Circle. They're both in Zone 1. Also in Zone 1 are most other tourist attractions. If your trip takes you into a second zone the price is $5.50, $6.90 for a third zone, $8.25 for a fourth, and so on. You're unlikely to travel more than three zones unless you're staying in some remote section of town.

So far, the fares are pretty low. Here's how they could add up: There's a $1.50 charge for each additional passenger after the first, so a $4 Zone 1 fare can become $8.50 for a family of four (though one child under six can ride free). There's also a rush-hour surcharge of $1 per trip between 7 to 9:30am and between 4 to 6:30pm weekdays. Surcharges are also added for large pieces of luggage and for arranging a pickup by telephone ($1.50).

The zone system is not used when your destination is an out-of-District address (such as an airport); in that case, the fare is based on mileage covered—$2 for the first half mile or part thereof and 70¢ for each additional half mile or part. You can call **202/331-1671** to find out the rate between any point in D.C. and an address in Virginia or Maryland. Call **202/645-6018** to inquire about fares within the District.

It's generally easy to hail a taxi. Unique to the city is the practice of allowing drivers to pick up as many passengers as they can comfortably fit, so expect to share (unrelated parties pay the same as they

Taxicab Zones

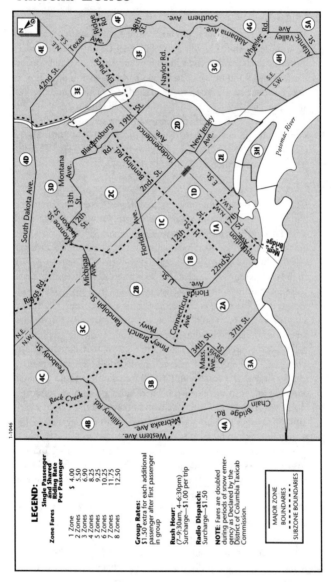

would if they were not sharing). You can also call a taxi, though there's that $1.50 charge. Try **Diamond Cab Company** (☎ 202/387-6200) or **Yellow Cab** (☎ 202/544-1212).

BY TOURMOBILE

You can save on shoe leather and see most Washington landmarks in comfort aboard Tourmobiles (☎ 202/544-5100), comfortable blue-and-white sightseeing trams that run along the Mall and as far out as Arlington National Cemetery and even (with coach service) Mount Vernon.

Washington/Arlington Cemetery Tour   You can take the Washington and Arlington Cemetery tour or tour Arlington Cemetery only. The former stops at 14 different sights on or near the Mall and three sights at Arlington Cemetery: the Kennedy grave sites, the Tomb of the Unknowns, and Arlington House.

Here's how the system works: You pay the driver when you first board the bus (you can also purchase a ticket inside the Arlington National Cemetery Visitor Center or, for a small surcharge, order your ticket in advance from TicketMaster (☎ 800/551-SEAT). Along the route, you may get off at any stop to visit monuments or buildings. When you're ready to move on, step aboard the next Tourmobile that comes along without extra charge. The buses travel in a loop, serving each stop about every 20 minutes. One **fare** allows you to use the buses for a full day. The charge for the Washington/Arlington Cemetery tour is $12 for adults, $6 for children 3 to 11. For Arlington Cemetery only, adults pay $4, children $2. Children under three ride free. Buses follow figure-eight circuits from the Capitol to Arlington Cemetery and back. You can also buy a regular-price ticket after 2pm that is valid for the rest of the afternoon plus the following day.

Tourmobiles operate daily year-round on the following schedules. From June 15 to Labor Day, they ply the Mall between 9am and 6:30pm. After Labor Day, the hours are 9:30am to 4:30pm. In Arlington Cemetery, between October and March, they start at 8:30am and end at 4:30pm. April through September, the hours are 8:30am to 6:30pm.

Other Tours   April through October, Tourmobiles also run round-trip to **Mount Vernon.** Coaches depart from the Arlington National Cemetery Visitor Center and the Washington Monument at 10am, noon, and 2pm. The price is $20 for adults, $10 for children, including admission to Mount Vernon. A combination

---

The Metro Way

An inexpensive alternative to the Tourmobile and Old Town Trolley is the **$5 One-Day Metro Pass,** which allows you to go as far as you want throughout the Metrorail system and get on and off trains as often as you like during the course of a day without paying any additional fares. It's valid from 9:30am on weekdays and all day on weekends. Since most sightseeing attractions are near Metro stops, this can be a money-saving way to get around if you plan your itinerary wisely. The one-day passes are sold in many Metro stations and at some hotels; call **202/637-7000** to find out your most convenient location.

---

tour of Washington, Arlington Cemetery, and Mount Vernon (good for two days) is $32 for adults, $16 for children. Another offering (June 15 to Labor Day) is the **Frederick Douglass National Historic Site Tour,** which includes a guided tour of Douglass's home, Cedar Hill. Departures are from Arlington National Cemetery and the Washington Monument at noon. Adults pay $6, children $3. A two-day **Combination Frederick Douglass Tour and Washington-Arlington National Cemetery Tour** is also available at $24 for adults, $12 for children. For both the Mount Vernon and Frederick Douglass tours, you must reserve in person at least an hour in advance.

BY OLD TOWN TROLLEY

A service similar to Tourmobile's is Old Town Trolley Tours of Washington (☎ **202/832-9800**). For a fixed price, you can get on and off these green-and-orange vehicles as often as you like for a full day. Following a loop, the trolleys stop at 17 locations in the District, including Georgetown; they also go out to Arlington National Cemetery. They operate daily from 9am to 5pm Memorial Day to Labor Day; the rest of the year, 9am to 4pm. The cost is $18 for adults, $9 for children 5 to 12, free for children under five. The full tour, which is narrated, takes two hours, and trolleys come by every 20 to 30 minutes. You can board without a ticket and purchase it en route. Old Town Trolley also offers a $2^{1}/_{2}$-hour "Washington After Hours" tour of illuminated federal buildings and memorials from mid-March to the end of December. Call for details.

FAST FACTS: Washington, D.C.

Airports/Airport Transportation   See "Getting There," in chapter 1.

Ambulances   See "Emergencies," below.

American Express   There's an American Express Travel Service office at 1150 Connecticut Ave. NW (☎ **202/457-1300**). It functions as a full travel agency and currency exchange; of course, you can also buy traveler's checks here.

Area Code   Within the District of Columbia, it's 202. In suburban Virginia, it's 703. In suburban Maryland, it's 410 or 301.

Crime   See "Safety," below.

Congresspersons   To locate a senator or congressional representative, call the Capitol switchboard (☎ **202/224-3121**).

Doctors/Dentists   **Prologue** (☎ **800/DOCTORS**), can refer you to any type of doctor or dentist you need. Its roster includes just about every specialty. Hours are Monday to Thursday 7:30am to 10pm, Friday 7:30am to 8pm, Saturday 9am to 5:30pm, and Sunday 11:30am to 7pm. You can also call the Dental Referral Service (☎ **202/547-7615** Monday to Friday 8am to 4pm).

Drugstores   CVS, Washington's major drugstore chain (with more than 40 stores), has two convenient 24-hour locations: 14th Street and Thomas Circle NW, at Vermont Avenue (☎ **202/ 628-0720**), and at Dupont Circle (☎ **202/785-1466**), both with round-the-clock pharmacies. Check your phone book for other convenient locations.

Emergencies   Dial **911** to contact the police or fire department or to call an ambulance. See also "Hospital Emergency Wards," below.

Hospital Emergency Wards   Georgetown University Hospital, 3800 Reservoir Rd. NW (make a left off Wisconsin Avenue; ☎ **202/784-2118**), and George Washington University Hospital, 901 23rd St. NW (entrance on Washington Circle; ☎ **202/ 994-3884**), are both excellent.

Liquor Laws   Minimum drinking age is 21. Liquor stores are closed on Sunday.

Poison Control Center   A 24-hour emergency hotline is **202/ 625-3333**.

Post Office   The city's main post office (☎ 202/523-2628) is located opposite Union Station at 2 Massachusetts Ave. NE (at G and North Capitol streets). It's open Monday to Friday 7am to midnight, and on weekends until 8pm.

Safety   In Washington, you're quite safe throughout the day in all the major tourist areas described in this book, and you can also safely visit the Lincoln Memorial after dark. None of the restaurants listed here will take you into dangerous or sparsely populated areas at night. Also, riding the Metro in Washington is quite safe.

Taxis   See "Getting Around," earlier in this chapter.

Tickets   See chapter 8 for details.

Tourist Information   Two major sources are the **White House Visitor Center,** Pennsylvania Ave, NW, between 14th and 15th Streets (☎ 202/208-1631) and the **Smithsonian Information Center,** 1000 Jefferson Dr. SW (☎ 202/357-2700). Details on both above and in chapter 5.

You can also call **Dial-a-Museum** (☎ 202/357-2020), the Smithsonian's number for recorded daily information on all its museum programs and activities, and **Dial-a-Park** (☎ 202/619-PARK) to find out about events in the National Capital Region parks.

Transit Information   See "Getting There," in chapter 1 and "Getting Around," earlier in this chapter.

Accommodations

*Y*our first priority on a Washington visit is finding a place to stay. Luckily, with some 64,000 hotel and motel rooms in the District and surrounding metropolitan area, there's no shortage of rooms. They exist in every category, from luxurious accommodations to budget guest houses—with many more, alas, in the upper bracket than in the lower. Presented below are those establishments in all price categories that offer the best value for your money.

HOW TO READ THE LISTINGS

The hotels listed below are grouped first by location, then alphabetically by price category within a given neighborhood. Hotels categorized as **very expensive** charge $200 or more for a double room, those charging $150 to $200 are listed as **expensive,** $100 to $149 as **moderate,** and $99 or less as **inexpensive.** Most of the recommendations in all price categories are located in the northwest sector, where you will also find a number of major sightseeing attractions and good restaurants. If you have a car, inquire about the cost of parking when you make your reservation; some hotels charge more than $20 a night!

Taxes   In the District, in addition to your hotel rate, you'll have to pay 13% in taxes plus $1.50 a night room tax.

GETTING THE MOST FOR YOUR DOLLAR

WEEKEND, OFF-SEASON & SPECIAL RATES   In Washington, the majority of hotels in all price categories slash their rates by almost half on the weekends, and sometimes weekdays as well during the off-season (generally July through August and late December through January). When telephoning to make arrangements, be sure to verify that your reservation is at weekend rates before you hang up, and check on it again when you register. At many hotels, you must register in advance to obtain weekend rates. *Note:* Weekend rates listed for hotels in this chapter are, generally, subject to availability.

Call the **D.C. Committee to Promote Washington** (☎ 800/422-8644), and request a copy of "Discover Washington, D.C." It lists weekend rates at more than 90 hotels in all price ranges.

Also inquire about special packages. Many hotels offer special rates as a matter of course to senior citizens, families, active-duty military personnel, and government employees.

A Reservations Service   Make use of a free service offered by **Capitol Reservations,** 1730 Rhode Island Ave. NW, Suite 1114, Washington, DC 20036 (☎ **800/VISIT-DC** or 202/452-1270; fax 202/452-0537). They'll find you a hotel that meets your specific requirements and is within your price range, and they'll do the bargaining for you. "Because of the high volume of room nights we book," explains owner Thom Hall, "many properties offer discounts available only through this service." Capitol Reservations listings begin at about $55 a night for a double. Hotels are screened for cleanliness and other desirability factors, and they're all in safe neighborhoods.

BED & BREAKFASTS

Many people find staying at B&B accommodations one of the most enjoyable ways to travel. Prices are reasonable, rooms are often charming, and you have an opportunity to meet local people and other travelers.

In addition to specific B&Bs (see below), I've listed two services that represent numerous homes that rent out rooms on this basis. Call as far in advance as possible, and be sure to specify your needs and preferences: For instance, discuss children, pets, smoking policy, preferred locations (do you require convenient public transportation?), and parking.

The **Bed and Breakfast League/Sweet Dreams and Toast,** P.O. Box 9490, Washington, DC 20016 (☎ **202/363-7767**), is a reservation service representing more than 70 B&Bs in the District. Through it, you might find a room in a mid-1800s Federal-style Capitol Hill mansion, a Georgetown home with a lovely garden, or a turn-of-the-century Dupont Circle town house filled with Victorian furnishings. The accommodations are all screened, and guest reports are given serious consideration. All listings are convenient to public transportation. Rates for most range from $40 to $120 for a single, $50 to $150 for a double, and $10 to $25 per additional person. There's a two-night minimum-stay requirement and a booking fee of $10 (per reservation, not per night). AE, DC, MC, V.

A similar service, **Bed & Breakfast Accommodations Ltd.,** P.O. Box 12011, Washington, DC 20005 (☎ **202/328-3510;** fax 202/332-3885), has more than 80 homes, inns, guest houses, and unhosted furnished apartments in its files. Most are in historic districts. Rates are $45 to $110 single, $55 to $150 double, $15 for an extra person, and from $65 for a full apartment. At guest houses and inns, rates run the gamut from $68 to $180 single, $78 to $250 double. AE, DC, MC, V.

1 Best Bets

- **Best Historic Hotel:** The grand dame of Washington hotels is the magnificent **Renaissance Mayflower,** 1127 Connecticut Ave. NW (☎ **202/347-3000**), which, when it was built in 1925, was considered not only the last word in luxury and beauty but "the second-best address" in town. Harry S. Truman preferred it even over the White House.

- **Best for Business Travelers:** Several Washington hotels cater largely to a business and convention clientele and are fully equipped to meet your business needs. But only the **Washington Hilton and Towers,** 1919 Connecticut Ave. NW (☎ **202/ 483-3000**), combines a full business center with extensive resort facilities.

- **Best for a Romantic Getaway:** The posh **Four Seasons,** 2800 Pennsylvania Ave. NW (☎ **202/342-0444**), at the edge of Georgetown, pampers guests with every luxury and sets a sumptuous stage for romance.

- **Best Trendy Hotel:** The **Four Seasons** (see address and telephone above) is the glamorous choice of many visiting celebrities; Michael Jackson had a special dance floor set up in his room, Richard Simmons did jumping jacks in the lobby, and Billy Joel once took over the Garden Terrace piano and entertained delighted guests for an hour.

- **Best Moderately Priced Hotel:** The newly renovated **Hotel Lombardy,** 2019 Pennsylvania Ave. NW (☎ **202/828-2600**), is conveniently located, its accommodations are spacious and attractively decorated, and its front desk offers concierge-like service.

- **Best Inexpensive Hotel:** The **Days Inn Downtown,** 1201 K St. NW (☎ **202/842-1020**), close to the Convention Center, even has a small rooftop pool. If you reserve far in advance, you may be able to get the special $59 per night "Super Saver" rate.

- **Best B&B:** The stunning **Morrison Clark Inn,** Massachusetts Avenue and 11th Street NW (☎ **202/898-1200**), housed in two beautifully restored Victorian town houses, has exquisite rooms and pampers its guests with every luxury.
- **Best Service:** The aristocratic **Hay-Adams,** 16th and H streets NW (☎ **202/638-6600**), offers the kind of service that harks back to the days when people traveled with steamer trunks.
- **Best Health Club:** Once again, The **Four Seasons** (see address and telephone above), where Lifecycles, Stairmasters, and treadmills are all equipped with TVs, VCRs, and radio/cassette Walkmans (movies, workout tapes, and music cassettes are available); there's also a full complement of Nautilus equipment, a skylit lap pool, a whirlpool, a sauna for women, and a steam room for men. Personal trainers and fitness evaluation are available. Workout clothes are provided. For business travelers, the club offers an on-premises fax, phones, and word processor. You can even get a suit pressed while you work out.
- **Best Views:** The **Channel Inn,** 650 Water St. SW (☎ **202/554-2400**), overlooks the boat-filled Washington Channel.
- **Best (Most Breathtaking) Interior:** The **Willard Inter-Continental,** 1401 Pennsylvania Ave. NW (☎ **202/628-9100**), is an architectural masterpiece and National Landmark that has been painstakingly restored to its original opulence (it's worth a look even if you don't stay here).
- **Best Resort Hotel:** The **Omni Shoreham,** 2500 Calvert St. NW (☎ **202/234-0700**), bordering beautiful Rock Creek Park, offers biking, hiking, and jogging trails (including a Perrier parcourse with exercise stations); tennis courts; an Olympic-size swimming pool; complete health club; and more.

2 Downtown

VERY EXPENSIVE

✪ **J. W. Marriott.** 1331 Pennsylvania Ave. NW (at E St.), Washington, DC 20004. ☎ **800/228-9290** or 202/393-2000. Fax 202/626-6991. 739 rms, 33 suites. A/C TV TEL. Weekdays $199–$209 double, $219–$229 concierge level double. Weekends $119–$159 double with full breakfast. Extra person free. AE, DC, DISC, JCB, MC, V. Parking $16. Metro: Metro Center.

This flagship Marriott property is adjacent to the National and Warner Theaters. Though conventioneers make up a lot of the its clientele, tourists (including families) and businesspeople traveling on their own will enjoy the extensive facilities here. Stunning public areas combine futuristic architecture with lush plantings to create an exciting but very livable environment. Residential-style rooms, decorated in pleasing color schemes (such as sage and rose), are furnished with cherrywood pieces in traditional styles. You'll also find an iron and full-sized ironing board in your room.

Dining/Entertainment: The hotel's most elegant facility is **Celadon,** a Chinoiserie setting for American/continental cuisine. The very pretty **National Café** serves American fare and, in warm weather, offers seating at umbrella-shaded tables; "early bird" dinners here are priced under $15. Alfresco dining is featured at **SRO,** a friendly pub. And for piano entertainment and nightly jazz bands, there's the skylit **Garden Terrace.**

Services: 24-hour room service.

Facilities: A connecting mall with 85 shops and restaurants, complete health club (with indoor swimming pool and hydrotherapy pool), video-game arcade, full business center, gift shop.

Renaissance Washington, D.C., Hotel. 999 9th St. NW (at K St.), Washington, DC 20001. ☎ **800/228-9898** or 202/898-9000. Fax 202/789-4213. 779 rms, 21 suites. A/C MINIBAR TV TEL. Weekdays $205–$225 double; Club Level $245 double. Weekends $99 double. Extra person free. AE, CB, DC, DISC, MC, V. Parking $14. Metro: Gallery Place.

Directly across the street from the D.C. Convention Center, this hotel is part of the $340 million World Technology Trade Center Complex. Although catering primarily to conventioneers and business travelers, it also delivers a lot of luxury and convenience to tourists. The spiffy rooms are done up in teal/mauve or sage/sienna color schemes, with oak furnishings and Southwest-look bedspreads and drapes.

Dining/Entertainment: Mahogany-paneled and crystal-chandeliered, **The Tavern** features American regional cuisine; a bar adjoins. Less formal is the cheerful **Café Florentine,** off the lobby, offering reasonably priced buffets and à la carte meals. The skylit **Marco Polo** piano bar resembles a Chinese pagoda. And the **Plaza Gourmet and Pastry Shop** offers take-out sandwiches, salads, and fresh-baked pastries.

Services: 24-hour room service, concierge.

Facilities: Gift shop, hairdresser, full business center, full health club.

✪ **Willard Inter-Continental.** 1401 Pennsylvania Ave. NW, Washington, DC 20004. ☎ **800/327-0200** or 202/628-9100. Fax 202/637-7326. 304 rms, 37 suites. A/C MINIBAR TV TEL. Weekdays $295–$380 double. Weekends $199

Georgetown & Downtown Accommodations

Capitol Hill Suites 18
Channel Inn 17
Days Inn Downtown 13
Four Seasons 3
Georgetown Dutch Inn 1
Georgetown Suites 2
Hay-Adams 10
Hostelling International 14
Hotel Lombardy 7
Howard Johnson's
  Premier Hotel 4
J. W. Marriott 12
Jefferson 9
Lincoln Suites Downtown 8
Morrison Clark Inn 15
Renaissance
  Washington, D.C.,Hotel 16
State Plaza Hotel 6
Watergate Hotel 5
Willard Inter-
  Continental 11

double. Extra person $30. Children under 12 stay free in parents' room. AE, DC, DISC, JCB, MC, V. Parking $20. Metro: Metro Center.

Billed as the "crown jewel of Pennsylvania Avenue," this is actually the crown jewel of all Washington hotels. Its upscale clientele is likely to include visiting premiers and presidents (more than 90 heads of state have stayed here in the last decade). Lincoln spent the eve of his inaugural here, and it was at the Willard that Julia Ward Howe penned the words to the "Battle Hymn of the Republic."

In 1901, Henry Janeway Hardenbergh, a noted hotel architect, was hired to design the French Second Empire beaux arts palace that occupies the hotel's original site today. Saved as a National Landmark in 1974, its restoration began in the 1980s, and a new building, designed to harmonize with the old, was constructed. In the original building, the exquisite plasterwork and scagliola marble were repaired or replicated, along with marble mosaic tile floors, carpeting, and chandeliers. Rooms are suitably sumptuous, furnished in Edwardian and Federal-period reproductions and adorned with beautiful gilt-framed French prints.

Dining/Entertainment: The **Willard Room** (the term *power lunch* originated here) is simply stunning (see chapter 4 for details). The circular **Round Robin Bar** is where Henry Clay mixed the first mint julep in Washington. The **Café Espresso** offers croissant sandwiches, pastas, pastries, and vintage wines by the glass, along with more substantial grilled entrées; full afternoon teas are served here weekday afternoons. And the **Nest Lounge** offers live jazz on weekends.

Services: Twice-daily maid service, nightly bed turndown, 24-hour room service, concierge, currency exchange, airline/train ticketing.

Facilities: Full business center, complete fitness center.

INEXPENSIVE

🟢 Days Inn Downtown. 1201 K St. NW, Washington, DC 20005. ☎ **800/ 562-3350**, 800/325-2525, or 202/842-1020. Fax 202/289-0336. 220 rms. A/C TV TEL. Weekdays $89–$109 double. Weekends $58–$89 double. Extra person $10. Children under 18 stay free in parents' room. Lower "Super Saver" rates (about $59) are sometimes available if you reserve in advance (the earlier the better) via the toll-free number, 800/325-2525—it's worth a try. AE, CB, DC, DISC, MC, V. Parking $11. Metro: McPherson Square.

Proximity to the Convention Center makes this Days Inn a perfect choice for visitors attending events there. A small rooftop pool and a video-game arcade will also appeal to families with young children. Newly renovated rooms are cheerfully decorated and equipped with hair dryers and coffeemakers; some also offer kitchenettes and/or cafes.

A pleasant restaurant specializes in reasonably priced steak, seafood, and pasta dishes, and its adjoining lounge airs sporting events on TV monitors over the bar. A car-rental agency is just across the street. City tours depart from the lobby. Inquire about special packages when you reserve.

⑤ Hostelling International—Washington, D.C. 1009 11th St. NW (at K St.), Washington, DC 20001. ☎ **202/737-2333.** 250 beds. A/C. $18 for AYH members, $21 for nonmembers. MC, V. Metro: Metro Center.

Your best bet among inexpensive accommodations is this spiffy youth hostel, which opened in late 1987. Situated in a fully renovated eight-story brick building, it offers freshly painted dorm rooms (with 4 to 14 beds) and clean baths down the hall. There's a huge self-service kitchen where you can cook your own meals (a supermarket is two blocks away), a dining room, a comfortable lounge, coin-op washers/dryers, storage lockers, and indoor parking for bicycles. HIW offers special activities for guests: volleyball games, cookouts, lectures, movies, travel seminars, and more.

The location is excellent: just three blocks from the Metro, six blocks from the Mall. And the clientele is monitored, so it's a perfectly safe place to send your college-age kids or, for that matter, your mother. All age groups are welcome, but since the dorms are for men or women only, couples are separated. (Subject to availability, there are a limited number of rooms for families and couples October to March; reserve them early.) Maximum stay is six nights, but that limit may be extended with permission, subject to available space. You must supply your own towels and soap (blankets, linens, and pillows are provided); sleeping bags are not allowed. Call as far in advance as possible to reserve, and assure your reservation with a 50% deposit.

BED & BREAKFAST

✪ Morrison Clark Inn. Massachusetts Ave. at 11th St. NW, Washington, DC 20001. ☎ **800/332-7898** or 202/898-1200. Fax 202/289-8576. 40 rms (all with bath), 14 suites. A/C TV TEL. Weekdays $155–$185 double. Weekends $85 double. Rates include continental breakfast. Extra person $20. Children under 12 stay free in parents' room. AE, CB, DC, DISC, MC, V. Parking $15. Metro: Metro Center.

Looking for a romantic setting for that special weekend? This magnificent inn, occupying twin 1865 Victorian brick town houses—with a newer wing in converted stables across an interior courtyard—is on the National Register of Historic Places. Guests enter via a turn-of-the-century parlor, with velvet-lace-upholstered Victorian furnishings and lace-curtained bay windows. Continental breakfast includes oven-fresh cakes, muffins, Danish, and croissants.

High-ceilinged guest rooms are exquisitely decorated. Color schemes use delicate hues like rose, muted gray/blue, and cream. Four rooms have private porches, and many have plant-filled balconies (with umbrella tables) overlooking a fountained courtyard garden.

Room service is available from the inn's highly acclaimed restaurant (see chapter 4). Other amenities here include twice-daily maid service with Belgian chocolates at bed turndown, complimentary daily newspapers, overnight shoeshine, a concierge, many business services, and fresh flowers in every room. A fitness center is on the premises.

3 Near the White House

VERY EXPENSIVE

✪ **Hay-Adams.** 16th and H sts. NW, Washington, DC 20006. ☎ **800/ 424-5054** or 202/638-6600. Fax 202/638-3803. 117 rms, 19 suites. A/C MINIBAR TV TEL. Weekdays $250–$425 double. Weekends $143–$210 per room. Extra person $30. Children under 12 stay free in parents' room. AE, CB, DC, JCB, MC, V. Parking (valet only) $20. Metro: Farragut West or McPherson Square.

In 1927, famed Washington builder Harry Wardman created the Hay-Adams. Its architecture evokes an Italian Renaissance palazzo with Doric, Ionic, and Corinthian orders and intricate ceiling motifs. Among the early guests were Amelia Earhart, Sinclair Lewis, and Ethel Barrymore. In the 1990s, the hotel is still as sedately elegant as ever. A typical room might feature 18th-century–style furnishings, silk-covered walls hung with botanical prints and fine art, a gorgeous molded plaster ceiling, and French silk floral-print bedspreads, upholstery, and curtains. Many rooms have ornamental fireplaces and/or French doors that open onto views of Lafayette Square and the White House.

Dining/Entertainment: The sunny **Lafayette Restaurant** (overlooking the White House) is an exquisite dining room; it serves contemporary American/continental fare at all meals, plus afternoon tea. The adjoining lounge features nightly piano-bar entertainment.

Services: 24-hour room and concierge service, nightly bed turndown, complimentary shoeshine.

> ## 👬 Family-Friendly Hotels
>
> **Channel Inn** *(see p. 54)* This lovely hotel has a swimming pool, and adults will love the rooms that overlook the boat-filled Washington Channel.
>
> **Howard Johnson's Premier Hotel** *(see p. 44)* Close to the Kennedy Center, this flagship HoJo has a rooftop pool, Ping-Pong room, video games, and coin-op washers and dryers. Rooms have small refrigerators and TVs equipped with Nintendo games.
>
> **Omni Shoreham** *(see p. 51)* Adjacent to Rock Creek Park, close to the zoo, and equipped with two outdoor pools—a large one for swimming laps and a kiddie pool—the Shoreham offers an extensive program of children's activities. Three lighted tennis courts are an additional attraction.
>
> **Washington Hilton and Towers** *(see p. 52)* A large heated outdoor pool, a wading pool, video-game arcade, three tennis courts, shuffleboard, and bike rental. What more do you need?

Facilities: Guest access to a local health club, secretarial and business services, in-room fax on request.

✪ **The Jefferson.** 1200 16th St. NW (at M St.), Washington, DC 20036. ☎ **800/368-5966** or 202/347-2200. Fax 202/223-9039. 70 rms, 30 suites. A/C MINIBAR TV TEL. Weekdays $245–$265 double. Weekends $175 double. Extra person $25. Children under 12 stay free in parents' room. AE, CB, DC, JCB, MC, V. Parking $20. Metro: Farragut North.

Opened in 1923 just four blocks from the White House, The Jefferson (along with the Hay-Adams—see above), is the city's most exclusive venue, proffering discreet hotel hospitality to political personages, royalty, literati, and other notables. With a very high staff-to-guest ratio, The Jefferson puts utmost emphasis on service; if you like, a butler will unpack your luggage and press clothes wrinkled in transit. Each room is uniquely decorated. Yours might have a four-poster bed with plump eyelet-trimmed comforter and pillow shams (many are topped with canopies), a cherrywood *bibliothèque* (bookstand) from the Napoleonic period filled with rare books, and a French Empire Louis XVI bureau.

Dining/Entertainment: Off the lobby is one of the city's premier dining rooms, offering the kind of haute fare and impeccable service you'd expect at such a prestigious establishment. American chef Andrew Roche was trained in the French tradition; his menus change seasonally. A marvelous high tea is served daily from 3 to 5pm in the reading room. There's also a cozy bar/lounge with a working fireplace, the setting for live jazz on Saturday night.

Services: 24-hour butler service, overnight shoeshine, nightly bed turndown with Godiva chocolate, morning newspaper delivery, 24-hour room and multilingual concierge service.

Facilities: Business/secretarial services; for a fee, guests have access to full health club facilities at the University Club across the street.

MODERATE

⑤ Lincoln Suites Downtown. 1823 L St. NW, Washington, DC 20036. ☎ **800/424-2970** or 202/223-4320. Fax 202/223-8546. 99 suites. A/C TV TEL. Weekdays $129–$149 suite for one person, $15 for each additional person. Weekends $69–$99 suite for two, extra person $15. Children under 16 stay free in parents' suite. AE, CB, DC, DISC, JCB, MC, V. Parking $10 (at nearby garage). Metro: Farragut North or Farragut West.

Fronted by an elegant green canopy, this property offers suite accommodations in the heart of the downtown business/shopping/restaurant area, just five blocks from the White House. Its large, comfortable suites were completely refurbished in 1995 during a multimillion-dollar renovation. Some offer full kitchens; others have refrigerators, wet bars, coffeemakers, and microwaves.

Samantha's, a plant-filled eatery with an outdoor cafe, offers reasonably priced American fare. Equally charming and affordable is the stone-walled **Beatrice,** a rather elegant grotto-like Italian restaurant open for all meals.

4 Foggy Bottom/Georgetown

VERY EXPENSIVE

❸ The Four Seasons. 2800 Pennsylvania Ave. NW, Washington, DC 20007. ☎ **800/332-3442** or 202/342-0444. Fax 202/944-2076. 166 rms, 30 suites. A/C MINIBAR TV TEL. Weekdays $325–$370 double. Weekends $245–$265 double. Extra person $30. Children under 18 stay free in parents' room. AE, CB, DC, JCB, MC, V. Parking $20. Metro: Foggy Bottom.

Since it opened in 1979, this most glamorous of Washington's haute hotels has hosted everyone from Billy Joel to King Hussein of Jordan. Open the front door and you enter a plush setting where thousands of plants and palm trees grow, and large floral arrangements enhance the gardenlike ambience. Exceptionally pretty accommodations, many of them overlooking Rock Creek Park or the C&O Canal, offer contrasting traditional dark-wood furnishings and charming print fabrics. Bedding is embellished with dust ruffles and scalloped spreads, and large desks and plump cushioned armchairs with hassocks contribute to the residential atmosphere.

Dining/Entertainment: At the elegant and highly acclaimed **Seasons**, dazzling culinary creations are complemented by an extensive and recherché wine list. The delightful **Garden Terrace** is bordered by tropical plants and flower beds and has a wall of windows overlooking the canal. It's open for lunch, a lavish Sunday jazz brunch, and classic English-style afternoon teas. And guests are given temporary membership at the warmly intimate **Desirée,** a private on-premises nightclub.

Services: Twice-daily maid service, 24-hour room service and concierge, complimentary limousine service weekdays within the District, gratis newspaper of your choice, car windows washed when you park overnight, complimentary shoeshine.

Facilities: Beauty salon, gift shop, jogging trail, business facilities, children's programs, extensive state-of-the-art fitness club (the best in town).

The Watergate Hotel. 2650 Virginia Ave. NW, Washington, DC 20037. ☎ **800/424-2736** or 202/965-2300. Fax 202/337-7915. 88 rms, 143 suites. A/C MINIBAR TV TEL. Weekdays $295–$320 double. Weekends $155 double. Suites from $420 double, with greatly reduced weekend rates. Extra person $25. Children under 18 stay free in parents' room AE, CB, DC, DISC, JCB, MC, V. Parking $10 (valet only). Metro: Foggy Bottom.

Everyone associates the Watergate with the notorious 1972 break-in that brought down the Nixon administration. But you'll forget that sordid scandal the minute you step into the hotel's sumptuous lobby, where antique furnishings grace intimate lamp-lit seating areas. The Watergate's clientele comprises high-level diplomats, business travelers, and Kennedy Center performers such as Kathleen Battle, Placido Domingo, Carol Channing, and Itzhak Perlman. Its spa facilities, indoor lap pool and sundeck, state-of-the-art health club, entertainment options, and dozens of adjacent shops also make it a fabulous choice for sophisticated travelers, including couples in search of a romantic weekend. Spacious rooms and suites are exquisitely appointed in the residential mode. Many accommodations have balconies overlooking the Potomac.

Dining/Entertainment: For many years, the Watergate was the D.C. home of celebrated French chef Jean-Louis Palladin. He recently defected to The Big Apple, and, at press time, another critically acclaimed D.C. chef, Robert Wiedemaier (who ran the

Four Seasons's premier restaurant for seven years), was set to take over and uphold this luxury hotel's reputation as a bastion of haute cuisine. The elegant **Potomac Lounge** serves British-style afternoon teas Tuesday through Sunday and features special early evening events such as caviar tastings, sushi/Japanese beer nights, and tapas/sherry nights. Friday evenings, enjoy live jazz and complimentary hors d'oeuvres in the **Crescent Bar.**

Services: 24-hour room service and concierge, full business services, nightly turndown, complimentary shoeshine and daily newspaper.

Facilities: Jacuzzi, steam, sauna, massage and spa treatments, barber/beauty salon, gift shop, jewelers (dozens of shops including designer boutiques, a supermarket, drugstore, and post office are in the adjacent complex).

MODERATE

✪ **The Georgetown Dutch Inn.** 1075 Thomas Jefferson St. NW (just below M St.), Washington, DC 20007. ☎ **800/388-2410** or 202/337-0900. Fax 202/333-6526. 47 suites. A/C TV TEL. Weekdays $125–$165 one-bedroom suite for two; $195–$300 two-bedroom duplex penthouse quad (sleeps six). Weekends $105 one-bedroom suite for two, $180–$250 penthouse suite. Rates include continental breakfast. Extra person $20. Children under 14 stay free in parents' room. AE, CB, DC, DISC, MC, V. Free parking. Metro: Foggy Bottom. Bus: M Street buses go to all major Washington tourist attractions.

Though a disproportionate number of the guests here are international embassy people, this is also a lovely choice for tourists. It's superbly located in the heart of Georgetown, just half a block from the C&O Canal (many rooms offer water views), on a charming brick-paved street lined with maple trees. Accommodations are spacious one- and two-bedroom suites, nine of them ultraluxurious duplex penthouses with 1¹/₂ baths. Staying here is like having your own Georgetown apartment, including a full living room, dining area, and kitchen (the maid does your dishes, and the hotel offers a food-shopping service). Though there's no on-premises restaurant, an extensive room-service menu is available, and there are dozens of eating places (and nightspots) within easy walking distance.

✪ **Georgetown Suites.** 1000 29th St. NW (between K and M sts.), Washington, DC 20007. ☎ **800/348-7203** or 202/298-1600. Fax 202/333-2019. 78 suites. A/C TV TEL. $139 studio suite (for two), $149 one-bedroom suite (for up to four). Weekends $99 studio suite, $109 one-bedroom suite. Rates include extended continental breakfast. Rollaways or sleep sofa $10 extra. AE, CB, DC, MC, V. Limited parking $12. Metro: Foggy Bottom.

This home-away-from-home property in the heart of Georgetown was designed to meet the needs of business travelers making extended visits, but it's marvelous even if you're spending only one night. The hotel is entered via a brick courtyard with flowering plants in terra-cotta pots and Victorian white wooden benches. Inside, off the lobby, is a comfortable lounge where tea and coffee are available throughout the day, and a substantial continental breakfast is served daily. And Monday to Thursday afternoons, complimentary beer, wine, and soft drinks are served with complimentary hors d'oeuvres between 5:30 and 7pm.

Accommodations—luxurious suites, with fully equipped kitchens, living rooms, and dining areas—offer large desks, cable TV with HBO, hair dryers, and irons and ironing boards. Among on-premises facilities are an outdoor barbecue grill for guest use, coin-op washers/dryers, and a small exercise room. Hotel services include complimentary grocery shopping and food delivery from nearby restaurants.

Georgetown Suites maintains another 136 suites (same phone, rates, and amenities) close by at 1111 30th St. NW, between K and M streets.

✪ **Hotel Lombardy.** 2019 Pennsylvania Ave. NW, Washington, DC 20006. ☎ **800/424-5486** or 202/828-2600. Fax 202/872-0503. 85 rms, 40 suites. A/C MINIBAR TV TEL. Weekdays $130–$140 double; $165–$185 suite for two. Weekends (and sometimes off-season weekdays) $69–$89 double; $119–$140 suite for two. Extra person $20. Children under 16 stay free in parents' room. AE, CB, DC, MC, V. Parking $15. Metro: Farragut West or Foggy Bottom.

From its handsome walnut-paneled lobby with carved Tudor ceilings to its appealing restaurant and rooms, the Lombardy offers a lot of luxury for the price and the location, about five blocks west of the White House. Though it serves a largely international/corporate clientele, tourists will also appreciate the Lombardy's warmly welcoming ambience. Spacious rooms are decorated in residential 1930s northern Italian mode, with animal-skin–motif throw rugs, ornate mirrors, decorative wrought-iron beds, and rich tapestried drapes; all but 20 rooms have fully equipped kitchens and dining nooks. Coin-op washers/dryers are located in the basement.

Moderately priced and open for all meals, The **Café Lombardy,** a sunny glass-enclosed restaurant and lounge, serves contemporary northern Italian fare that is prepared with considerable panache. It's frequented by many local businesspeople.

S **Howard Johnson's Premier Hotel.** 2601 Virginia Ave. NW (at New Hampshire Ave.), Washington, DC 20037. ☎ **800/965-6869** or 202/965-2700. Fax 202/337-5417. 192 rms. A/C TV TEL. $89–$139 double, concierge floor $20 additional. Extra person $10. Children under 18 stay free in parents' room. AE, DC, DISC, JCB, MC, V. Parking $9 (maximum height 6'2"). Metro: Foggy Bottom.

Just two blocks from the Kennedy Center, with a nicely landscaped porte cochere entrance, this flagship HoJo property—the first of its more upscale "Premier" group—recently underwent a $2.5 million renovation of rooms and public areas. Not only is it looking very spiffy, it now offers many assets unusual in its price range, including a concierge and a business center. Though its clientele is about 60% government and corporate, pluses for families include a large L-shaped rooftop pool with a sundeck, a workout room, a Ping-Pong room, video games, coin-op washers and dryers, sightseeing bus tours, and a gift shop. Rooms are attractively decorated in rich earth tones (half with balconies) and offer desks, small refrigerators, and safes. Local calls are free. **America's Best,** an upscale contemporary diner with an exhibition kitchen, serves all meals and provides room service; a bar/lounge adjoins.

☼ **State Plaza Hotel**. 2117 E. St. NW, Washington, DC 20037. ☎ **800/424-2859** or 202/861-8200. Fax 202/659-8601. 221 suites. A/C MINIBAR TV TEL. Weekdays $125–$150 efficiency suite for one or two people. $175–$225 a large one-bedroom suite (with dining room) for up to four people. Weekend (also, subject to availability, off-season weeknights) $69–$109. (Rates include continental breakfast.) Extra person $20. Children under 18 stay free in parents' room. AE, DC, MC, V. Parking $12. Metro: Foggy Bottom.

This all-suite hotel is deservedly popular with those traveling on government business (it's close to the World Bank and the State Department), as well as performers from the nearby Kennedy Center. It's also a good choice for tourists, especially those planning to attend plays and concerts while in town. And traveling business-people will appreciate the free local phone calls and no-fee long-distance access.

I was charmed from the moment I entered the State Plaza's antique-furnished, flower-filled lobby. The spacious accommodations (all with kitchen) are just lovely, decorated in pastel hues and pretty chintz fabrics, with Federal-style mahogany beds, Queen Anne chests, and framed botanical prints embellishing the walls. Among your amenities are coin-op washers and dryers and a fully equipped fitness center. The pristine **Garden Café,** with an awning-covered patio for alfresco dining, features American regional cuisine, highlighting market-fresh fare.

5   Dupont Circle

VERY EXPENSIVE

✪ **Renaissance Mayflower.** 1127 Connecticut Ave. NW (between L and M sts.) Washington, DC 20036. ☎ **800/HOTELS-1** or 202/347-3000. Fax 202/776-9182. 581 rms. 78 suites. A/C MINIBAR TV TEL. Weekdays $275–$335 double. Weekends $125–$170 double. Extra person $25. Children under 18 stay free in parents' room. Inquire about "summer value rates." AE, CB, DC, DISC, JCB, MC, V. Parking $12. Metro: Farragut North.

The Stouffer Renaissance–owned Mayflower (opened in 1925) is the grande dame of Washington hotels. A major restoration in the 1980s uncovered large skylights and renewed the lobby's pink marble bas-relief frieze and the spectacular block-long promenade. Ceilings and columns were regilded and Italianate murals rediscovered. In the graciously appointed guest rooms, hardwood crown moldings adorn high ceilings. Cream moiré wall coverings are complemented by accents of claret and teal, and mahogany furnishings are period reproductions (Queen Anne, Sheraton, Chippendale, Hepplewhite).

Dining/Entertainment: Washington lawyers and lobbyists gather for power breakfasts in the **Café Promenade.** Under a beautiful domed skylight, the restaurant is adorned with Edward Laning's murals, crystal chandeliers, ficus trees, marble columns, and lovely flower arrangements. A full English tea is served here afternoons Monday to Saturday.

The clubby, mahogany-paneled **Town and Country** is the setting for light buffet lunches and complimentary cocktail-hour hors d'oeuvres. The **Lobby Court,** a Starbucks espresso bar just opposite the front desk, features coffee and fresh-baked pastries each morning, piano bar and cocktails later in the day.

Services: Coffee and newspaper with wake-up call, 24-hour room service, twice-daily maid service, complimentary overnight shoeshine, concierge.

Facilities: Business center, full on-premises fitness center, florist, gift shop, Cartier jeweler.

✪ **The Ritz-Carlton.** 2100 Massachusetts Ave. NW, Washington, DC 20008. ☎ **800/241-3333** or 202/293-2100. Fax 202/293-0641. 206 rms, 32 suites. A/C MINIBAR TV TEL. Weekdays $265–$325 double, $375 Club double. Weekends $195 double. Extra person free. AE, CB, DC, MC, V. Valet parking $20. Metro: Dupont Circle.

Built in 1924 and totally renovated in 1995, this D.C. haunt of the rich and famous is a gem, from its richly walnut-paneled lobby to its pristine Oriental-carpeted hallways and lovely residential rooms with marble baths. The latter, decorated in muted tones, are handsomely furnished with traditional dark-wood pieces. Windows are framed by elegant tasseled draperies, walls hung with French architectural watercolor renderings.

Dining/Entertainment: The cheerful, pubby **Jockey Club** has long been one of Washington's most prominent restaurants; executive chef Hidemasa Yamamoto brings Eastern nuance to classic continental cookery. The elegant **Fairfax Club,** with a working fireplace, is an intimate setting for cocktails, light fare, piano bar, jazz, and dance music nightly; it's a private club to which hotel guests are admitted as temporary members.

Services: Complimentary morning newspaper delivery and shoeshine, nightly turndown with imported chocolates, 24-hour concierge and room service.

Facilities: Fitness room, business center.

EXPENSIVE

Canterbury Hotel. 1733 N St. NW, Washington, DC 20036. ☎ **800/ 424-2950** or 202/393-3000. Fax 202/785-9581. 99 junior suites. A/C MINIBAR TV TEL. Weekdays $160–$400 suite for two (most are under $200). Weekends and off-season weekdays $109–$140 per room. Extra person $20. Children under 12 stay free in parents' room. AE, CB, DC, DISC, MC, V. Parking $14. Metro: Dupont Circle.

Located on a lovely residential street, this small, European-style hostelry is central to almost all major tourist attractions. Its prestigious address was once the home of both Theodore Roosevelt and Franklin D. Roosevelt; although the hotel building is not the actual town house they occupied, it does attempt to recapture the elegance of an earlier era. Each room is actually a junior suite, with a sofa/ sitting area, dressing room, and kitchenette or full kitchen. Attractively decorated in residential style, these spacious accommodations offer 18th-century mahogany English-reproduction furnishings (a few have four-poster beds).

Dining/Entertainment: A new restaurant called **Brighton-on-N** serves continental fare at all meals. And the Tudor-beamed **Union Jack Pub,** complete with dartboard and a menu featuring fish-and-chips, is the perfect place to relax after a busy day on the town.

Services: Nightly turndown with fine chocolate, room service, morning delivery of the *Washington Post,* complimentary *Wall Street Journal* available in lobby and restaurant.

Facilities: Guests enjoy gratis use of the nearby YMCA/National Capital Health Center's extensive workout facilities, including an indoor lap pool.

Adams-Morgan & Dupont Circle Accommodations

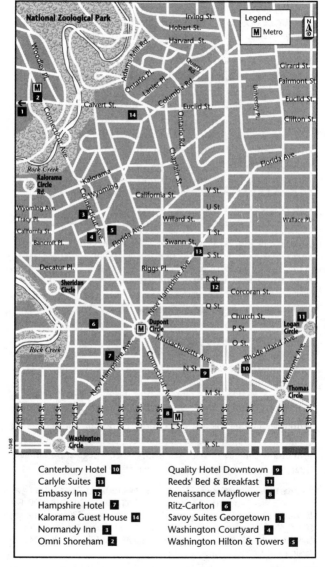

Canterbury Hotel 10
Carlyle Suites 13
Embassy Inn 12
Hampshire Hotel 7
Kalorama Guest House 14
Normandy Inn 3
Omni Shoreham 2

Quality Hotel Downtown 9
Reeds' Bed & Breakfast 11
Renaissance Mayflower 8
Ritz-Carlton 6
Savoy Suites Georgetown 1
Washington Courtyard 4
Washington Hilton & Towers 5

MODERATE

Hampshire Hotel. 1310 New Hampshire Ave. NW (at N St.), Washington, DC 20036. ☎ **800/368-5691** or 202/296-7600. Fax 202/293-2476. 82 junior suites. A/C MINIBAR TV TEL. Weekdays $129–$159 suite for two. Weekends and off-season weekdays $89–$119 per suite. Inquire, too, about low summer rates. Extra person $15. Children under 12 stay free in parents' room. AE, CB, DC, DISC, JCB, MC, V. Parking $12. Metro: Dupont Circle.

Though it's on a quiet tree-lined street, the Hampshire is within easy walking distance of Georgetown and two blocks from Dupont Circle—convenient to numerous restaurants and nightspots. Spacious junior-suite accommodations, perfect for families, are furnished with 18th-century mahogany reproductions and offer lots of closet space, big dressing rooms, couches, coffee tables, and desks; most also have kitchenettes.

The delightful **Peacock Bistro,** its assets including an outdoor cafe and a fresh juice bar, serves up deli sandwiches, salads, pastas, and more at all meals; a good choice of fresh-baked muffins and bagels at breakfast is a plus for guests. A bar/lounge adjoins.

✪ **Normandy Inn.** 2118 Wyoming Ave. NW (at Connecticut Ave.), Washington, DC 20008. ☎ **800/424-3729** or 202/483-1350. Fax 202/387-8241. 75 rms. A/C TV TEL. Weekdays $113 double. Weekends $79 double. Extra person $10. Children under 12 stay free in parents' room. AE, CB, DC, MC, V. Parking $10. Metro: Dupont Circle.

This gracious small hotel—perfect for travelers who prefer a quiet, low-key environment—blends in perfectly with neighboring embassies. Pristinely charming rooms have tapestry-upholstered mahogany furnishings in 18th-century styles, floral-print bedspreads, and gilt-framed botanical prints gracing the walls. Amenities include refrigerators and coffeemakers.

Continental breakfast is available in the comfortable **Tea Room** off the lobby for $5.50. Coffee and tea are served throughout the day from an antique oak sideboard in the Tea Room, and cookies are put out at 3pm. In nice weather you can take these snacks outside to umbrella tables on a garden patio. Tuesday nights, complimentary wine and cheese are served to guests.

Quality Hotel Downtown. 1315 16th St. NW (between Rhode Island Ave. and O St.), Washington, DC 20036. ☎ **800/368-5689** or 202/232-8000. Fax 202/667-9827. 125 rms, 10 suites. A/C TV TEL. Weekdays $89–$129 double; $99–$140 one-bedroom suite. Weekends $79–$99 double. Extra person $15. Children under 18 stay free in parents' room. AE, CB, DC, DISC, JCB, MC, V. Parking $10.50. Metro: Dupont Circle.

The very central and pleasantly plush-looking Quality offers a lot of bang for your buck. For openers, all of the rooms here are actually large suites, with a kitchen; they feature French country pine or dark-wood furnishings in traditional styles. Most contain dining areas and sofas, and all have dressing rooms. A few rooms feature Murphy beds—an innovation appreciated by people who conduct business in their hotel rooms. Room service, a gift shop, coin-op washers/dryers, and a full-service business center are additional pluses. Gray Line tours depart from the lobby.

The Quality's restaurant, **Wondi's Cafe,** is pleasant and bright. Open for all meals, it serves Asian specialties in addition to American and continental fare. **Bleeker's Lounge,** a cozy pub off the lobby, has a billiards table.

Washington Courtyard by Marriott. 1900 Connecticut Ave. NW (at Leroy Place), Washington, DC 20009. ☎ **800/842-4211** or 202/332-9300. Fax 202/328-7039. 147 rms. A/C TV TEL. Weekdays $120–$170 double. Weekends $69–$120 double. Extra person $15. Children under 18 stay free in parents' room. AE, CB, DC, DISC, MC, V. Parking $10. Metro: Dupont Circle.

The Courtyard has the well-heeled look of a much more expensive hostelry with the amenities to match. You'll be pleased from the minute you step into the chandeliered lobby, where classical music is always playing. Guest rooms, off charming hallways, are equipped with coffeemakers and hair dryers. Accommodations on higher floors provide panoramic views, and some rooms have stocked minibars.

In addition to an outdoor pool and sundeck, facilities include **Claret's,** a rather elegant restaurant serving moderately priced American fare at breakfast and dinner. **Bailey's,** a clubby bar, adjoins. There's a small exercise room on the premises, and, for a fee, guests can use the very well-equipped Washington Sports Club just across the street. Sightseeing tours can be picked up across the street at the deluxe Washington Hilton and Towers.

INEXPENSIVE

Carlyle Suites. 1731 New Hampshire Ave. NW (between R and S sts.), Washington, DC 20009. ☎ **800/964-5377** or 202/234-3200. Fax 202/387-0085. 176 suites. A/C TV TEL. Weekdays $69–$139 studio suite for two; $150–$180 one-bedroom suite. Weekends $64.50 suite for two. Extra person $10. Children under 18 stay free in parents' suite. AE, DC, MC, V. Free limited parking. Metro: Dupont Circle.

Spacious accommodations with small but complete kitchens and dining nooks (a huge Safeway is conveniently located two blocks away) make Carlyle Suites a good family choice. The property occupies a converted art deco landmark building on a quiet residential street near Dupont Circle.

Unlike public areas, suites eschew the art deco motif, decorated instead in cheerful pastel hues. They come equipped with huge closets and cozy seating areas with sofas.

The art deco **Neon Cafe** serves American/continental fare and features live music weekend nights. There are coin-op washers/dryers on the premises, and guests enjoy free access to a well-equipped health club nearby.

BED & BREAKFASTS

Embassy Inn. 1627 16th St. NW (between Q and R sts.), Washington, DC 20009. ☎ **800/423-9111** or 202/234-7800. Fax 202/234-3309. 38 rms (all with bath). A/C TV TEL. Weekdays $79–$99 double. Weekends $59 double. Rates include continental breakfast. Extra person $10. Children under 14 stay free in parents' room. AE, CB, DC, MC, V. Metro: Dupont Circle.

This 1910 Federal-style brick building, a former inn, was rescued from demolition some years back, spruced up, and transformed once more into a quaintly charming small hotel—a great place for a romantic getaway. The comfortably furnished lobby doubles as a parlor where breakfast (including fresh-baked muffins and croissants) is served daily, and fresh coffee brews all day; it's complimentary, along with tea, cocoa, and evening sherry. You can buy Tourmobile tickets here, pick up maps and brochures, or request sundries you may have forgotten (toothbrush, razor, and the like).

Rooms are furnished with 18th-century–style mahogany pieces. Bedspreads and curtains in attractive floral prints, pale-lemon walls hung with turn-of-the-century lithographs and historic prints of Washington, and new carpeting combine to create a homey atmosphere. Baths have showers only (no tubs). *Note:* There is no elevator, and there's street parking only.

✪ **The Reeds' Bed & Breakfast.** P.O. Box 12011, Washington, DC 20005. ☎ **202/238-3510**. 6 rms (with shared bath), 1 apt (with bath). A/C TV TEL. $60–$85 double with breakfast. Apt (no breakfast) $75–$85 for two. Extra person $15. Children 18 and under $10; crib $5 extra. AE, DC, MC, V. Parking $5. Metro: McPherson Square or Dupont Circle (about six blocks from either).

Even by the most exacting standards, the Reeds' restored Victorian mansion is a masterpiece of good taste. When Charles and Jackie Reed bought the place in 1975, they combed antique shops and auction houses for period/reproduction furnishings and art, landscaped the garden, and added fountains. Today, the house is a gorgeous Victorian/art nouveau showplace with carved fireplace mantels and rich oak and mahogany paneling. Breakfast is served at a Victorian banquet table in a formal dining room complete with 19th-century stained-glass windows and a working fireplace.

The rooms, reached by a grand carved-oak staircase with intricate fretwork, are charmingly decorated in period styles. Completely separate from the main building is a one-bedroom apartment with a private bath and a fully equipped kitchen; it easily accommodates five people. Guests are encouraged to use the gorgeous Victorian-style lattice porch, fountained patio, and barbecue facilities. Breakfast is continental (featuring fresh-baked breads and muffins) on weekdays, a full bacon-and-eggs meal on weekends. A computer and a treadmill are available on request, and there's a washer and dryer for guest use. No charge for local calls here.

Because the Reeds' doesn't take walk-ins, the address above is a P.O. box. You must call to reserve.

6 North Washington/Adams-Morgan

VERY EXPENSIVE

Omni Shoreham. 2500 Calvert St. NW (at Connecticut Ave.), Washington, DC 20008. ☎ **800/228-2121** or 202/234-0700. Fax 202/265-5333. 745 rms, 55 suites. A/C TV TEL. Weekdays $205–$285 double. Off-season and weekends $89 double. Extra person $20. Children under 18 stay free in parents' room. AE, CB, DC, DISC, JCB, MC, V. Parking $14. Metro: Woodley Park–Zoo.

Though the Shoreham is primarily a meeting and convention venue, leisure travelers should consider it for its numerous recreational facilities: jogging trails, three tennis courts, an Olympic-size swimming pool and a kiddie pool, and an excellent health club. An extensive children's activity program is a plus for families. Set on 11 acres adjacent to verdant Rock Creek Park, the Shoreham is a deluxe resort hotel right in the heart of the city. Built in 1930, it has been the scene of inaugural balls for every president since FDR. Spacious guest rooms are beautifully decorated.

Dining/Entertainment: The elegant **Monique Café et Brasserie,** reminiscent of the famed La Coupole in Paris, specializes in continental/American fare with an emphasis on steak and seafood. Rock Creek Park provides a fitting backdrop for the lushly planted **Garden Court,** a popular cocktail lounge under a 35-foot vaulted ceiling. The hotel's nightlife centers on the art deco **Marquee Cabaret** (details in chapter 8).

Services: Room service, concierge.

Facilities: Shops; travel/sightseeing desk; business center; 10 miles of jogging, hiking, and bicycle trails (winding off into Rock Creek Park), plus a $1^1/2$-mile Perrier parcourse with 18 exercise stations.

Washington Hilton & Towers. 1919 Connecticut Ave. NW (at T St.), Washington, DC 20009. ☎ **800/HILTONS** or 202/483-3000. Fax 202/797-5755. 1,041 rms, 82 suites. A/C MINIBAR TV TEL. Weekdays $230–$270 double; Towers rooms $265–$305 double. Weekends (and selected weekdays and holidays) $105 per room, $135 for Towers rooms. Extra person $20. Children of any age stay free in parents' room. AE, CB, DC, DISC, JCB, MC, V. Parking $12. Metro: Dupont Circle.

This is a kind of superhotel/resort offering every imaginable amenity. The Hilton hosts numerous conventions and functions: inaugural balls, debutante cotillions, state banquets, and society shindigs. Rooms are cheerful, attractively furnished, and equipped with bathroom scales, irons, and ironing boards; many offer panoramic views of Washington.

Dining/Entertainment: The handsome mahogany-paneled **1919 Grill** specializes in steaks, seafoods, and pasta dinners. The cheerful **Capital Café,** serves buffet meals and coffee shop fare. A poolside eatery serves light fare under a striped tent top in season. The sports-themed **McClellan's,** a clubby lounge with a handsome brass-railed mahogany bar and commodious leather chairs, offers sporting events aired on four TV monitors. And **Capital Court,** an elegant lobby lounge, features a nightly piano bar.

Services: Room service during restaurant hours, nightly bed turndown, transportation/sightseeing desk.

Facilities: Extensive health club facilities, a large nightlit heated outdoor pool, children's pool, three nightlit tennis courts, shuffleboard, bike rental, jogging path, lobby shops, comprehensive business center, shoeshine stand, car-rental desk, ATM machine with foreign-currency capability.

INEXPENSIVE

Savoy Suites Georgetown. 2505 Wisconsin Ave. NW (above Calvert St.), Washington, DC 20007. ☎ **800/944-5377** or 202/337-9700. Fax 202/337-3644. 150 rms. A/C TV TEL. Weekdays $69–$139 double. Weekends $64.50 double. Extra person $10. Children under 18 stay free in parents' room. AE, DC, MC, V. Free parking. Even-numbered buses stop in front of the hotel and connect to Georgetown, Dupont Circle, and the Mall.

This inexpensive luxury hotel in a sedate embassy district (just five minutes from the heart of Georgetown by bus or car) offers a lot in its price range. Many restaurants are within walking distance, and Washington National Cathedral is just four blocks away.

Accommodations, half of them suites with fully stocked kitchens and dining areas, are decorated with French provincial pieces. Many have in-room steam baths or Jacuzzis, and about half offer panoramic city views over the treetops.

A stunning art nouveau lobby is the setting for a garden-motif restaurant called **On Wisconsin,** which features American/continental fare. In warm weather the Savoy also has a tree-shaded outdoor cafe serving light fare. Other on-premises amenities include a small sundeck and coin-op washers/dryers. There's a complimentary shuttle bus to and from the Woodley Park Metro stop. Guests also enjoy free use of a well-equipped nearby health club with an Olympic-size pool.

BED & BREAKFASTS

⑤ Kalorama Guest House. 1854 Mintwood Place NW (between 19th St. and Columbia Rd.), Washington, DC 20009. ☎ **202/667-6369.** Fax 202/319-1262. 31 rms (12 with bath). A/C. $45–$75 double with shared bath, $60–$105 double with bath; $95 two-room suite ($5 each additional occupant). Rates include continental breakfast. AE, CB, DC, DISC, MC, V. Limited parking $7. Metro: Woodley Park–Zoo.

This San Francisco–style B&B guest house was so successful, it expanded in a short time from a six-bedroom Victorian town house (at 1854 Mintwood) to include four houses on Mintwood Place and two on Cathedral Avenue NW between 26th and 27th streets (☎ **202/328-0860;** fax 202/328-8730). The Mintwood Place location is near Metro stations, dozens of restaurants, nightspots, and shops. And the Cathedral Avenue houses, even closer to the Metro, offer proximity to Rock Creek Park and the National Zoo.

Owner Roberta Pieczenik regularly haunts antique stores, flea markets, and auctions to find beautiful furnishings and accouterments for her rooms and public areas. At 1854 is the cheerful breakfast room with plant-filled windows. The morning meal includes bagels, croissants, and English muffins. Other amenities here: a seldom-used TV, a phone (local calls are free), a phone for long-distance credit- or charge-card calls, a washing machine and dryer, and a refrigerator. Upstairs in the parlor, which has a working fireplace, there's a decanter of sherry on the buffet; magazines, games, and current newspapers are provided. There's a garden behind the house with umbrella tables. Though the rooms have no phones, incoming calls are answered around the clock, so people can leave messages for you. *Note:* Some of the buildings are non-smoking.

7 Capitol Hill/Mall

EXPENSIVE

🄢 **Capitol Hill Suites.** 200 C St. SE, Washington, DC 20003. ☎ **800/ 424-9165** or 202/543-6000. Fax 202/547-2608. 152 suites. A/C TV TEL. Weekdays $159–$199 double. Weekends $99–$119 double. Extra person $20. Children under 18 stay free in parents' room. AE, CB, DC, DISC, MC, V. Valet parking $12. Metro: Capitol South.

This well-run all-suite property comprises two converted apartment houses on a residential street close to the Library of Congress, the Capitol, and Mall attractions. The spacious accommodations are ideal for families; all rooms offer full kitchens or kitchenettes and dining areas—complete living and dining rooms in one-bedroom units. Decor is residential, with 18th-century mahogany reproduction furnishings and museum art prints adorning the walls.

There are no on-premises dining facilities, but a food market and about 20 restaurants are close by (many of them deliver to the hotel). Weekdays, gratis drinks and snacks are served in the hotel lobby at cocktail hour. The *Washington Post* is delivered to your door Monday to Saturday. There are coin-op washers/dryers, and guests enjoy free use of extensive facilities at the nearby Washington Sports Club.

MODERATE

✪ **Channel Inn.** 650 Water St. SW (at 7th St. and Maine Ave.), Washington, DC 20024. ☎ **800/368-5668** or 202/554-2400. Fax 202/863-1164. 100 rms. A/C TV TEL. Weekdays $110–$125 double. Weekends $80–$90 double. Extra person $10. Children under 12 stay free in parents' room. Call toll-free number for best rates. AE, CB, DC, DISC, JCB, MC, V. Free parking. Metro: Waterfront.

Washington's only waterfront hotel, the Channel Inn caters largely to government employees, but it's also a great choice for leisure travelers, close to a Metro stop and within easy walking distance of the Mall. Most rooms offer wonderful views of the boat-filled Washington Channel. They are beautifully decorated with 18th-century–style mahogany furnishings and floral chintz bedspreads and drapes. Some have high cathedral ceilings; all have balconies.

Pier 7, an inviting continental/seafood restaurant with marina views, serves moderately priced fare. A sunny glass-walled coffee shop offers cafeteria-style breakfasts. And the immense **Engine Room** lounge offers a happy hour buffet of free hors d'oeuvres and a low-priced raw bar.

There is a concierge, and room service is available during restaurant hours. Guests enjoy complimentary access to the fully equipped Waterside Fitness Club and outdoor pool/sundeck; a golf course and indoor/outdoor tennis courts are within walking distance; and the waterfront is an ideal place for jogging.

Dining

*T*he District supports dozens of first-rate restaurants with nationally renowned chefs who are not only up on the latest culinary trends, but are creating them as well. In a city filled with foreign embassies, numerous eateries also cater to the international contingent, offering everything from Spanish tapas to Ethiopian doro watt. It all adds up to an excitingly diverse dining scene—one where you're likely to rub shoulders with senators and Supreme Court justices over gravlax and champagne.

Washington's upper-crust diners lost one of their favorite haute-cuisine bastions in 1996, when flamboyant French chef Jean Louis Palladin closed his eponymous restaurant at the Watergate; his movable feast has traveled north to the Big Apple.

HOW TO READ THE LISTINGS

The restaurants listed below are grouped first by location, then alphabetically by price. I've used the following price categories: **very expensive** (the average main course at dinner is more than $20), **expensive** ($16 to $20), **moderate** ($10 to $15), and **inexpensive** ($10 and under).

Keep in mind that the above categories refer to *dinner* prices, but some very expensive restaurants offer affordable lunches and/or early bird dinners. Also, I'm assuming that you're not going to stint when you order. Some restaurants, for instance, offer entrées ranging from $12 to $20. In most cases you can dine for less if you order carefully.

Note: A Metro station is indicated when it's within walking distance of a restaurant. If you need bus-routing information, call **202/637-7000.**

Although my favorite restaurants are marked with a star, I must admit that every restaurant listed here is actually a favorite of mine. And this is only a sampling of the District's superb cuisine; for more comprehensive coverage of restaurants, consult the complete *Frommer's Washington D.C.*

1 Best Bets

- **Best Spot for a Romantic Dinner:** When the weather is balmy, enjoy a tête-à-tête under the grape and wisteria arbor at the **Iron Gate,** 1734 N St. NW (☎ **202/737-1370**); if it's cold, snuggle by the blazing fireplace within.
- **Best Spot for a Business Lunch:** No setting can match the ambience of success and affluence at the **Willard Room,** 1401 Pennsylvania Ave. NW (☎ **202/637-7440**), where, in fact, the term *power lunch* was coined. Large tables are well spaced for privacy. The food's great, too.
- **Best Spot for a Celebration: Citronelle,** 3000 M St. NW (☎ **202/625-2150**), where every dish is an exquisite little culinary celebration, is fancy enough for special occasions but casual enough to be fun.
- **Best Spot for a Night on the Town:** For an exuberant evening, dine to a Brazilian beat at **Coco Loco,** 810 7th St. NW (☎ **202/ 289-2626**), and stay on to dance the night away.
- **Best View:** Washington Harbour, with its stunning flower-bedded esplanade, is the setting for **Sequoia,** 3000 K St. NW (☎ **202/944-4200**), where a multilevel garden terrace offers a panoramic vista of the Potomac and verdant Theodore Roosevelt Island beyond; if you're dining inside, ask for the bar-level alcove that overlooks the Harbour's spectacular fountain as well as the Potomac—best seat in the house.
- **Best Pizza:** At **Pizzeria Paradiso's,** 2029 P St. NW (☎ **202/ 223-1245**), peerless chewy-crusted pizzas are baked in an oak-burning oven and crowned with delicious toppings; you'll find great salads and sandwiches on fresh-baked foccacia here, too.
- **Best Southern Cuisine: Vidalia,** 1990 M St. NW (☎ **202/ 659-1990**). Chef Jeff Buben calls his cuisine "provincial American," a euphemism for fancy fare that includes cheese grits and biscuits in cream gravy.
- **Best Southwestern Cuisine:** It doesn't get more exciting than **Red Sage,** 605 14th St. NW (☎ **202/638-4444**), where superstar chef Mark Miller brings contemporary culinary panache to traditional Southwestern cookery; keep his **Cafe and Chili Bar** in mind for Red Sage cuisine and ambience at lower prices.
- **Best Desserts:** Hot chocolate cake with orange ginger sauce at **Citronelle** (see address and telephone above), or, for that matter,

any dessert at Citronelle, domain of award-winning patissier Michel Richard.

- **Best Diet Meal:** At **Legal Sea Foods,** 2020 K St. NW (☎ 202/496-1111), follow up a cup of light clam chowder (made without butter, cream, or flour) with an entrée of grilled fresh fish and vegetables and a superb sorbet for dessert.

- **Best Late-Night Dining:** Washington's not a late-night restaurant town unless you count the action at 5 or 6am when the workaholic population gets into gear for early office arrival. D.C.'s top chefs hang out after hours at **Bistro Français,** 3124 M St. in Georgetown (☎ 202/338-3830), exchanging culinary gossip over coquilles St. Jacques; it's open until 3am Sunday through Thursday, 4am Friday and Saturday.

- **Best for Families:** Take the kids to the **Dirksen South Buffet Room,** 1st and C streets NW (☎ 202/224-4249), which involves a subway ride inside the Capitol; the affordable fixed-price buffet includes a make-your-own-sundae bar.

- **Best Brunch:** Combine a Kennedy Center tour or Sunday matinee with a lavish brunch at its on-premises **Roof Terrace Restaurant** (☎ 202/416-8555). This ornate establishment invites guests into the kitchen where a stunning array of food is laid out. Your meal includes a glass of champagne or a mimosa, and musicians (flute and guitar) entertain while you dine. Price is $22.95, hours Sunday 11:30am to 3pm. An à la carte menu is also available.

- **Best Afternoon Tea:** With lush plantings and windowed walls overlooking the C&O Canal, the divine **Garden Terrace** at the Four Seasons Hotel (☎ 202/342-0444), provides soothing piano music during afternoon tea Monday through Saturday from 3 to 5pm and Sunday from 3:30 to 5pm. For $15 you can enjoy a selection of finger sandwiches, fresh fruit tartlets, assorted English tea breads and biscuits, a Scottish sultana scone with double Devonshire cream and homemade preserves, and a pot of fresh-brewed tea. Vintage ports, sherries, and champagne are also available.

- **Best Breakfast:** The plush **Old Ebbitt Grill,** 675 15th St. NW (☎ 202/347-4801), opens for breakfast at 7:30am weekdays and 8am Saturday and features reasonably priced items ranging from cranberry muffins to thick slabs of French toast with sausage and maple syrup.

2 Restaurants by Cuisine

AFRICAN (SEE ALSO ETHIOPIAN)

Bukom Café (Adams-Morgan, *I*)

AMERICAN

America (Union Station, *M*)

Café des Artistes at the Corcoran (the Corcoran, *I*)

Cafeteria (Library of Congress, *I*)

Cashion's Eat Place (Adams-Morgan, *M*)

Clyde's (Foggy Bottom/Georgetown, *M*)

Concourse Buffet (National Gallery of Art, *I*)

Dirksen Senate Office Building South Buffet Room (the Capitol, *I*)

Encore Cafe (Kennedy Center, *I*)

Flight Line (National Air and Space Museum, *I*)

Food Court (Union Station, *I*)

House of Representatives Restaurant (the Capitol, *I*)

Kramerbooks and Afterwords, A Café (Dupont Circle, *M*)

Montpelier Room (Library of Congress, *I*)

Old Ebbitt Grill (Downtown/Capitol Hill, *M*)

Reeve's Restaurant and Bakery (Downtown/Capitol Hill, *I*)

Roof Terrace Restaurant (Kennedy Center, *VE*)

Sequoia (Foggy Bottom/Georgetown, *M*)

1789 (Foggy Bottom/Georgetown, *VE*)

Sholl's Cafeteria (Near the White House, *I*)

Supreme Court Cafeteria (Supreme Court, *I*)

Trio (Dupont Circle, *I*)

The Tombs (Foggy Bottom/Georgetown, *I*)

Vidalia (Dupont Circle, *E*)

The Willard Room (Downtown/Capitol Hill, *VE*)

The Wright Place (National Air and Space Museum, *I*)

ASIAN

Asia Nora (Dupont Circle, *E*)

Raku (Dupont Circle, *I*)

CHILEAN

Julia's (Adams-Morgan, *I*)

CHINESE

City Lights of China (Dupont Circle, *M*)

Sichuan Pavilion (Near the White House, *M*)

CONTINENTAL/INTERNATIONAL

Cities (Adams-Morgan, *E*)

National Gallery Restaurants (National Gallery of Art, *I*)

Key to Abbreviations: *E*=Expensive; *I*=Inexpensive; *M*=Moderate; *VE*=Very Expensive

Seasons (Foggy Bottom
Georgetown, *VE*)

ETHIOPIAN

Meskerem (Adams-
Morgan, *I*)
Zed's (Foggy Bottom/
Georgetown, *I*)

FRENCH

Citronelle (Foggy Bottom
Georgetown, *VE*)
Le Lion d'Or (Near the
White House, *VE*)

INDIAN

Aditi (Foggy Bottom/
Georgetown, *M*)
Bombay Palace (Near the
White House, *M*)

ITALIAN

Pizzeria Paradiso (Dupont
Circle, *I*)

LATIN AMERICAN

Gabriel (Dupont Circle, *E*)

MEDITERRANEAN

Iron Gate Restaurant
and Garden (Dupont
Circle, *E*)

MEXICAN

Coco Loco (Downtown/
Capitol Hill, *M*)
Mixtec (Adams-Morgan, *I*)

ORGANIC

Nora (Dupont Circle, *VE*)

SANDWICHES/SALADS/PASTRY

Chesapeake Bagel Bakery
(Downtown/Capitol
Hill, *I*)
Georgetown Bagelry (Foggy
Bottom/Georgetown, *I*)
Patisserie Café Didier (Foggy
Bottom/Georgetown, *I*)
Uptown Bakers (Near the
National Zoo, *I*)

SEAFOOD

Legal Sea Foods (Near the
White House, *E*)
The Sea Catch (Foggy
Bottom/Georgetown, *E*)

SOUTHWESTERN/SOUTHERN/WESTERN

B. Smith's (Union
Station, *E*)
Peyote Cafe (Adams-
Morgan, *M*)
Red Sage (Downtown/
Capitol Hill, *VE*)

STEAKS/CHOPS

Prime Rib (Near the White
House, *VE*)

VIETNAMESE

Miss Saigon (Adams-
Morgan, *M*)

3 Downtown/Capitol Hill

VERY EXPENSIVE

✪ **Red Sage.** 605 14th St. NW (at F St.). ☎ **202/638-4444.** Reservations recommended. Main courses $11–$16 at lunch, $16–$31.95 at dinner; Cafe/Chili Bar items are almost all under $10. AE, CB, DC, MC, V. Restaurant Mon–Fri

11:30am–2:15pm and 5:30–10:30pm, Sat 5:30–10:30pm, Sun 5–10pm. Cafe/Chili Bar Mon–Sat 11:30am–11:30pm, Sun 4:30–11:30pm. Metro: Metro Center. WESTERN/CONTEMPORARY AMERICAN.

Red Sage is the creation of nationally renowned chef Mark Miller. Down a curved stairway, the main dining room comprises a warren of cozy, candlelit alcoves under a curved ponderosa log-beamed ceiling. Upstairs are the more casual (albeit gorgeous) **Cafe** and high-ceilinged **Chili Bar,** which serve inexpensive light fare. Exquisite food presentations at Red Sage are as intricately nuanced as the dishes themselves. A filet mignon–like entrée of oak-grilled rare tuna glazed with a merlot/habenero chile reduction is served atop cowboy beans (pintos studded with nuggets of smoked bacon, chipped garlic, and roasted jalapeños) and accompanied by spicy sautéed spinach, fried parsnips, and tomatoes in a lemony sage dressing. The wine list is extensive and well researched.

The Willard Room. In the Willard Inter-Continental Hotel, 1401 Pennsylvania Ave. NW. ☎ **202/637-7440.** Reservations recommended. Main courses $9.75–$16.75 at lunch, $17–$25.50 at dinner; three-course fixed-price lunch $24; fixed-price dinners $36–$45 ($49–$65 with wines); afternoon tea $14.50. AE, DC, DISC, JCB, MC, V. Mon–Fri 7:30–10am and 11:30am–2pm (afternoon tea 2:30–4pm); nightly 6–10pm. Metro: Metro Center. AMERICAN REGIONAL/CLASSIC EUROPEAN.

The clientele here includes upper-crust Washingtonians, visiting presidents and premiers, and often a king or two. The dining room has been restored to its original turn-of-the-century splendor, with gorgeous carved oak paneling, chandeliers, and a faux-bois beamed ceiling. The menu changes with the seasons, but Chef Guy Reinbolt, like many great *cuisiniers,* trained in Alsace; he added creole and Southern dishes to his repertoire during stints in Memphis and New Orleans. A list of more than 250 fine wines mentions Thomas Jefferson's notes from his voyages in the vineyards of France.

MODERATE

✪ **Coco Loco.** 810 7th St. NW (between H and I sts.). ☎ **202/289-2626.** Reservations recommended. Tapas mostly $3.95–$7.95; churrascaria with antipasti bar $15.95 lunch, $24.95 dinner; antipasti bar only $9.95 lunch, $15.95 dinner. AE, DC, MC, V. Mon–Fri 11:30am–2:30pm; Sun–Wed 5:30–10pm, Thurs–Sat 5:30–11pm. Valet parking $4 evenings. Metro: Gallery Place. CONTEMPORARY MEXICAN/TAPAS/BRAZILIAN CHURRASCARIA.

Superbly talented French chef Yannick Cam (see Provence below) is one of the owners of—and the culinary inspiration behind—this immense and immensely popular Washington restaurant. Coco Loco crackles with excitement, especially at night when it pulsates

Georgetown & Downtown Dining

Aditi ❸
America ㉓
B. Smith's ㉓
Bombay Palace ❿
Café des Artistes at
   the Corcoran ⓯
Chesapeake Bagel Bakery ㉖
Citronelle ❻
Clyde's ❸
Coco Loco ⓴
Dirksen Senate Office
   Building South
   Buffet Room ㉔
Encore Cafe ❾
Flight Line ㉑
Georgetown Bagelry ❸
House of Representatives
   Restaurant ㉒
Legal Sea Foods ❿
Le Lion d'Or ⓭
Library of Congress
   Cafeteria ㉕

Montpelier Room ㉕
Old Ebbitt Grill ⓰
Patisserie Café Didier ❹
Prime Rib ❿
Red Sage ⓱
Reeve's Restaurant
   and Bakery ⓲
Roof Terrace
   Restaurant ❾
The Sea Catch ❺
Seasons ❽
Sequoia ❼
1789 ❶
Sholl's Cafeteria ⓫
Sichuan Pavilion ⓬
The Tombs ❶
Union Station
   Food Court ㉓
Willard Room ⓲
The Wright Place ㉑
Zed's ❷

63

to the beat of Brazilian music. A lively precinct is the U-shaped bar, but if you want a quieter setting, opt for the window-walled front room or the garden patio. Tapas here combine diverse textures and subtle flavors. Pan-roasted shrimp, for instance, is served on a bed of chewy black (squid-infused) Chinese jasmine rice flavored with smoked bacon and pork. And red snapper is accompanied by sweet fried plantains in a rich coconut milk sauce nuanced with caramelized onions, red pepper strips, and jalapeños. The wine list is small but well chosen.

Ⓢ Old Ebbitt Grill. 675 15th St. NW (between F and G sts.). ☎ **202/ 347-4801.** Reservations recommended. Main courses $4.50–$6.95 at breakfast, $5.95–$9.95 at brunch, $6.95–$10.95 at lunch, $9.95–$14.95 at dinner; burgers and sandwiches $6.25–$10.95. AE, DC, DISC, MC, V. Mon–Fri 7:30am– midnight, Sat 8am–midnight, Sun 9:30am–midnight. Bar Sun–Thurs to 2am, Fri–Sat to 3am. Metro: McPherson Square or Metro Center. Complimentary valet parking from 6pm Mon–Sat, from noon Sun. AMERICAN.

Located two blocks from the White House, this is the city's oldest saloon, founded in 1856—but it's hardly a fusty old tavern. Fronted by a grandiose beaux arts facade, the existing facility is a plush reconstruction, with Persian rugs, beveled mirrors, flickering gaslights, and other turn-of-the-century details. Keep the Ebbitt in mind for yummy breakfasts and Sunday brunches. Its excellent oyster bar (serving safe shellfish from certifiably clean waters) is also note-worthy. At lunch or dinner, enjoy the luxe ambience at low cost by ordering items such as a cheeseburger with fries or hummus with grilled pita and vegetables. More serious entrée listings at dinner might include herb-crusted roast leg of lamb served with applemint chutney, asparagus, and oven-roasted potatoes.

INEXPENSIVE

Chesapeake Bagel Bakery. 215 Pennsylvania Ave. SE. ☎ **202/546-0994.** Salads $1.50–$4.50, bagel and croissant sandwiches $1.40–$5. No credit cards. Mon–Fri 6:30am–8pm, Sat 7am–6pm, Sun 7am–5pm. Metro: Capitol South. SANDWICHES/SALADS.

Its hard to beat this pleasant minicafeteria for a quick meal. Twelve kinds of bagels are baked from scratch on the premises; sandwich fillings range from cream cheese with walnuts, raisins, and carrots to chicken salad. There's a Dupont Circle location at 1636 Connecticut Ave. NW, between Q and R streets (☎ **202/328-7985**), and another at 818 18th St. NW (☎ **202/775-4690**).

Ⓢ Reeve's Restaurant & Bakery. 1306 G St. NW. ☎ **202/628-6350.** Main courses $5.50–$8; sandwiches $3.50–$6; buffet breakfast $5.25 Mon–Fri,

$6.25 Sat and holidays. MC, V. Mon–Sat 7am–6pm. Metro: Metro Center. AMERICAN.

There's no place like Reeve's, a Washington institution since 1886. J. Edgar Hoover used to send a G-man here to pick up chicken sandwiches. It's fronted by a long bakery counter filled with scrumptious pies and cakes. Everything is homemade with top-quality ingredients—the potato salad, the bread, even the mayonnaise. At breakfast, you can't beat the all-you-can-eat buffet. Hot entrées run the gamut from golden-brown Maryland crab cakes to country-fried chicken with mashed potatoes and gravy. And leave room for one of those fabulous pies. No alcoholic beverages are served.

4 Near the White House/K Street Restaurant Row

VERY EXPENSIVE

✪ **Le Lion d'Or.** 1150 Connecticut Ave. NW (at M St.). ☎ **202/296-7972.** Reservations required. Main courses $20–$32. AE, CB, DC, MC, V. Mon–Sat 6–10pm. Metro: Farragut North. FRENCH.

Le Lion d'Or is one of Washington's most highly esteemed bastions of haute cuisine. It has a delightful French country ambience, with seating in dark-brown tufted-leather banquettes under tented silk canopies. The food is classic French cuisine at its best, beautifully presented and graciously served. A not-to-be-missed hors d'oeuvre is the ravioli de foie gras: a large poached pasta pocket stuffed with fresh duck foie gras marinated in white port wine and served in a canard glaze with small diced vegetables. And tender, juicy roast rack of lamb is coated just before completion with a Dijon-mustard meringue, crushed green peppercorns, and herbed bread crumbs; it's served with an array of fresh seasonal vegetables.

Prime Rib. 2020 K St. NW. ☎ **202/466-8811.** Reservations recommended. Main courses $10–$16.50 at lunch, $18–$28 at dinner. AE, CB, DC, MC, V. Mon–Fri 11:30am–3pm; Mon–Thurs 5–11pm, Fri–Sat 5–11:30pm. Free valet parking after 6pm. Metro: Farragut West. STEAKS/CHOPS/SEAFOOD.

Washington Post restaurant critic Phyllis Richman calls the Prime Rib "Washington's most glamorous setting for plain old steak and roast beef." It is indeed glamorous, with black-tie waiters, brass-trimmed black walls, and white-linened tables softly lit by shaded brass lamps. The beef is thick, tender, and juicy; aged for four to five weeks. For less carnivorous diners there are about a dozen seafood entrées. A bountiful basket of fried potato skins with a big bowl of sour cream is a must. Bar drinks here, by the way, are made with fresh-squeezed juices and Evian water.

EXPENSIVE

Legal Sea Foods. 2020 K St. NW. ☎ **202/496-1111.** Reservations recommended, especially at lunch. Main courses $9.95–$15.95 at lunch (sandwiches $6.95–$8.95), $12.95–$23.95 at dinner. AE, DC, DISC, MC, V. Mon–Thurs 11am–10:30pm, Fri 11am–11pm, Sat noon–11pm; Sun noon–10pm. Metro: Farragut North or Farragut West. Valet parking $3. SEAFOOD.

This famous family-run Boston-based seafood empire, whose motto is "If it's not fresh, it's not Legal," made its Washington debut in August 1995 and immediately became a power-lunch haunt for K Street lawyers and executives. Sporting events, especially Boston games, are aired on a TV over the handsome marble bar/raw bar. Legal's buttery rich clam chowder is a classic; other worthy treats include garlicky golden-brown farm-raised mussels au gratin and fluffy pan-fried Maryland lump crab cakes served with zesty corn relish and mayo-mustard sauce.

MODERATE

Bombay Palace. 2020 K St. NW. ☎ **202/331-4200.** Reservations recommended. Main courses $6.50–$16.95 (most are under $12), fixed-price three-course lunch (Mon–Fri) $10.95–$13.95, lunch buffet (Sat–Sun) $9.95. AE, MC, V. Mon–Fri 11:30am–2:30pm, Sat–Sun noon–2:30pm; Sun–Thurs 5:30–10pm, Fri–Sat 5:30–10:30pm. Metro: Farragut North or Farragut West. NORTH INDIAN.

Bombay Palace features the Mughlai cooking of northern India, famous for its subtle mélanges of full-flavored spices and creamy yogurt-based marinades. Indian music and bas-relief sculptures of Hindu deities provide the requisite exotic-interior note. Start off with aloo papri chat (a medley of chickpeas and potato and flour crisps topped with chutney-yogurt dressing). One of my favorite dishes is makhani (butter) chicken, tandoor-baked and served in a fragrant, spiced tomato cream sauce. And make sure to order one of the tandoor-baked breads with your meal—perhaps chewy naan stuffed with cashews and dried fruits.

Sichuan Pavilion. 1820 K St. NW. ☎ **202/466-7790.** Reservations recommended. Main courses $6.95–$14.95 at lunch, $7.95–$15.95 at dinner; fixed-price brunch (Sat–Sun) $10.95. AE, DC, DISC, MC, V. Mon–Fri 11:30am–3pm, Sat–Sun noon–4pm; nightly 5–10:30pm. Metro: Farragut North or Farragut West. SZECHUAN.

Sichuan Pavilion recruits its chefs from the highest ranks of the People's Republic of China's Chengdu Service Bureau, which prepares sumptuous state banquets. And it shows; keep in mind that though some of the dishes sound familiar—moo shu pork, Kung Pao chicken, twice-cooked shredded duck—their subtle flavors distinguish them from Szechuan fare you've had elsewhere. The chef's specialties include tinkling bells with 10 ingredients (sliced shrimp, crab, beef, and chicken sautéed with vegetables and topped with Szechuan dumplings).

INEXPENSIVE

☉ Sholl's Cafeteria. In the Esplanade Mall, 1990 K St. NW. ☎ **202/ 296-3065.** Main courses $1.65–$5.25. No credit cards. Mon–Sat 7am–8pm, Sun 8:30am–6pm. Metro: Farragut West. AMERICAN.

In March 1928, Pennsylvania Dutchman Evan A. Sholl opened this Washington cafeteria, offering fresh, wholesome, inexpensive fare, prayers, and patriotism. The current owner, Sholl's nephew, upholds these traditions. On every table is a sheet announcing the weekly special, along with a biblical quote, Sholl's motto ("Live well for less money with quality food at more reasonable prices"), and perhaps an inspirational poem as well. At breakfast, load up your tray with scrambled eggs, bacon, biscuits, coffee, orange juice, and home fries for under $3.50. Lunch or dinner entrées might include braised beef and rice, roast turkey and dressing, or beef stew with potatoes, carrots, celery, and onions. Add a vegetable or a scoop of mashed potatoes for another 75¢ to 85¢, a piece of homemade peach or pumpkin pie for $1.05.

5 Foggy Bottom/Georgetown

VERY EXPENSIVE

✪ Citronelle. In the Latham hotel, 3000 M St. NW. ☎ **202/625-2150.** Reservations recommended. Main courses mostly $10.50–$14.95 at lunch/ brunch, $23–$29 at dinner; three-course pretheater dinner (until 6:30pm) $35, five- and six-course fixed-price dinners $55 and $65, respectively ($100 for the latter with wines); six-course Chef's Table served in the kitchen $85 ($125 with wines). AE, CB, DC, DISC, JCB, MC, V. Daily 6:30–10:30am, 11am–3pm, and 5:30–10:30pm. Complimentary valet parking at dinner. CONTEMPORARY FRENCH.

Citronelle is an East Coast branch of Los Angeles's famed Citrus, the creation of exuberant French chef Michel Richard. The bilevel atrium setting is charming—updated French country, with oak plank floors, a stone wall, and candlelit tables amid potted greenery. At Citronelle, each dish provides a wondrous explosion of tastes and crispy-crunchy textures. Menus vary seasonally, but sautéed foie gras remains a signature appetizer, most recently presented in the form of a roulade filled with warm shiitake mushrooms, crispy julienned fried potatoes, frisée, truffles, and shallots in a balsamic vinaigrette. Citronelle's extensive wine list offers 17 premium by-the-glass selections.

✪ **Seasons.** In the Four Seasons hotel, 2800 Pennsylvania Ave. NW. ☎ **202/944-2000.** Reservations recommended. Main courses $12.75–$18 at lunch, $16–$29 at dinner. AE, CB, DC, JCB, MC, V. Mon–Fri noon–2:30pm; nightly 6–10:30pm. Free valet parking. CONTINENTAL.

Although Seasons is the signature restaurant of one of Washington's most upscale hotels, it takes a casual approach to formal dining. There's no dress code, and the wait staff is friendly and unintimidating. Seasons is candlelit at night; during the day, it's a sunlit wall of windows overlooking the C&O Canal. Scottish chef William Douglas McNeill's cuisine focuses on fresh market fare. A recent menu featured entrées ranging from crisp-fried sea bass served on a bed of julienned and gingered Oriental vegetables to roast rack of lamb encrusted with Indian spices. A vast and carefully researched wine list encompasses major wine-growing regions of France and California; vintage ports are also available.

✪ **1789.** 1226 36th St. NW (at Prospect St.). ☎ **202/965-1789.** Reservations recommended. Main courses $18–$29, fixed-price pretheater menu $25. AE, DC, DISC, MC, V. Sun–Thurs 6–10pm, Fri 6–11pm, Sat 5–11pm. Complimentary valet parking. AMERICAN REGIONAL.

The restaurant 1789, located in a Federal town house in Georgetown, is as cozy as a country inn, complete with working fireplace and framed Currier and Ives prints. Noted chef Ris Lacoste varies her menus seasonally. Appetizer options might include sherry- and garlic-marinated sautéed shrimp served atop cheese grits studded with nuggets of caramelized onion. And typical entrées range from pumpkin seed-crusted roasted red snapper (served atop black beans with hominy, chorizo sausage, and a sweet potato tamale) to roast rack of lamb with creamy feta potatoes au gratin in a red pepper purée-infused merlot sauce. The wine list is long and distinguished. A great bargain here: The pretheater menu offered nightly through 6:45pm includes appetizer, entrée, dessert, and coffee for just $25!

EXPENSIVE

The Sea Catch. 1054 31st St. NW (just below M St.). ☎ **202/337-8855.** Reservations recommended. Main courses $8.25–$14.95 at lunch, $8.95–$13 at brunch, $14.75–$21.95 at dinner. Three-course pretheater menu served 5:30–7pm is $19.95. AE, CB, DC, MC, V. Mon–Sat noon–3pm and 5:30–10:30pm. Complimentary valet parking. SEAFOOD.

Since I love the C&O Canal, I'm especially fond of this stunning restaurant on its bank. Marble-topped tables are romantically candle-lit in the evening; by day, watch ducks and punters glide by while you dine. The innlike main dining room is charming as well. For openers, plump farm-raised oysters, clams, and other raw-bar offerings merit consideration. The kitchen willingly prepares fresh fish and seafood dishes to your specifications, including live lobster from the tanks. An extensive wine list highlights French, Italian, and American selections. Fresh-baked desserts usually include an excellent key lime pie.

MODERATE

Aditi. 3299 M St. NW. ☎ **202/625-6825.** Reservations recommended. Main courses $4.95–$7.50 at lunch, $6.95–$13.95 at dinner. AE, DC, DISC, MC, V. Mon–Sat 11:30am–2:30pm, Sun noon–2:30pm; Sun–Thurs 5:30–10pm, Fri–Sat 5:30–10:30pm. INDIAN.

This is first-rate Indian cookery, the kind where everything is made from scratch and each dish is uniquely spiced. Linen-covered tables are set with fresh flowers and candles, while above the bar is a display of Kathakali figurines, representing the classic dance forms of southern India. A "must" here is the platter of assorted appetizers—bhajia (a deep-fried vegetable fritter), deep-fried cheese and shrimp pakoras, and crispy vegetable samosas stuffed with spiced potatoes and peas. I also love the chicken pasanda (in a mild yogurt-cream sauce seasoned with onion, cumin, fresh cilantro, and almond paste). Sauces are on the mild side, so if you like your food fiery, inform your waiter.

Clyde's. 3236 M St. NW. ☎ **202/333-9180.** Reservations recommended. Main courses mostly $6.95–$10.95 at lunch/brunch, $9.95–$16.95 at dinner (most under $12); burgers and sandwiches under $7 all day. AE, DC, DISC, MC, V. Mon–Thurs 11:30am–2am, Fri 11:30am–3am, Sat 9am–3am, Sun 9am–2am; brunch Sat–Sun 9am–4pm. AMERICAN.

Clyde's has been a favorite watering hole for an eclectic mix of Washingtonians—college students, Hill staffers, even football stars—since 1963. At any time of day, you can order burgers, sandwiches, and salads. Lunch and dinner entrées change daily, but always seem to include several pastas as well as Maryland-style crab cakes. An Afternoon Delights menu (inspired by the song of the same name, which was written at Clyde's by the Starland Vocal

Band) features light fare ranging from buffalo wings to smoked chicken quesadillas. And beverage choices range from draft beers and microbrews to Ben and Jerry milkshakes.

Sequoia. 3000 K St. NW (at Washington Harbour). ☎ **202/944-4200.** Reservations recommended (not accepted for outdoor seating). Main courses $10.95–$20.95, salads and sandwiches $7.95–$14.95. AE, DISC, MC, V. Sun–Thurs 11:30am–midnight, Fri–Sat 11:30am–1am. Paid parking available at the Harbour, discounted to restaurant patrons at dinner on weekends. AMERICAN REGIONAL.

In the restaurant-with-a-view category, no setting is more spectacular than Sequoia's terrace, where umbrella-shaded tables overlook the boat-filled Potomac between two bridges. You can enjoy the same river vista from the soaring window-walled interior, an elegant balconied setting where candlelit tables are adorned with sprays of fresh flowers. It's a casual place; feel free to arrive in jeans. Although the view clearly outshines the food, the extensive menu runs the gamut from burgers and sandwiches to pastas, salads, and pizzas. For a heartier meal, you might select mint-marinated lamb chops with garlic smashed potatoes and napa cabbage. Save room for one of Sequoia's excellent desserts, perhaps toasted pecan/whiskey pie.

INEXPENSIVE

Georgetown Bagelry. 3245 M St. NW. ☎ **202/965-1011.** Sandwiches $3–$4.50. No credit cards. Mon–Sat 6am–9pm, Sun 7am–6pm. SANDWICHES.

Here, ex–New Yorker Erik Koefoed turns out about 5,000 bagels a day, not to mention bialys. You can get them spread with cream cheese and lox or an array of other fillings such as homemade chicken salad, hummus and sprouts, even hot pastrami. Come by early in the morning to enjoy an oven-fresh bagel together with fresh-squeezed orange juice and coffee while you read the morning paper (it's sold here, too). Though there's counter seating only (no chairs and tables), it's nice to sit by the big windows and watch Georgetown coming to life.

✪ **Patisserie Café Didier.** 3206 Grace St. NW (off Wisconsin Ave. just below M St.). ☎ **202/342-9083.** Main courses $7.99–$8.99; breakfast pastries, muffins, croissants, and desserts $1.10–$4.95. DC, DISC, MC, V. Tues–Sat 8am–7pm, Sun 8am–5pm. CONTINENTAL/PATISSERIE.

This is the most delightful place in town for continental breakfasts, light lunches, and afternoon teas. Dieter Schorner, former pastry chef at New York's Le Cirque and La Côte Basque, came to D.C. in 1988. His cafe is charming—light and sunny, adorned with

---

ii Family-Friendly Restaurants

Dirksen Senate Office Building South Buffet Room *(see p. 80)* Getting here involves a subway ride through the belly of the Capitol; there's a reduced price for children, and, for dessert, a make-your-own-sundae bar.

Flight Line *(see p. 81)* At this airy, very pleasant cafeteria the kids can dig into burgers and pizza, while adults enjoy many other options, even wine. Before you arrive, pick up astronaut freeze-dried ice cream for the kids at any museum shop—an intriguing dessert.

Union Station Food Court *(see p. 83)* Something for everyone, and the setting is very pleasant.

Sholl's Cafeteria *(see p. 67)* Pleasant surroundings, a wide choice of freshly made high-quality fare, and low, low prices. You can't beat it with a stick.

18th-century lithographs and fresh flowers. The tempting pastries are displayed in a glass case: croissants worthy of Paris, classic tart tatins, sumptuous creations such as a rich Swiss chocolate cake lavishly iced and filled with chocolate ganache. For lunch, enjoy homemade soups, quiches, soufflés, sandwiches, salads, small European-style pizzas, cold platters, and hot items such as crab cakes, lamb couscous, or grilled trout served with fresh vegetables and new potatoes.

$ The Tombs. 1226 36th St. NW (at Prospect St.). ☎ **202/337-6668.** No reservations. Burgers, sandwiches, salads $3.95–$7.95; main courses $6.95–$10.95. AE, DISC, MC, V. Mon–Thurs 11:30am–2am, Fri 11:30am–3am, Sat 11am–3am, Sun 9:30am–2am; brunch Sun 10am–3pm. *Note:* the kitchen closes a few hours before the bar. AMERICAN.

For good food, good prices, and convivial ambience, you can't beat this Georgetown watering hole, directly below the upscale 1789 restaurant. There's a central bar with surrounding tables, but I prefer the less rambunctious room called "the Sweeps." Offerings include burgers, sandwiches, and salads, along with a few serious entrées such as charcoal-grilled sirloin with baked potato and vegetable. Menus are supplemented by low-priced specials. Beer prices are low to accommodate the student crowd, lager is a specialty, and a few premium wines are offered by the glass each night. Arrive at off-peak hours to avoid waiting for a table.

✪ **Zed's.** 3318 M St. NW. ☎ **202/333-4710.** Reservations accepted for large parties only. Main courses $5.95–$10.75 at lunch, mostly $6.95–$12.95 at dinner. AE, MC, V. Sun–Thurs 11am–11pm, Fri–Sat 11am–1am. ETHIOPIAN.

Everyone thinks the best Ethiopian restaurants are in ethnic Adams-Morgan, but none can match Zed's, in Georgetown, a charming little place with indigenous paintings, posters, and artifacts adorning pine-paneled walls. Ethiopian food is eaten sans utensils; a sourdough crepelike pancake called injera is used to scoop up food. I love the doro watt: chicken stewed in a tangy hot red chili pepper sauce. Equally scrumptious is infillay: strips of tender chicken breast flavored with seasoned butter and honey wine and served with a delicious chopped spinach and rice side dish. You get a choice of one vegetable with each entrée, but consider ordering extras such as garlicky chopped collard greens, red lentil purée in spicy red pepper sauce, or a purée (served chilled) of roasted yellow split peas mixed with onions, peppers, and garlic.

6 Dupont Circle

VERY EXPENSIVE

✪ **Nora.** 2132 Florida Ave. NW (at R St.). ☎ **202/462-5143.** Reservations recommended. Main courses $19.95–$24.95. MC, V. Mon–Thurs 6–10pm, Fri–Sat 6–10:30pm. Metro: Dupont Circle. ORGANIC/MULTIETHNIC.

Owner-chef Nora Pouillon brings haute panache to healthful organic cookery at Nora, a favorite haunt of the Clintons and the Gores. The skylit main dining room is a converted stable, with a weathered-looking pine ceiling; especially lovely is the intimate brick-walled patio. The chemical-free, organically grown, free-range fare varies nightly; featured entrées might include grilled Copper River king salmon (served with tomato-onion relish, sweet corn succotash, and fiddlehead ferns) and roasted free-range chicken stuffed with goat cheese and toasted pumpkin seeds. An extensive wine list includes, but is not limited to, selections made with organically grown grapes. I promise you won't miss any of the bad-for-you ingredients at Nora.

EXPENSIVE

Asia Nora. 2213 M St. NW. ☎ **202/797-4860.** Reservations recommended. Main courses $17.50–$22.50. MC, V. Mon–Thurs 5:45–10pm, Fri–Sat 5:45–10:30pm. Metro: Dupont Circle or Foggy Bottom. ASIAN FUSION.

Long-time gourmet-organic restaurant queen Nora Pouillon (see Nora, above) expanded her food concept in 1994 with Asia Nora.

The setting evokes the adventure-movie glamour of the 1930s. Gold-flecked jade walls display Asian artifacts, and the wait staff is attired in black silk pajamas. Try the appetizer of Japanese paper-thin salmon sashimi, served with crunchy Thai cucumber/peanut salad. I'd also recommend the thali tray entrée of lamb curry, basmati rice, chutney, dal, vegetables, raita, and Indian breads. Although the wine list has been constructed to complement boldly flavored Asian dishes, I find hot sake goes well with everything.

✪ **Gabriel.** In the Radisson Barceló Hotel, 2121 P St. NW. ☎ **202/956-6690.** Reservations recommended. Main courses $8–$14 at lunch, $15–$22 at dinner; tapas $2.75–$6.50; Mon–Fri lunch buffet $9.50, Sunday brunch buffet $16.75, Mon–Fri happy hour buffet $7.50. AE, CB, DC, DISC, MC, V. Mon–Thurs 11:30am–10pm, Fri–Sat 11:30am–10:30pm; Sun 11am–9:30pm (brunch 11am–3pm; tapas and bar daily 11:30am–midnight). Metro: Dupont Circle. LATIN AMERICAN/MEDITERRANEAN.

Gabriel features Latin-accented fare in a sophisticated, inviting, earth-toned interior. Noted Washington chef Greggory Hill spent months studying with major chefs in Spain and Mexico before creating Gabriel's dazzlingly innovative and ever-changing menu. You can sample a variety of tapas at the bar or begin a meal with them— plump chorizo-stuffed black figs or chile-flavored corn/potato pancakes served with large grilled scallops and spicy chorizo sausage in a creamy smoked garlic/cilantro sauce with a zesty sprinkle of lime juice. There's a well-chosen wine list, with several by-the-glass selections including dry and sweet sherries—the ideal complement to tapas.

✪ **Iron Gate Restaurant & Garden.** 1734 N St. NW. ☎ **202/737-1370.** Reservations recommended. Main courses $8.50–$13.50 at lunch, $15.50–$19 at dinner. AE, MC, V. Mon–Fri 11:30am–5pm; Mon–Sat 5–10pm, Sun 5–9pm. Closed Sun July–Aug. Metro: Dupont Circle. MEDITERRANEAN.

Housed in a converted 19th-century stable, the Iron Gate is Washington's most romantic dining venue. In winter, a big fire blazes in an immense brick fireplace hung with gleaming copper pots. And spring through fall, you can dine alfresco under a grape-and-wisteria arbor in an enchanting brick-walled garden. An excellent starter is the baked goat-cheese torte with charred-pepper coulis. A totally satisfying pasta dish is tagliatelle tossed with grilled shrimp, pancetta, and sugar peas. Save room for dessert—it's divine. There's a nice choice of wines and even fresh-squeezed lemonade. Keep the Iron Gate in mind not only for meals, but as the perfect place for leisurely afternoon tea/espresso/cappuccino or cocktails.

✪ **Vidalia.** 1990 M St. NW. ☎ **202/659-1990.** Reservations recommended. Main courses $12.50–$16.85 at lunch, $16–$20 at dinner. AE, DC, MC, V. Mon–Fri 11:30am–2:30pm; Mon–Thurs 5:30–10pm, Fri–Sat 5:30–10:30pm. Complimentary valet parking at dinner. Metro: Dupont Circle. PROVINCIAL AMERICAN.

The charmingly country-cozy Vidalia is softly lit, and its cream stucco walls are hung with gorgeous dried-flower wreaths and works by local artists. The lovely setting is enhanced by exquisite flower arrangements, big terra-cotta pots of chrysanthemums, and bowls of fruit. Chef Jeff Buben's menus (focusing on Southern-accented regional specialties) change frequently, but his highly recommended crisp East Coast lump crab cakes (the lightest, fluffiest ever, with a piquant dash of capers and cayenne) are a constant among appetizer choices. At lunch, there are hearty sandwiches such as seared tuna on sourdough bread with arugula, bacon, and saffron aioli. Either meal, save room for a dessert of buttery-crusted lemon chess pie with strawberry sauce.

MODERATE

✪ **City Lights of China.** 1731 Connecticut Ave. NW (between R and S sts.). ☎ **202/265-6688.** Reservations recommended. Main courses mostly $5.95–$9.95 at lunch, $6.95–$11.95 at dinner (a few are pricier). AE, CB, DC, DISC, MC, V. Mon–Thurs 11:30am–10:30pm, Fri 11:30am–11pm, Sat noon–11pm, Sun noon–10:30pm; dinner from 3pm daily. Metro: Dupont Circle. SZECHUAN/ HUNAN/MANDARIN.

I'm hooked on the irresistible Chinese regional dishes prepared by talented Taiwanese chef (and part owner) Kuo-Tai Soug. The setting is pretty but unpretentious: a three-tiered dining room with much of the seating in comfortable pale-green leather booths and banquettes. There are wonderful appetizers such as crisp-fried Cornish hen prepared in a cinnamon-soy marinade and served with a tasty dipping sauce; as for entrées, the pièce de résistance is the crisp fried shredded beef: a delicate mix of finely julienned beef, carrot, scallion, and celery in a crunchy peppercorn hot-caramel sweet glaze. There's a full bar.

Kramerbooks & Afterwords, A Café. 1517 Connecticut Ave. NW, (between Q St. and Dupont Circle). ☎ **202/387-1462.** No reservations. Main courses mostly $8.75–$12.25. AE, DISC, MC, V. Mon–Thurs 7:30am–1am, around the clock Fri 7:30am–Mon 1am. Metro: Dupont Circle. AMERICAN.

This schmoozy bookstore-cum-cafe is the kind of place you go for cappuccino after the movies, for an intense discussion of your love life over a platter of fettuccine, or to linger over a good book and a cognac on a sunny afternoon. The cafe opens early, serving

Adams–Morgan & Dupont Circle Dining

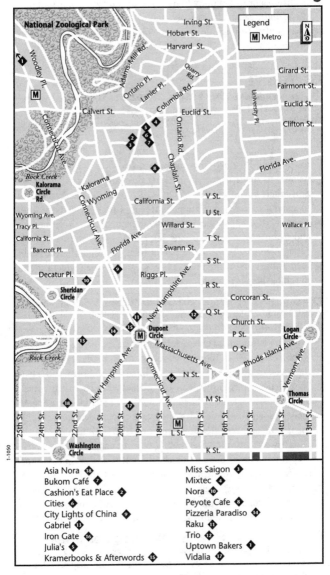

Legend

M Metro

National Zoological Park

Irving St.
Hobart St.
Harvard St.

Girard St.
Fairmont St.
Euclid St.
Clifton St.

Woodley Pl.

Adams-Mill Rd.

Ontario Pl.
Lanier Pl.
Columbia Rd.
Euclid St.

Quarry Rd.

University Pl.

Calvert St.

Connecticut Ave.

Ontario Rd.

Chaplain St.

Florida Ave.

Rock Creek
Kalorama Circle Rd.

Kalorama
Wyoming

California St.

V St.
U St.

Wallace Pl.

Wyoming Ave.
Tracy Pl.
California St.
Bancroft Pl.

Connecticut Ave.

Florida Ave.

Willard St.

Swann St.

T St.
S St.

Decatur Pl.

Riggs Pl.

New Hampshire Ave.

R St.

Corcoran St.

Sheridan Circle

Church St.

P St.

Logan Circle

Dupont Circle

New Hampshire Ave.

Massachusetts Ave.

Connecticut Ave.

O St.
Rhode Island Ave.

N St.

Vermont Ave.

Thomas Circle

Rock Creek

M St.

25th St.
24th St.
23rd St.
22nd St.
21st St.
20th St.
19th St.
18th St.
17th St.
16th St.
15th St.
14th St.
13th St.

L St.

Washington Circle

K St.

1-1050

Asia Nora **18**		Miss Saigon **3**	
Bukom Café **7**		Mixtec **4**	
Cashion's Eat Place **2**		Nora **10**	
Cities **6**		Peyote Cafe **8**	
City Lights of China **9**		Pizzeria Paradiso **14**	
Gabriel **13**		Raku **11**	
Iron Gate **16**		Trio **12**	
Julia's **5**		Uptown Bakers **1**	
Kramerbooks & Afterwords **15**		Vidalia **17**	

75

traditional breakfast fare; at weekend brunches (served all day) a glass of champagne or a Bloody Mary is just $1.25. Fare at lunch or dinner includes salads, sandwiches, and interesting hot entrées such as Thai jambalaya linguine in green chile coconut curry. Wednesday through Saturday nights there's live entertainment, mostly blues and jazz.

INEXPENSIVE

✪ **Pizzeria Paradiso.** 2029 P St. NW. ☎ **202/223-1245.** No reservations. Pizzas $6.50–$15.75, sandwiches and salads $3.95–$5.95. DC, MC, V. Mon–Thurs 11am–11pm, Fri–Sat 11am–midnight, Sun noon–10pm. Metro: Dupont Circle. ITALIAN REGIONAL/PIZZA AND PANINI

Pizzeria Paradiso is housed on the second floor of a Dupont Circle town house. Pristinely charming, its arched trompe l'oeil ceiling is painted to suggest blue sky peeking through ancient stone walls. Since there are only about 16 tables, it is best to come early or late to avoid a wait. My favorite pizza toppings are the Genovese (thin slices of red skin potatoes drizzled with pesto and fresh Parmesan), and quattro formaggi (four cheese), studded with chunks of fresh garlic. Also on the menu are panini (sandwiches) and great salads such as tuna and white bean. There's a small Italian wine list, and the coffee here is rich and freshly brewed.

✪ **Raku.** 1900 Q St. NW. ☎ **202/265-RAKU.** No reservations. All menu items $3.95–$7.75. MC, V. Mon–Thurs 11:30am–midnight, Fri–Sat 11:30am–2am, Sun noon–10pm. Metro: Dupont Circle. STREET FOODS OF ASIA.

To create Raku, noted chefs Mark Miller (see Red Sage, above) and Robbin Haas spent months traveling around Asia, familiarizing themselves with the street foods of China, Japan, Korea, and Thailand. Order several dishes, and ask your waiter to pace their arrival; otherwise service tends to be too brisk. My favorites include a Saigon satay of soy-glazed minced shrimp and chicken wrapped around sugar cane and served with cucumber salad and piquant peanut sauce; sweet and spicy Bangkok (a bowl of coconut curry replete with shrimp, bean sprouts, bok choy, cilantro, and pea shoots); and firecracker dumplings (filled with chile-spiked chicken and pork, corn, and scallions). Beverages include tea, beer, wine, and sake. Favorite decor aspect: the TV monitors that air campy videos (anything from *Godzilla* to instructions on the correct use of chopsticks).

❸ **Trio.** 1537 17th St. NW (at Q St.). ☎ **202/232-6305.** No reservations. Main courses $5.75–$9.50 at lunch and dinner; burgers and sandwiches $1.75–$5.75; full breakfasts $2.75–$5.95. AE, MC, V. Daily 7:30am–midnight. Metro: Dupont Circle (Q Street exit). AMERICAN.

This art deco coffee shop has been around for four decades, and is now something of a Washington legend. The food is fresh and you can't beat the prices. The same menu is offered throughout the day, but there are very low priced lunch specials such as crab cakes with tartar sauce, grilled pork chops with applesauce, turkey with corn bread dressing and cranberry sauce, and fried oysters—all served with two side dishes (perhaps roasted red bliss potatoes and buttered fresh carrots). Similar specials are featured at dinner. There's a full bar and a soda fountain turns out hot-fudge sundaes and milkshakes.

7 Adams-Morgan

Though the action centers on just two or three blocks, this is one of D.C.'s liveliest neighborhoods, filled with ethnic and trendy restaurants and happening nightclubs. The best way to get here is via taxi; parking is very difficult, and the closest Metro stop is a bit of a hike.

EXPENSIVE

Cities. 2424 18th St. NW. (near Columbia Rd.). ☎ **202/328-7194.** Reservations recommended. Main courses $12.95–$22.95. AE, DC, MC, V. Mon–Thurs 6–11pm, Fri–Sat 6–11:30pm. Bar, Sun–Thurs 5pm–2am, Fri–Sat 5pm–3am. Metro: Woodley Park–Zoo. INTERNATIONAL.

Housed in a century-old former five-and-dime store, Cities is a restaurant-cum-travelogue. Once a year, following a comprehensive research expedition by the owner and chef, the restaurant is revamped to reflect the cuisine, character, and culture of a different city. For instance, when Florence was featured, the decor included copies of Botticelli's *Birth of Venus* and other Renaissance masterpieces as well as classic Italian tapestries. And the menu listed pastas, risottos, and entrées such as grilled veal chop. Of course, by the time you read this, the cuisine and setting will be entirely different—that's part of the fun.

MODERATE

Cashion's Eat Place. 1819 Columbia Rd. NW (between 18th St. and Mintwood Pl.). ☎ **202/797-1819.** Limited reservations accepted. Main courses $12.75–$15.95 at dinner, $6.95–$11.25 at brunch. MC, V. Tues–Sat 5:30–11pm, Sun 11:30am–2:30pm and 5:30–10pm. Metro: Woodley Park–Zoo. Valet parking $5. AMERICAN WITH EUROPEAN INFLUENCES.

In this trendy new restaurant, pine walls are hung with vintage black-and-white family photographs, creating a nostalgic Americana ambience that's reflected in Chef Anne Cashion's down-home cooking—it's like Mom's, if your mom was a whiz in the kitchen. A recent menu (they change daily) offered an appetizer of whole wheat fettuccine tossed in butter and olive oil with sautéed hen-of-the-woods mushrooms, shallots, morsels of prosciutto, and finely chopped parsley. For my entrée, I selected tender slices of roast pork in tomato-sage sauce; it came with a colorful array of oven-roasted vegetables and mashed sweet potatoes. At Sunday brunch, order up a basket of fresh-baked breakfast pastries along with entrées ranging from challah French toast to grilled Shenandoah trout with tomato-mustard beurre blanc and haricots verts.

✪ **Miss Saigon.** 1847 Columbia Rd. NW (at Mintwood Pl.). ☎ **202/ 667-1900.** Reservations recommended, especially weekend nights. Main courses $5.50–$7.95 at lunch, $6.95–$14.95 at dinner. AE, MC, V. Mon–Thurs noon–10:30pm, Fri–Sat noon–11pm, Sun 5–10pm. Metro: Woodley Park–Zoo. VIETNAMESE.

The food here is delicious and authentic, though the service can be a trifle slow when the restaurant is busy. To begin, there are crispy spring rolls stuffed with cellophane noodles, mushrooms, pork, onions, and vegetables. Yielding a wonderful mélange of tastes and textures is the Saigon combo entrée: skewers of crunchy grilled shrimp, scallops, and tender beef punctuated by chunks of tomato, onion, and green pepper; it's served atop a mound of rice vermicelli studded with caramelized onion. There's a full bar. Not to be missed is drip pot coffee, brewed tableside and served iced over sweetened condensed milk.

Peyote Cafe. 2319 18th St. NW (between Belmont and Kalorama rds.). ☎ **202/462-8330.** Reservations recommended. Sandwiches, salads, burgers $3.50–$7.95; main courses $5.95–$14.95 at dinner, mostly $3.95–$7.95 at brunch. AE, CB, DC, MC, V. Mon–Fri 5–11pm, Sat–Sun 11:30am–midnight. Bar, Sun–Thurs to 2am, Fri–Sat to 3am. Metro: Woodley Park–Zoo. SOUTHWESTERN/TEX-MEX.

The Peyote Cafe evokes a Southwestern roadside eatery with Texas-themed ornament lights over the bar, neon beer signs, and a juke-box stocked with country tunes. Popular with young locals and families, this is a casual neighborhood hangout, but there's nothing casual about the kitchen. The cafe's chili is Lone Star State quality—thick and stewlike with tender chunks of sirloin, tomatoes, and pinto beans, its spicy sauce spiked with Dos Equis beer. Everything here is good, but especially irresistible is the Tex-Mex mixed grill (pork chop, chicken breast, and chorizo sausage) accompanied by skin-on mashed potatoes (the best ever, topped with ancho chile gravy), corn on the cob, and chunky homemade applesauce. There's a full bar (including a wide choice of tequilas).

INEXPENSIVE

Bukom Café. 2442 18th St. NW (between Columbia and Belmont rds.). ☎ **202/265-4600.** Main courses $7.95–$9.25. AE, DISC, MC, V. Tues 4pm–midnight, Wed–Thurs and Sun 4pm–2am, Fri–Sat 4pm–4am. Metro: Woodley Park–Zoo. WEST AFRICAN.

Arrive early for dinner at this festive and friendly African restaurant/club; as the evening wears on, the place becomes mobbed and smoke-filled, though the live music is great. The menu features several West African cuisines. From the Ivory Coast, there's a hearty stew of okra, smoked bluefish, crayfish, tomatoes, onions, garlic, and hot peppers. Senegalese dishes include sautéed chicken in peanut/tomato/onion sauce. Or you might try a Nigerian egusi: slices of spicy, tender boiled goat meat in a broth of ground melon seeds and spinach. A full bar includes beers from Togo, Nigeria, and Kenya.

Julia's. 2452 18th St. NW (just off Columbia Rd.). ☎ **202/328-6232.** All menu items under $3. No credit cards. Sun–Thurs 10:30am–10pm, Fri–Sat 10:30pm–3am. Metro: Woodley Park–Zoo. CHILEAN.

Julia Hohman, from Chile, runs this casual snack bar that offers limited counter seating and one table. The golden-crusted, fresh-baked empanadas are delicious. Among the fillings: spinach, cheeses, pine nuts, and spices; Jamaican-style curried beef, onion, and potato; and chicken, potato, green peas, hard-boiled egg, green olives, and onion. Beverages include tropical juices.

⊛ Mixtec. 1792 Columbia Rd. (just off 18th St.). ☎ **202/332-1011.** Main courses $4.75–$9.95, full breakfast $6.25–$8.75. MC, V. Mon–Thurs 7am–11:30pm, Fri–Sat 7am–4am, Sun 7am–11pm. Metro: Woodley Park–Zoo. MEXICAN REGIONAL.

This cheerful Adams-Morgan eatery boasts the delicious authenticity of its regional Mexican cuisines. Delicious made-from-scratch corn and flour tortillas enhance whatever they're stuffed with. Freshly prepared guacamole and Mexican pizzas are also excellent here. The house specialty, a full entrée served with rice and beans, is mole Mexicano–broiled chicken in a rich sauce of five peppers (the kitchen uses some 200 different spices!), sunflower and sesame seeds, onions, garlic, almonds, cinnamon, and chocolate. Beverage options include more than 30 kinds of tequila, a nice choice of Mexican beers, and fresh fruit juices.

8 At Sightseeing Attractions

THE CAPITOL

You can rub elbows with senators and representatives if you dine in the Capitol. The ⑤ **Dirksen Senate Office Building South Buffet Room,** 1st and C streets NE (☎ **202/224-4249**), has a lavish all-you-can-eat buffet for $8.75 ($6 for children under 12). The marble-colonnaded art deco setting is most attractive, and you can help yourself to unlimited viands from the carving station (perhaps roast beef or leg of lamb). One way to get here is to take a free subway that runs through the underbelly of the Capitol, a fun trip; ask Capitol police for directions. Open Monday through Friday from 11:30am to 2:30pm. The **House of Representatives Restaurant,** Room H118, at the south end of the Capitol (☎ **202/225-6300**), has lofty ceilings, chandeliers, and gilt-framed mirrors. Prices are very reasonable for such a posh setting. A hearty breakfast of eggs, biscuits, sausage, fresh-squeezed orange juice, and coffee is about $5. At lunch, the "house" specialty, bean soup, is $1.50. There are also deli sandwiches, salads, and burgers, and daily specials always include one low-cholesterol/low-salt entrée. Open Monday through Friday from 8 to 11am and 1 to 2:30pm, only when Congress is in session.

THE CORCORAN

The ✪ **Café des Artistes at the Corcoran,** 17th Street NW, between E Street and New York Avenue (☎ **202/638-1590**), couldn't be more lovely. Neoclassic marble statuary and flower-bedecked tables rest under a skylight ceiling. Fare includes sandwiches (such as smoked turkey with herbed stuffing, applewood bacon, and cranberry orange relish on country bread) and salads such a trio of smoked fish served with mixed greens, horseradish-caper cream cheese, and a baked garlic crostini. Do stop by on Sunday for a buffet brunch, with live gospel music. Open Wednesday through Monday from 11am to 3pm, and Thursday till 8:30pm; brunch is served Sunday from 11am to 2pm.

KENNEDY CENTER

An inexpensive choice is the **Encore Cafe,** New Hampshire Ave. NW, at Rock Creek Parkway (☎ **202/416-8560**), an attractive self-service restaurant with windows that provide gorgeous city views. Sandwiches, homemade soups, pizza, salads, wine, and beer are available. From 5 to 8pm you can order a fresh-carved prime-rib dinner here, with baked potato and vegetable, for $14.95. It's open daily from 11am to 8pm. A meal at the **Roof Terrace Restaurant,** New Hampshire Avenue NW, at Rock Creek Parkway (☎ **202/ 416-8560**), adds a glamorous note to an evening at the theater. It's extremely plush, with ornate crystal candelabra chandeliers and Louis XV–style chairs at crisply linened tables. Menus change seasonally, but typical lunch items might run the gamut from chicken pot pie to a spinach salad with grilled chicken, slivered apples, and Stilton cheese in walnut vinaigrette. And Sunday brunch features a vast buffet. After-theater munchies and cocktails are served in the adjoining and equally plush **Hors d'Oeuvrerie.** I love to stop here after a show for a glass of wine or champagne and a light late supper. It's gourmet snack fare. Desserts and coffee are also available. The Roof Terrace is open matinee days only from 11:30am to 3pm, nightly from 5:30 to 9pm, and Sunday from 11:30am to 3pm. Hors d'Oeuvrerie is open daily from 5pm to half an hour after the last show. *Note:* The Roof Terrace is occasionally closed when there are few shows; call before you go.

LIBRARY OF CONGRESS

The James Madison Memorial Building of the Library of Congress has a classy sixth-floor **۞ Cafeteria,** 101 Independence Ave. SE (☎ 202/707-8300), that serves fresh, homemade food. Hot entrées change daily; they might include old-fashioned beef stew, Swedish meatballs over noodles, homemade pizza, or crab cakes with tartar sauce. Sandwiches, fresh-baked pies and cakes, and a full array of breakfast foods round out the offerings here. It's open Monday through Friday from 9 to 10:30am and 12:30 to 2pm; light fare is available Monday through Friday from 2 to 3:30pm. Adjoining the James Madison cafeteria is the **۞ Montpelier Room,** which offers a marvelous midday buffet. The $8.50 fixed-price lunch served here is one of the best deals in town. Menus change daily. Wine and beer are available by the glass. Friday is the Montpelier's prime rib day; open Monday through Friday from 11:30am to 2pm. Closed August to mid-September.

NATIONAL AIR & SPACE MUSEUM

This major Mall museum features a 39,400-square-foot restaurant complex that occupies a conservatory-like glass building, with floor-to-ceiling windows on both levels offering panoramic views of the Mall and Capitol. **Flight Line,** Independence Avenue at 4th Street SW (☎ 202/371-8750) is encased under a Tinker-Toy assemblage of white-steel tubing. The self-service fare is reasonably priced, fresh, and tasty, with buffet stations for salads, hot entrées, vegetables, pastas and pizzas, fresh fruit, sandwiches, wine and beer, and even bottled waters. It's open daily from 10am to 5pm. Upstairs from Flight Line is **The Wright Place,** a plush, full-service restaurant. Entrées run the gamut from pulled-pork sandwiches with barbecue sauce to grilled flank steak. Gourmet pizzas with toppings such as grilled chicken pesto are additional options. Open daily from 11:30am to 3pm.

NATIONAL GALLERY

There are two charming full-service restaurants within the National Gallery, on the Mall between 3rd and 7th streets NW. (☎ **202/ 347-9401**), both of which provide a restful setting and good food. An attractive lunch spot with waiter service is nothing to scorn when you've been trudging around museums all day. The **Terrace Café,** in the East Building, overlooks the Mall, and the fern- and flower-bordered **Garden Café,** in the West Building, has a skylight and its tables surround a marble fountain that features a late Renaissance bronze *Venus and Cupid.*

The Terrace and Garden Cafés, with similar menus, offer about six items each day. They change from time to time (often reflecting current exhibits), but might include a plate of chilled poached salmon served on a bed of spinach pasta with a basket of bread, a salmagundi salad (greens with Cheddar cheese, eggs, black olives, anchovies, and Virginia ham), a cheese-and-fruit plate served with pâté and a glass of wine, and English spring lamb stew. Fresh-baked pastries and fresh fruit are among your dessert options at both eateries, as are wine, beer, and cappuccino/espresso.

Overlooking an indoor waterfall, the **Cascade,** an espresso/ cappuccino/wine bar, features sandwiches served with fresh fruit, salads, fruit and cheese plates, and exquisite desserts. Patrons sit at marble tables amid potted palms. Cascade is open Mon–Sat noon–4:30pm, Sun noon–5:30pm. Terrace Café is open Mon–Sat 11:30am–3pm, Sun noon–4pm. Garden Café is open Mon–Sat 11:30am–3pm, Sun noon–4pm. Sometimes the hours are extended; call ahead.

NEAR THE NATIONAL ZOO

Although there are eateries in the zoo, their fast-food menus are less than inspiring. A better bet is an alfresco lunch at one of the zoo's nice picnic areas. Get the fixings at **Uptown Bakers,** 3313

Connecticut Ave. NW, just north of Macomb Street (☎ **202/ 362-6262**). Among the offerings: sandwiches on scrumptious fresh-baked breads with yummy fillings such as smoked ham with chutney and honey mustard; roasted eggplant and red peppers with pesto vinaigrette; and Caesar salad with grilled chicken. Focaccia pizzas are also good; open Monday through Saturday from 7am to 9pm, and Sunday 7am to 7:30pm.

UNION STATION

Since it was renovated in the late 1980s, the architecturally stunning Union Station has become an extremely popular dining choice for both locals and tourists. It offers dozens of restaurants and food vendors in different price ranges, and when you're through dining you can browse the diverse shops (see chapter 7) or take in a movie at the nine-screen cinema complex on the lower level. On the lower level is a vast **Food Court,** offering an incredible array of low- to medium-priced options. It's all cafeteria-style, with food vendors selling everything from blintzes to falafel to sushi.

Union Station's most upscale restaurant is **B. Smith's** (☎ **202/ 289-6188**), which occupies the station's most exalted precinct, the Presidential Suite, where, in the heyday of rail travel, presidents officially greeted visiting monarchs and dignitaries. The magnificent main dining room, shaped like the White House Oval Office, has 29-foot ceilings, imposing mahogany doors, white marble floors, gold-leafed moldings, and towering Ionic columns. At Sunday brunch and Wednesday and Saturday nights there's laid-back live jazz. Chef Robert Holmes's menu offers Cajun-influenced appetizers such as jambalaya or red beans and rice studded with andouille sausage and tasso (spicy smoked pork). Among the main dishes, I love his sautéed Virginia trout piled high with crabmeat/vegetable "stuffing" and served atop mesclun with rice and a medley of roasted vegetables. Desserts include dense pecan diamonds topped with praline ice cream, and an almost all-American wine list features many by-the-glass selections. The brunch menu adds breakfast items such as Southern cornmeal pancakes served with honey-maple syrup and sausage. It's open daily from 11:30am to 4pm; Sunday 5 to 10pm, Monday through Thursday from 5 to 11pm, Friday and Saturday 5pm to midnight.

Like all Union Station restaurants, ❺ **America** (☎ **202/ 682-9555**) attracts senators, congresspeople, and justices from the nearby Capitol and Supreme Court, as well as media people and, of course, tourists. Its essentially art deco interior includes WPA-style murals, a large painting of the American West, and a whimsical frieze depicting surfers, athletes, astronauts, and superheroes in outer space. A vast American-classic menu comprises hundreds of items: delicious baked macaroni and cheese, sandwiches ranging from a Philadelphia cheese steak to a New Orleans oyster po-boy, burgers, salads, and entrées running the gamut from Maryland crab cakes to Rhode Island roast turkey with stuffing and orange-cranberry compote. All bar drinks are available, along with a wide selection of domestic beers and microbrews. Many wines are offered by the glass, and nonalcoholic beverages range from milkshakes to lemonade. Hours are Sunday through Thursday from 11:30am to midnight, and Friday and Saturday from 11:30am to 1am. The bar stays open a few hours later.

What to See & Do in Washington, D.C.

*P*eople often come to Washington for a weekend expecting to see all the sights. Talk about life in the fast lane! The Smithsonian Institution alone consists of more than a dozen museums plus the National Zoo. Then there are the monuments and memorials, the White House, the Capitol, the Supreme Court, the Library of Congress, the FBI, the Kennedy Center, the Holocaust Museum, the National Archives, and Washington National Cathedral—major sights one and all. About a dozen other very interesting attractions will also vie for your sightseeing time.

There's so much to see that you should consider spending at least a week. Even then, remember that you can't see everything, and it's more rewarding to see a few attractions thoroughly than to race through dozens. To make the most of your time, read the following listings and plan a reasonably relaxed sightseeing itinerary focusing on the sights that interest you most. As you plan, keep in mind geographic proximity (don't waste energy zigzagging back and forth across town); days and hours attractions are open; and applicable warnings about arriving early to avoid long lines or secure necessary tickets. "Special Tickets for VIP Congressional Tours," in chapter 1 tells you how to obtain tickets ahead of time for VIP tours to some attractions.

Most museums offer highlight tours (call in advance for the exact hours), a good way to get a useful overview in a short time. The good news: Almost everything is free.

1 The Three Major Houses of Government

Three of the most visited sights in Washington are the buildings housing the executive, legislative, and judicial branches of the U.S. government. All stunning edifices, they offer considerable insight into the workings of our system.

✪ **The White House.** 1600 Pennsylvania Ave. NW (visitor entrance gate on E. Executive Ave.). ☎ **202/456-7041** or 202/208-1631. Free admission. Tues–Sat 10am–noon. Closed some days for official functions; check before leaving your hotel by calling the 24-hour number. Metro: McPherson Square.

"I never forget," said Franklin Delano Roosevelt in one of his fire-side chats, "that I live in a house owned by all the American people." Not only do Americans own the White House, but they're welcome to visit, making it almost unique among world residences of heads of state. Its interior is a repository of art and furnishings, reflecting the tastes of our chief executives and first ladies from the earliest years of the American Republic to the present. Highlights of the tour include the following rooms:

The gold-and-white **East Room,** where Lynda Bird Johnson was married, heads of state have been entertained, and seven of the eight presidents who died in office (all but Garfield) laid in state. Note the famous Gilbert Stuart portrait of George Washington that Dolley Madison saved from the British torch during the War of 1812.

The **Green Room,** today used as a sitting room, was Thomas Jefferson's dining room. Walls here are covered in green watered-silk fabric, and some of the early 19th-century furnishings are attributed to the famous cabinetmaker Duncan Phyfe.

The oval **Blue Room,** where presidents and first ladies have officially received guests since the Jefferson administration, is today decorated in the French Empire style chosen by James Monroe in 1817. Grover Cleveland, the only president ever to wed in the White House, was married here. Every year it's the setting for the White House Christmas tree.

Several portraits of past presidents—plus Albert Bierstadt's *View of the Rocky Mountains* and a Gilbert Stuart portrait of Dolley Madison—hang in the **Red Room.** It's used as a reception room, usually for afternoon teas. The satin-covered walls and most of the Empire furnishings are red.

The **State Dining Room** is a superb setting for state dinners and luncheons. Its architecture is modeled after late 18th-century neo-classical English houses. Theodore Roosevelt, a big-game hunter, had a large moose head over the fireplace and other trophies on the walls.

Touring Tips: More than 1.2 million people line up annually to see the Executive Mansion. Your best bet is to obtain tickets in advance from your congressperson or senator for the VIP tours at 8:15, 8:30, and 8:45am (see chapter 1 for details). This will ensure your entrance, even during the tourist season when more than 6,000 people try to squeeze in during the two hours each day the White House is open. It will also entitle you to a more extensive, and guided, tour; during the regular visiting hours, there are guides on hand to answer questions, but no actual tour is given.

The White House is open to tourists mornings only, Tuesday through Saturday. Most of the year, if you don't have VIP tour tickets, you just line up at the southeast gate at E Street and Executive Avenue (just south of the White House) where park rangers are on hand to assist visitors.

From about mid-March (sometimes a bit earlier) through Labor Day weekend, tickets are required. They are distributed, free of charge, at the White House Visitor Center, Pennsylvania Avenue between 14th and 15th streets NW (☎ **202/208-1631,** or 202/456-7041 for recorded information). Tickets are timed for tours between 10am and noon, issued on the day of the tour only on a first-come, first-served basis starting at 7am. One person may obtain up to six tickets. The number of tickets for each day is limited (approximately 4,500 are distributed), and the ticket counter closes when the supply for that day is gone. Hence, it is essential that you arrive early (even before 7am, to ensure admission). Tickets are valid only for the day and time issued. Tours depart from bleachers on the Ellipse, the park area south of the White House.

Note: During those months when tickets are not required, you still need to arrive early. Also, all visitors, even those with VIP congressional tour passes, should call 202/456-7041 before setting out in the morning; occasionally the White House is closed to tourists on short notice because of unforeseen events.

✪ **The Capitol.** At the east end of the Mall, entrance on E. Capitol St. and 1st St. NW. ☎ **202/225-6827.** Free admission. Daily 9am–4:30pm (tours 9am–3:45pm). The Rotunda is open till 8pm Memorial Day to Labor Day most years (this is decided each year). Closed Jan 1, Thanksgiving Day, and Dec 25. Parking at Union Station. Metro: Capitol South.

As our most tangible national symbol since its first wing was completed in 1800, and the place where all our laws are debated, the Capitol is perhaps the most important edifice in the United States. It's also one of the most beautiful.

The **Rotunda**—a huge circular hall some 96 feet across and under a 180-foot dome—is the hub of the Capitol. Nine presidents have lain in state here. On the circular walls are eight immense oil paintings of events in American history, such as the presentation of the Declaration of Independence and the surrender of Cornwallis at

Yorktown. In the dome is an allegorical fresco masterpiece by Constantino Brumidi, *Apotheosis of Washington,* a symbolic portrayal of George Washington surrounded by Roman gods and goddesses watching over the progress of the nation. There's also a life-size marble statue of Lincoln.

The south and north wings are occupied by the House and Senate chambers, respectively. The House of Representatives chamber is the largest legislative chamber in the world. The president delivers his annual State of the Union address there.

Touring Tips: As at the White House, VIP tour tickets from a representative or senator for the morning tours (departing at intervals between 8 and 8:45am) are a definite advantage (see chapter 1 for details). Also request visitors' passes for each member of your party to view a session of the House and/or Senate. If you don't get advance tickets, free 30-minute guided tours leave from the Rotunda every 15 minutes (more often in spring and summer) between 9am and 3:45pm. And if you don't receive visitors' passes in the mail (not every senator or representative sends them), they're obtainable at your senator's office (on the Constitution Avenue side of the building) or your representative's office (on the Independence Avenue side). Noncitizens can present a passport at the first-floor appointment desk on the Senate side or at the third-floor House gallery and ask for a pass. You'll know when the House or Senate is in session when you see flags flying over their respective wings of the Capitol.

✪ **Supreme Court.** East of the Capitol on 1st St. NE (between E. Capitol St. and Maryland Ave). ☎ **202/479-3000.** Free admission. Mon–Fri 9am–4:30pm. Closed weekends and all federal holidays. Metro: Capitol South or Union Station.

In these oft-turbulent times, I find it reassuring to visit the massive Corinthian marble palace that houses the Supreme Court, its serene classical dignity reinforced by the pledge etched in a frieze over the colonnaded entrance: "Equal Justice Under Law." The highest tribunal in the nation, the Supreme Court is charged with deciding whether actions of Congress, the president, the states, and lower courts are in accord with the Constitution and with interpreting that document's enduring principles and applying them to new situations and changing conditions. It has the power of "judicial review"— authority to invalidate legislation or executive action that conflicts with the Constitution.

If you're in town when the Court is in session, try to see a case being argued (call ahead for details). The Court meets Monday

Capitol Hill

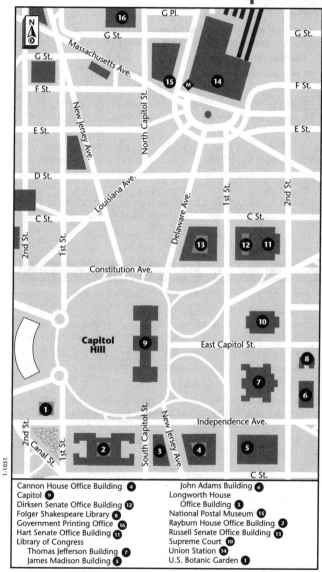

Cannon House Office Building ④
Capitol ⑨
Dirksen Senate Office Building ⑫
Folger Shakespeare Library ⑧
Government Printing Office ⑯
Hart Senate Office Building ⑪
Library of Congress
   Thomas Jefferson Building ⑦
   James Madison Building ⑤

John Adams Building ⑥
Longworth House
   Office Building ③
National Postal Museum ⑮
Rayburn House Office Building ②
Russell Senate Office Building ⑬
Supreme Court ⑩
Union Station ⑭
U.S. Botanic Garden ①

1-1051

through Wednesday starting at 10am from the first Monday in October through late April, alternating, in approximately two-week intervals, between "sittings" to hear cases and deliver opinions and "recesses" for consideration of business before the Court. Mid-May to late June, you can attend brief sessions (about 15 minutes) at 10am on Monday, when the justices release orders and opinions. Arrive at least an hour early, even earlier for a highly publicized case, to line up for seats, about 150 of which are allotted to the general public.

Touring Tips: If the Court is not in session during your visit, you can attend a free **lecture** in the courtroom about Court procedure and the building's architecture. Lectures are given from 9:30am to 3:30pm every hour on the half hour. After the talk, explore the Great Hall and go down a flight of steps to see the 20-minute film on the workings of the Court. The ground floor is a good vantage point to view one of two grand spiral staircases here similar to those at the Vatican and the Paris Opéra.

2　The Presidential Memorials

Few American presidents have been singled out for recognition with great monuments in Washington, D.C. Until recently, there were only three; the last, to Thomas Jefferson, was dedicated in 1943 during cherry-blossom time. In 1994, ground was broken at a 7½-acre site on the Tidal Basin for a fourth presidential memorial, to Franklin Delano Roosevelt. It is scheduled for completion soon.

✪ **Washington Monument.** Directly south of the White House (at 15th St. and Constitution Ave. NW). ☎ **202/426-6839.** Free admission. Easter Sunday to Labor Day, daily 8am–11:45pm; the rest of the year, daily 9am–4:45pm. Last elevators depart 15 minutes before closing (arrive earlier). Closed Dec 25, open till noon July 4. Metro: Smithsonian; then a 10-minute walk.

Note: To combat the problem of unbelievably long lines during the tourist season (early April through Labor Day), in 1996 the Washington Monument began issuing free admission tickets for half-hour timed intervals between 8am and 8pm. During the rest of the year and after 8pm no tickets are required. You can obtain these tickets on the day of the tour at a booth on 15th Street NW between Independence and Constitution avenues. Or save yourself the trouble and get them in advance (up to six tickets per person) via Ticket-Master (☎ 800/505-5040); this entails a nominal fee of $1.50 per ticket plus a 50¢ service charge per transaction.

The 555-foot stark marble obelisk that shimmers in the sun and glows under floodlights at night is the city's most visible landmark. It is, like the Eiffel Tower in Paris or London's Big Ben, a symbol of the city.

The idea of a tribute to George Washington first arose 16 years before his death at the Continental Congress of 1783. An equestrian statue was planned, and Washington himself approved the site for it, on the Mall, west of the future Capitol and south of the "President's Palace." However, more than a century elapsed before a very different monument was completed. The new nation had more pressing problems, and funds were not readily available. It wasn't until the early 1830s, with the 100th anniversary of Washington's birth approaching, that any action was taken. In 1833, prominent citizens organized the Washington National Monument Society. The cornerstone was laid on July 4, 1848; for the next 37 years, watching the monument grow, or not grow, was a local pastime. Declining contributions and the Civil War brought construction to a halt at an awkward 150 feet. The unsightly stump remained until 1876, when President Grant approved federal monies to complete the project. Dedicated in 1885, it was opened to the public in 1888.

The 360° views are spectacular. To the east are the Capitol and Smithsonian buildings; to the north, the White House; to the west, the Lincoln and Vietnam Memorials, and Arlington National Cemetery beyond; and to the south, the gleaming-white shrine to Thomas Jefferson and the Potomac River. It's a marvelous orientation to the city.

Touring Tips: June through September, 30-minute talks are given by rangers throughout the day. Climbing the 897 steps is verboten, but a large elevator whisks visitors to the top in just 70 seconds. If, however, you're avid to see more of the interior, **"Down the Steps" tours** are given, subject to staff availability, weekends at 10am and 2pm (more often in summer). For details, call before you go or ask a ranger on duty.

✪ **Lincoln Memorial.** Directly west of the Mall in Potomac Park (at 23rd St. NW, between Constitution and Independence aves.). ☎ **202/426-6895.** Free admission. Park staff on duty 8am–midnight daily. Metro: Foggy Bottom; then about a 20-minute walk.

The Lincoln Memorial attracts some six million visitors annually. It's a beautiful and moving testament to a great American, its marble walls seeming to embody not only the spirit and integrity of Lincoln,

Washington, D.C., Attractions

Arts and Industries Building ㉑
Arthur M. Sackler Gallery ⑲
Bureau of Engraving and Printing ⑰
Capitol ㊱
Constitution Hall ⑪
Corcoran Gallery ⑫
Dumbarton Oaks ②
Enid A. Haupt Garden ⑱A
FDR Memorial ⑥A
Federal Bureau of Investigation ㉗
Folger Shakespeare Library ㉞
Ford's Theatre ㉘
Freer Gallery of Art ⑱
Hirshhorn Museum ㉓
Jefferson Memorial ⑨
Kennedy Center ⑤
Korean War Veterans Memorial ⑧
Library of Congress ㉟
Lincoln Memorial ⑥
Nat'l Air and Space Museum ㉔
National Archives ㉖
National Gallery of Art ㉕
Nat'l Geographic Society's Explorers Hall ⑭

National Museum of African Art ⑳
Nat'l Museum of American Art ⑩
Nat'l Museum of American History ⑮
Nat'l Museum of Natural History ㉒
Nat'l Musuem of Women in the Arts ⑭A
National Portrait Gallery ㉙
National Postal Museum ㉛
National Zoological Park ③
Phillips Collection ④
Renwick Gallery ⑬A
Supreme Court ㉝
Union Station ㉜
U.S. Botanic Garden ㊲
U.S. Holocaust Memorial Museum ⑯
U.S. Navy Memorial ㉕A
Vietnam Veterans Memorial ⑦
Washington National Cathedral ①
Washington Monument ⑩
White House ⑬

but all that has ever been good about America. Visitors are silently awed in its presence.

The monument was a long time in the making. Although it was planned as early as 1867, two years after Lincoln's death, it was not until 1912 that Henry Bacon's design was completed, and the memorial itself was dedicated in 1922.

A beautiful neoclassical templelike structure, similar in architectural design to the Parthenon in Greece, the memorial has 36 fluted Doric columns representing the states of the Union at the time of Lincoln's death, plus two at the entrance. The memorial chamber, under 60-foot ceilings, has limestone walls inscribed with the Gettysburg Address and Lincoln's Second Inaugural Address. Two 60-foot murals by Jules Guerin on the north and south walls depict, allegorically, Lincoln's principles and achievements. Most powerful, however, is Daniel Chester French's 19-foot-high seated statue of Lincoln in deep contemplation in the central chamber. Its effect is best evoked by these words of Walt Whitman: "He was a mountain in grandeur of soul, he was a sea in deep undervoice of mystic loneliness, he was star in steadfast purity of purpose and service and he abides."

Touring Tips: An information booth and bookstore are on the premises. June through September, 20- to 30-minute ranger programs are presented throughout the day. The rest of the year, ranger talks are given on request. Free parking is available at Constitution Avenue and Ohio Drive.

✪ **Jefferson Memorial.** South of the Washington Monument on Ohio Dr. (at the south shore of the Tidal Basin). ☎ **202/426-6822.** Free admission. Park staff on duty 8am–midnight daily. Transportation: Tourmobile.

The site for the Jefferson Memorial, in relation to the Washington and Lincoln Memorials, was of extraordinary importance. The Capitol, the White House, and the Mall were already located in accordance with L'Enfant's plan, and there was no spot for such a project if the symmetry that guided L'Enfant was to be maintained. So the memorial was built on land reclaimed from the Potomac River, now known as the Tidal Basin. Franklin Roosevelt had all the trees between the Jefferson Memorial and the White House cut down, so that he could see it every morning and draw inspiration from it.

It's a beautiful memorial, a columned rotunda in the style of the Pantheon in Rome, which Jefferson so admired. On the Tidal Basin side, the sculptural group above the entrance depicts Jefferson with Benjamin Franklin, John Adams, Roger Sherman, and Robert Livingston, who worked on drafting the Declaration of Independence. The domed interior of the memorial contains the 19-foot bronze statue of Jefferson standing on a six-foot pedestal of black Minnesota granite. The sculpture is the work of Rudulph Evans, who was chosen from more than 100 artists in a nationwide competition. Jefferson is depicted wearing a fur-collared coat given to him by his close friend, the Polish general, Tadeusz Kosciuszko. Inscriptions from Jefferson's writing engraved on the interior walls expand on Jefferson's philosophy.

Touring Tips: June through September, 20- to 30-minute ranger programs are presented throughout the day. The rest of the year, rangers give short talks to visitors on request. Spring through fall, a refreshment kiosk at the Tourmobile stop offers snack fare. A bookshop is on the premises. There's free one-hour parking.

Franklin Delano Roosevelt Memorial. In West Potomac Park about midway between the Lincoln and Jefferson Memorials, on the west shore of the Tidal Basin. ☎ **202/426-6841.** Free admission. Park staff on duty 8am–midnight daily. Transportation: Tourmobile.

This latest D.C. presidential memorial, designed by architect Lawrence Halprin, is nearing completion at press time. Visitors will enter a sequence of four "outdoor rooms," each devoted to one of Roosevelt's four terms in office (1933 to 1945). Ten bronze sculptures (by Leonard Baskin, John Benson, Neil Estern, Robert Graham, Thomas Hardy, and George Segal) will not only honor Franklin (and Eleanor) Roosevelt, but memorialize the institution of the presidency, the struggles of the Great Depression, and America's rise to world leadership. Roosevelt's inspirational words will be carved into red Dakota granite amid waterfalls and quiet pools.

3 The Smithsonian Museums

The Smithsonian's collection of more than 140 million objects encompasses the entire world and its history, as well as its peoples and animals (past and present) and our attempts to probe into the future. The sprawling institution comprises 14 museums (nine of them on the Mall) as well as the National Zoological Park in Washington, D.C., plus two additional museums in New York City.

It all began with a $500,000 bequest from James Smithson, an English scientist who had never visited this country. When he died in 1829, he willed his entire fortune to the United States "to found at Washington . . . an establishment for the increase and diffusion of knowledge." Since then, other munificent private donations have swelled Smithson's original legacy many times over. Major gallery and museum construction through the years stands as testament to thoughtful donors.

In 1987 the **Sackler Gallery** (Asian and Near Eastern art) and the **National Museum of African Art** were added to the Smithsonian's Mall attractions. The **National Postal Museum** opened in 1993. And future plans call for moving the **National Museum of the American Indian** (currently in New York) here by the end of the decade.

If you want to know what's happening at any of the Smithsonian museums, just get on the phone; **Dial-a-Museum** (☎ **202/ 357-2020**), a recorded information line, will bring you news of daily activities and special events. For other information, call 202/ 357-2700.

Smithsonian Information Center. 1000 Jefferson Dr. SW. ☎ **202/ 357-2700.** Daily 9am–5:30pm. Closed Dec. 25. Metro: Smithsonian.

Make your first stop the impressively high-tech and very comprehensive Smithsonian Information Center, located in the institution's original Norman-style red sandstone building, popularly known as the "Castle."

The main information area here is the Great Hall, where a 20-minute video overview of the institution runs throughout the day in two theaters. There are two large schematic models of the Mall (as well as a third in Braille), and two large electronic maps of Washington allow visitors to locate 69 popular attractions and Metro and Tourmobile stops. Interactive videos, some of them at children's heights, offer extensive information about the Smithsonian and other capital attractions and transportation (the menus seem infinite).

The entire facility is handicapped-accessible, and information is available in a number of foreign languages. Daily Smithsonian events are displayed on monitors, and, between 9am and 4pm, the information desk's volunteer staff (some of whom speak foreign languages) can answer questions and help you plan a Smithsonian sightseeing itinerary. Most of the museums are within easy walking distance of the facility. And be sure to stroll through the stunning Enid A. Haupt Garden behind the south entrance when you leave. James Smithson's crypt is also on the premises. *Note:* The Information Center opens one hour earlier than the museums.

✪ **National Museum of American History.** On the north side of the Mall (between 12th and 14th sts. NW), with entrances on Constitution Ave. and Madison Dr. ☎ **202/357-2700.** Free admission. Daily 10am–5:30pm. Summer hours, sometimes extended, are determined annually. Closed Dec 25. Metro: Smithsonian or Federal Triangle.

The National Museum of American History deals with "everyday life in the American past" and the external forces that have helped to shape our national character. Its massive contents run the gamut from Gen. George Washington's Revolutionary War tent to Archie Bunker's chair.

Exhibits on the **first floor** (enter on Constitution Avenue) include: "Engines of Change: The American Industrial Revolution 1790–1860," which tells the story of America's transformation from an agricultural to an industrial society; and "Information Age: People, Information and Technology," which looks at the ways information technology has changed society during the past 150 years.

If you enter from the Mall, you'll find yourself on the **second floor** facing the original Star-Spangled Banner, 30 by 42 feet, that inspired Francis Scott Key to write the U.S. national anthem in 1814. (*Note:* it may be down for repairs in 1997.) "Field to Factory: Afro-American Migration, 1915–40," is an in-depth study of America's social and demographic history from an African-American perspective. Perhaps the most fascinating exhibit is the Foucault Pendulum, a copy of the original model that was exhibited in Paris in 1851. Also on this is the display of first ladies' gowns.

A vast collection of ship models, uniforms, weapons, and other military artifacts is located on the **third floor,** where major exhibits focus on the experiences of GIs in World War II (and the postwar world) as well as the wartime internment of Japanese Americans.

Inquire at the information desks about highlight tours, demonstration center hands-on activities for children and adults, films, lectures, and concerts. There is a cafeteria on the premises.

✪ **National Museum of Natural History.** On the north side of the Mall (between 9th and 12th sts. NW), with entrances on Madison Dr. and Constitution Ave. ☎ **202/357-2700.** Free admission. Daily 10am–5:30pm, with extended hours in summer some years. Closed Dec 25. Metro: Smithsonian or Federal Triangle.

The National Museum of Natural History contains more than 120 million artifacts and specimens, everything from Ice Age mammoths to the legendary Hope Diamond.

Free highlight **tours** are given daily at 10:30am and 1:30pm, but if you have the time, the self-guided audio tour provides the most comprehensive commentary on exhibits. It's available at the Rotunda information desk for a nominal fee. A **Discovery Room,** filled with creative hands-on exhibits for children four and up, is on the first floor. Call ahead or inquire at the information desk about hours. Children under 12 must be accompanied by an adult. If you have kids, this is a must.

On the **Mall Level,** off the Rotunda, evolution is traced back billions of years in fossils, comprising such exhibits as a 3.5-billion-year-old stromatolite (blue-green algae clump) fossil—one of the earliest signs of life on earth—and a 70-million-year-old dinosaur egg. Dinosaurs, of course, loom large—giant skeletons of creatures that dominated the earth for 140 million years before their extinction about 65 million years ago. Suspended from the ceiling over Dinosaur Hall are exhibits on ancient birds, including a life-size model of the pterosaur, which had a 40-foot wingspan. Here, too, is the "Exploring Marine Ecosystems" exhibit, including a spectacular living coral reef in a 3,000-gallon tank. A second 1,800-gallon tank houses a subarctic sea environment typical of the Maine coast. And an exhibit called "Giant Squid" focuses on the world's largest invertebrates.

On the **second floor** is the Gems and Minerals Hall, where, along with the Hope Diamond, such dazzling gems as the 182-carat Star of Bombay sapphire that belonged to Mary Pickford and Marie Antoinette's diamond earrings are on display. Nearby are geological specimens ranging from meteorites to moon rocks. Numerous skeletons are displayed in "Bones," from the gigantic extinct Stellar sea cow to the tiny pocket mouse.

There's a plant-filled cafeteria off the Rotunda. *Note:* Due to renovations, the Gems and Minerals Hall, some museum shops, and the restaurant may be closed during your visit.

✪ **National Air & Space Museum.** On the south side of the Mall (between 4th and 7th sts. SW), with entrances on Jefferson Dr. or Independence Ave. ☎ **202/357-2700,** or 202/357-1686 for IMAX ticket information. Free admission. Daily 10am–5:30pm (some years the museum has extended hours during summer). Closed Dec 25. Metro: L'Enfant Plaza (Smithsonian Museums/Maryland Avenue exit).

The National Air and Space Museum chronicles the story of our mastery of flight, from Kitty Hawk to outer space, in 23 galleries filled with exciting exhibits. Plan to devote at least three or four hours exploring these exhibits and, especially during the tourist season and on holidays, arrive before 10am to make a rush for the film-ticket line when the doors open. The not-to-be-missed **IMAX films** shown in the Samuel P. Langley Theater here, on a screen five stories high and seven stories wide, are immensely popular; tickets tend to sell out quickly. There are five or more films playing each day, most with aeronautical or space-exploration themes. See as many as you have time for. Tickets cost $4 for adults, $2.75 for ages 2 to 21 and seniors over 55; they're free for children under two. You can also see IMAX films most evenings after closing (call for details and ticket prices). At the same time, purchase tickets (same prices) for a show at the **Albert Einstein Planetarium.**

In between shows, you can view the exhibits; free 1¹/₂-hour highlight **tours** are given daily at 10:15am and 1pm. Audio tours are also available for rental. Interactive computers and slide and video shows enhance the exhibits throughout.

Highlights of the **first floor** include famous airplanes (such as the *Spirit of St. Louis*) and spacecraft (the *Apollo 11* Command Module); the world's only touchable moon rock; galleries in which you can design your own jet plane and study astronomy; and rockets, lunar-exploration vehicles, manned spacecraft, and guided missiles. And "How Things Fly," a gallery that opened in 1996 to celebrate the museum's 20th anniversary, includes wind and smoke tunnels, a boardable Cessna 150 airplane, and dozens of interactive exhibits that demonstrate principles of flight, aerodynamics, and propulsion.

Kids love the "walk-through" Skylab orbital workshop on the **second floor.** Other galleries here highlight the solar system, U.S. manned space flights, sea-air operations, and aviation during both world wars.

National Museum of American Art. 8th and G sts. NW. ☎ **202/ 357-2700.** Free admission. Daily 10am–5:30pm. Closed Dec 25. Metro: Gallery Place/Chinatown.

The National Museum of American Art owns more than 37,500 works representing two centuries of our national art history. About 1,000 of these works are on display at any given time, along with special exhibitions highlighting various aspects of American art. The collection, along with the National Portrait Gallery (described below), is housed in the palatial quarters of the 19th-century Greek Revival Old Patent Office Building.

Twentieth-century art occupies the most exalted setting, the third-floor Lincoln Gallery, with vaulted ceilings and marble columns. On view are works of post–World War II artists (de Kooning,

Kline, Noguchi, and others). Other 20th-century works on this floor include paintings commissioned during the New Deal era.

Mid- to late-19th-century artists such as Winslow Homer, Mary Cassatt, Albert Pinkham Ryder, and John Singer Sargent are on the second floor, as is a suite of galleries devoted to the Gilded Age. Here, too, are works by such early American masters as Charles Willson Peale, Benjamin West, and Samuel F. B. Morse.

When you enter, pick up a map and calendar of events and ask about current temporary exhibits at the information desk. Free walk-in tours are given at noon weekdays and at 2pm Saturday and Sunday. There is a lovely courtyard cafe on the premises.

The National Portrait Gallery. 8th and F sts. NW. ☎ **202/357-2700.** Free admission. Daily 10am–5:30pm. Closed Dec 25. Metro: Gallery Place/ Chinatown.

The "heroes and villains, thinkers and doers, conservatives and radicals" who have made "significant contributions to the history, development, and culture of the United States" are represented here in paintings, sculpture, photography, and other forms of portraiture. Although the museum didn't open until 1968, the concept of a national portrait gallery first arose in the mid-19th century when Congress commissioned G. P. A. Healy to paint a series of presidential portraits for the White House. It's great fun to wander the corridors here, matching faces to famous names for the first time.

In addition to the Hall of Presidents (on the second floor), notable exhibits include Gilbert Stuart's famed "Lansdowne" portrait of George Washington, a portrait of *Mary Cassatt* by Degas, 19th-century silhouettes by French-born artist August Edouart, Jo Davidson's sculpture portraits (including a Buddha-like Gertrude Stein), and photographs by Mathew Brady. On the mezzanine, the Civil War is documented in portraiture, including one of the last photographs ever taken of Abraham Lincoln. Take a look at the magnificent Great Hall on the third floor. Originally designed as a showcase for patent models, it later became a Civil War hospital, where Walt Whitman came frequently to "soothe and relieve wounded troops."

Pick up a calendar of events at the information desk to find out about the museum's comprehensive schedule of temporary exhibits, lunchtime lectures, concerts, films, and dramatic presentations. Walk-in tours are given at varying hours; inquire at the information desk.

Renwick Gallery of the National Museum of American Art. Pennsylvania Ave. and 17th St. NW. ☎ **202/357-2700.** Free admission. Daily 10am–5:30pm. Closed Dec 25. Metro: Farragut West or Farragut North.

A department of the National Museum of American Art, the Renwick, a showcase for American creativity in crafts, is housed in a historic mid-1800s landmark building of the French Second Empire style. The original home of the Corcoran Gallery, it was saved from demolition by First Lady Jacqueline Kennedy in 1963, when she recommended that it be renovated as part of the Lafayette Square restoration. Although the setting—especially the magnificent Victorian Grand Salon with its wainscoted plum walls and 38-foot skylight ceiling—evokes another era, the museum's contents are mostly contemporary. The rich and diverse display of objects here includes both changing crafts exhibitions and contemporary works from the museum's permanent collection. Typical exhibits run the gamut from "Uncommon Beauty: The Legacy of African-American Craft Art" to "Masterpieces of Louis Comfort Tiffany."

The Renwick offers a comprehensive schedule of crafts demonstrations, lectures, and films. Inquire at the information desk. And check out the museum shop near the entrance for books on crafts, design, and decorative arts, as well as craft items, many of them for children.

✪ Hirshhorn Museum & Sculpture Garden. On the south side of the Mall (at Independence Ave. and 7th St. SW.). ☎ **202/357-2700.** Free admission. Daily 10am–5:30pm, Sculpture Garden 7:30am–dusk. Closed Dec. 25. Metro: L'Enfant Plaza (Smithsonian Museums/Maryland Avenue exit).

This museum of modern and contemporary art is named after Latvian-born Joseph H. Hirshhorn, who, in 1966, donated his vast art collection—more than 4,000 drawings and paintings and some 2,000 pieces of sculpture—to the United States "as a small repayment for what this nation has done for me and others like me who arrived here as immigrants." At his death in 1981, Hirshhorn bequeathed an additional 5,500 artworks to the museum, and numerous other donors have since greatly expanded his legacy.

Constructed 14 feet above the ground on sculptured supports, the museum's contemporary cylindrical concrete-and-granite building shelters a verdant plaza courtyard where sculpture is displayed. The light and airy interior follows a simple circular route that makes it easy to see every exhibit without getting lost in a honeycomb of galleries. Natural light from floor-to-ceiling windows makes the inner galleries the perfect venue for viewing sculpture, second only, perhaps, to the magnificently beautiful tree-shaded sunken Sculpture Garden across the street.

A rotating show of about 600 pieces is on view at all times. The collection features just about every well-known 20th-century artist and touches on most of the major trends in Western art since the late 19th century, with particular emphasis on our contemporary period. Among the best-known pieces are Rodin's *The Burghers of Calais,* Hopper's *First Row Orchestra,* de Kooning's *Two Women in the Country,* and Warhol's *Marilyn Monroe's Lips.*

Pick up a free calendar when you come in to find out about free films, lectures, concerts, and temporary exhibits. Free docent **tours** of the collection are given daily at noon, with an additional 2pm tour on weekends.

✪ **Arthur M. Sackler Gallery.** 1050 Independence Ave. SW. ☎ **202/ 357-2700.** Free admission. Daily 10am–5:30pm. Closed Dec. 25. Metro: Smithsonian.

Opened in 1987, the Sackler, a national museum of Asian art, presents traveling exhibitions from major cultural institutions in Asia, Europe, and the United States. In the recent past, these have focused on such wide-ranging areas as 15th-century Persian art and culture, ancient Buddhist and Hindu sculpture from Sri Lanka, 20th-century painting from China and Japan, and the opulent court arts of Indonesia. Art from the permanent collection includes Chinese bronzes from the Shang (1523–1027 B.C.) through the Han (A.D. 206–220) dynasties; Chinese jade figures spanning the millennia from 3000 B.C. to the 20th century; ancient Near Eastern works in silver, gold, bronze, and clay; and stone and bronze sculptures from South and Southeast Asia.

The Sackler is part of a museum complex that also houses the National Museum of African Art. And it shares its staff and research facilities with the adjacent Freer Gallery, to which it is connected via an underground exhibition space. For information about museum programs (including many wonderful experiences for children and families), highlight tours (highly recommended), films, events, and temporary exhibits, inquire at the information desk.

National Museum of African Art. 950 Independence Ave. SW. ☎ **202/ 357-2700.** Free admission. Daily 10am–5:30pm. Closed Dec. 25. Metro: Smithsonian.

This is the only national art museum in the United States devoted to research in, and the collection and exhibition of, African art.

Founded in 1964, and part of the Smithsonian since 1979, it moved to the Mall in 1987 to share a subterranean space with the Sackler Gallery (see above) and the Ripley Center. Its above-ground domed pavilions reflect the arch motif of the neighboring Freer.

Although the museum collects and exhibits ancient and contemporary art from the entire African continent, its permanent collection of more than 7,000 objects (shown in rotating exhibits) highlights the traditional arts of the vast sub-Saharan region. Most of the collection dates from the 19th and 20th centuries. Also among the museum's holdings are the Eliot Elisofon Photographic Archives, comprising 300,000 photographic prints and transparencies and 120,000 feet of film on African arts and culture. Permanent exhibits include "The Ancient Nubian City of Kerma, 2500–1500 B.C." (ceramics, jewelry, and ivory animals), and "Purpose and Perfection: Pottery as a Woman's Art in Central Africa." Specific objects or themes are explored in depth in a small exhibition space called the Point of View Gallery.

Inquire at the desk about special exhibits, workshops (including excellent children's programs), storytelling, lectures, docent-led tours, films, and demonstrations. A comprehensive events schedule here (together with exhibitions) provides a unique opportunity to learn about the diverse cultures and visual traditions of Africa.

Enid A. Haupt Garden. 10th St. and Independence Ave. SW. ☎ **202/ 357-2700.** Free admission. Memorial Day to Labor Day, daily 7am–8pm; the rest of the year, daily 7am–5:45pm. Closed Dec 25. Metro: Smithsonian.

Named for its donor, a noted supporter of horticultural projects, this stunning garden is enhanced by elaborate flower beds and borders, plant-filled turn-of-the-century urns, 1870s cast-iron furnishings, and lush baskets hung from 19th-century–style lampposts. Although on ground level, it's really a rooftop garden above the subterranean Sackler and African Art Museums. A magnolia-lined parterre, framed by four floral swags, centers on a floral bed patterned after the rose window in the Commons of the "Castle"; it is composed of 30,000 green and yellow Alternanthera, supplemented by seasonal displays of spring pansies, begonias, or cabbage and kale. Additional features include wisteria-covered dome-shaped trellises, clusters of trees (Zumi crabapples, ginkgoes, and American hollies), a weeping European beech, and rose gardens. Elaborate cast-iron carriage gates made according to a 19th-century design by James Renwick, flanked by four red sandstone pillars, have been installed at the Independence Avenue entrance to the garden.

National Postal Museum. 2 Massachusetts Ave. NE (at 1st St.). ☎ **202/357-2700.** Free admission. Daily 10am–5:30pm. Closed Dec 25. Metro: Union Station.

Opened in 1993, this most recent addition to the Smithsonian complex appropriately occupies the palatial beaux arts quarters of the City Post Office Building designed by brilliant architect Daniel Burnham. Created to house and display the Smithsonian's national philatelic and postal history collection of more than 16 million objects, it is, somewhat surprisingly, a great deal of fun to visit. Dozens of intriguing interactive exhibits range from nickelodeon "films" about train wrecks and robberies to postal-themed video games. The museum documents America's postal history from 1673 (about 170 years before the advent of stamps, envelopes, and mailboxes) to the present. In addition, the museum houses a vast research library for philatelic researchers and scholars, a stamp store, and a museum shop. Inquire about free walk-in tours at the information desk.

Freer Gallery of Art. On the south side of the Mall (at Jefferson Dr. and 12th St. SW). ☎ **202/357-2700.** Free admission. Daily 10am–5:30pm. Closed Dec 25. Metro: Smithsonian (Mall or Independence Avenue exit).

A gift to the nation of 9,000 works from Charles Lang Freer, a collector of Asian art and American art from the 19th and early 20th centuries, the Freer Gallery opened in 1923. The collection includes Chinese and Japanese sculpture, printing, lacquer, metalwork, and ceramics; early Christian illuminated manuscripts; Japanese screens and wood-block prints; Chinese jades and bronzes; Korean ceramics; Iranian manuscripts, metalwork, and miniatures; ancient Near Eastern metalware; and South Asian sculpture and paintings.

Among the American works are more than 1,200 pieces (the world's largest collection) by Whistler. Other American painters represented in the collections are Thomas Wilmer Dewing, Dwight William Tryon, Abbott Henderson Thayer, John Singer Sargent, and Childe Hassam.

Housed in an Italian Renaissance–style granite-and-marble building, the Freer has lovely skylit galleries. In 1993, a $4^{1}/_{2}$-year, $26 million expansion and renovation project was completed. The main exhibit floor centers on a garden court open to the sky. An underground exhibit space connects the Freer to the neighboring Sackler Gallery, and both museums share The Meyer Auditorium, which is used for free chamber music concerts, dance performances, Asian feature films, and other programs. Inquire about these, as well as children's activities, at the information desk.

Arts & Industries Building. 900 Jefferson Dr. SW (on the South Side of the Mall). ☎ **202/357-2700.** Free admission. Daily 10am–5:30pm. Closed Dec 25. Metro: Smithsonian.

Completed in 1881 as the first U.S. National Museum, this redbrick and sandstone structure was the scene of President Garfield's Inaugural Ball. From 1976 through the mid-1990s, it housed exhibits from the 1876 United States International Exposition in Philadelphia—a celebration of America's 100th birthday that featured the latest advances in technology. Some of these are still on display, but, at this writing, the museum is in transition and offering changing exhibitions. You can find out what's happening here at the Smithsonian Information Center.

Singers, dancers, puppeteers, and mimes perform in the **Discovery Theater** (October to July, Tuesday to Saturday—call **202/ 357-1500** for show times and ticket information; admission is charged). Don't miss the charming Victorian-motif shop on the first floor. Weather permitting, there's a 19th-century carousel in operation across the street.

✪ **National Zoological Park.** Adjacent to Rock Creek Park, main entrance in the 3000 block of Connecticut Ave. NW. ☎ **202/673-4800** (recording) or 202/673-4717. Free admission. Apr 15–Oct 15, daily (weather permitting): grounds, 8am–8pm; animal buildings, 9am–4:30pm. Oct 16–Apr 14, daily: grounds, 8am–6pm; animal buildings, 9am–4:30pm. Closed Dec 25. Metro: Cleveland Park or Woodley Park–Zoo.

Established in 1889, the National Zoo is home to several thousand animals of some 500 species, many of them rare and/or endangered. A leader in the care, breeding, and exhibition of animals, it occupies 163 beautifully landscaped and wooded acres and is one of the country's most delightful zoos. Star resident is Hsing-Hsing, a rare giant panda donated by the People's Republic of China. He's best observed at feeding times, 11am and 3pm, and he's generally livelier at the morning feeding.

Enter the zoo at the Connecticut Avenue entrance; you will be right by the Education Building, where you can pick up a map and find out about feeding times and special activities taking place during your visit.

Zoo animals live in large open enclosures—simulations of their natural habitats—along two easy-to-follow numbered paths, **Olmsted Walk** and the **Valley Trail.** You can't get lost, and you won't unintentionally miss anything. Signs indicate the presence of baby animals born on the premises. Among the highlights are the **Great Ape House;** the **Reptile Discovery Center,** home to

Indonesian Komodo dragons, the world's largest lizards; and **Amazonia,** a lush rain forest habitat that includes a cascading tropical "Amazon River" and a re-creation of a tropical biology field station. Occupying a futuristic building under a 50-foot dome, it is home to 358 species of plants, dozens of animals and tropical birds, and immense naturalistic aquariums that simulate deep river pools.

Zoo facilities include stroller-rental stations, a number of gift shops, a bookstore, and several paid-parking lots. The lots fill up quickly, especially on weekends, so arrive early or take the Metro.

Anacostia Museum. 1901 Fort Place SE (off Martin Luther King Jr. Ave.). ☎ **202/287-3382** or 202/357-2700. Free admission. Daily 10am–5pm. Closed Dec 25. Metro: Anacostia; then take a W1 or W2 bus directly to the museum.

This unique Smithsonian establishment was created in 1967 as a neighborhood museum. Expanding its horizons over the years, the museum is today a national resource devoted to the identification, documentation, protection, and interpretation of the African-American experience, focusing on Washington, D.C., and the Upper South. The permanent collection includes about 5,000 items, ranging from videotapes of African-American church services to art, sheet music, and historic documents. In addition, the Anacostia produces a varying number of shows each year and offers a comprehensive schedule of free educational programs and activities in conjunction with exhibit themes. Call for an events calendar (which always includes children's activities) or pick one up when you visit.

4   Other Top Attractions

✪ **Library of Congress.** 1st St. SE (between Independence Ave. and E. Capitol St.). ☎ **202/707-8000.** Free admission. Madison Building Mon–Fri 8:30am–9:30pm, Sat 8:30am–6pm. Jefferson Building Mon–Sat 10am–5:30pm. Call ahead for tour information. Closed Sun and most major holidays. Metro: Capitol South.

Note: The Library's original Thomas Jefferson Building is set to reopen to the public in April 1997 following a 10-year renovation. At that time, it will once again become the focus of tours. If you are visiting after April, enter the building from First Street where you'll find the new Visitor's Center on the ground level. Free tickets will be available at the information desk in the Great Hall. Because the tour policy was still being worked out at this writing, call **202/707-8000** before you go for up-to-the-minute information.

This is the nation's library, established in 1800 "for the purchase of such books as may be necessary for the use of Congress." Over the years, it has expanded to serve all Americans, from the blind, for whom books are recorded on cassette and/or translated into braille, to research scholars and college students. Today the collection contains a mind-boggling 110 million items, with new materials being acquired at the rate of 10 items per minute!

As impressive as the scope of the library's effects and activities is its original home, the ornate Italian Renaissance-style **Thomas Jefferson Building.** It was erected between 1888 and 1897 to hold the burgeoning collection. Especially impressive are the exquisite marble Great Hall and the Main Reading Room, the latter under a 160-foot dome. Originally intended to hold the fruits of at least 150 years of collecting, the building was, in fact, filled up in 13. It is now supplemented by the **James Madison Memorial Building** and the **John Adams Building.** Pick up a calendar of events when you visit. The Madison Building offers interesting exhibits and features classic, rare, and unusual films in its Mary Pickford Theater. It also houses a noteworthy restaurant and cafeteria, though picnic tables out front provide a tempting alternative.

✪ **National Archives.** Constitution Ave. NW (between 7th and 9th sts.). ☎ **202/501-5000** for information on exhibits and films, 202/501-5400 for research information. Free admission. Exhibition Hall, Apr to Labor Day, daily 10am–9pm; day after Labor Day to Mar, daily 10am–5:30pm. Call for research hours. Closed Dec 25. Metro: Archives.

Keeper of America's documentary heritage, the National Archives displays our most cherished treasures in appropriately awe-inspiring surroundings. Housed in the Rotunda of the Exhibition Hall are the nation's three charter documents—the Declaration of Independence, the Constitution of the United States, and its Bill of Rights—which are on view daily to the public.

High above and flanking the documents are two larger-than-life murals painted by Barry Faulkner. One, entitled *The Declaration of Independence,* shows Thomas Jefferson presenting a draft of the Declaration to John Hancock, the presiding officer of the Continental Congress; the other, entitled *The Constitution,* shows James Madison submitting the Constitution to George Washington and the Constitutional Convention. In the display cases on either side of the Declaration of Independence are changing exhibits. The 1297 version of the Magna Carta, one of the bases for fundamental English privileges and rights, is on display in the Rotunda indefinitely.

The Archives serves as much more than a museum of cherished documents. Famous as a center for genealogical research—Alex Haley began his work on *Roots* here—it is sometimes called "the nation's memory." This federal institution is charged with sifting through the accumulated papers of a nation's official life—billions of pieces a year—and determining what to save and what to destroy. If you're casually thinking about tracing your roots, stop by Room 400 where a staff member can advise you about the time and effort that will be involved, and, if you decide to pursue it, exactly how to proceed. Free docent **tours** are given weekdays at 10:15am and 1:15pm by appointment only; call 202/501-5205 for details. Pick up a schedule of events (lectures, films, genealogy workshops) when you visit.

✪ **National Gallery of Art.** On the north side of the Mall (between 3rd and 7th sts. NW), with entrances at 6th St. and Constitution Ave. or Madison Dr., also at 4th and 7th sts. between Madison Dr. and Constitution Ave. ☎ **202/ 737-4215.** Free admission. Mon–Sat 10am–5pm, Sun 11am–6pm. Closed Jan 1 and Dec 25. Metro: Archives or Judiciary Square.

Most people don't realize it, but the National Gallery of Art is not really part of the Smithsonian complex; hence its listing here apart from the other Mall museums.

Housing one of the world's foremost collections of Western painting, sculpture, and graphic arts from the Middle Ages through the 20th century, the National Gallery has a dual personality. The original West Building, designed by John Russell Pope (architect of the Jefferson Memorial and the National Archives), is a neoclassic marble masterpiece with a domed rotunda over a colonnaded fountain and high-ceilinged corridors leading to delightful garden courts.

The West Building: On the main floor of the West Building, about 1,000 paintings are always on display. To the left (as you enter off the Mall) is the Art Information Room, housing the Micro Gallery, where those so inclined can design their own tours of the permanent collection and enhance their knowledge of art via user-friendly computers. Among the highlights: works by El Greco, Ribera, and Velázquez in the Spanish galleries; a stunning array of 18th- to 19th-century French paintings (including one of the world's greatest impressionist collections); and what is generally considered the finest Renaissance collection outside Italy (look at the only painting by Leonardo da Vinci outside Europe, *Ginevra de' Benci*).

The East Building: The scene of major changing exhibits, the East Building also houses an important collection of 20th-century art, including a massive aluminum Calder mobile under a seven-story skylight and, outside the front entrance, an immense bronze sculpture by Henry Moore.

In addition to its permanent collection, the National Gallery hosts a wide range of important temporary exhibits. Recent shows have ranged from "Michelangelo and His Influence" to "Picasso: The Early Years."

Pick up a floor plan and calendar of events at an information desk to find out about exhibits, films, tours, lectures, and concerts. Highly recommended are the free highlight **tours** (call for exact times) and audio tours. There are several dining options here (see "At Sightseeing Attractions" in chapter 4 for details).

✪ **Federal Bureau of Investigation.** J. Edgar Hoover FBI Building, E St. NW (between 9th and 10th sts.). ☎ **202/324-3447.** Free admission. Mon–Fri 8:45am–4:15pm. Closed Jan 1, Dec 25, and other federal holidays. Metro: Metro Center or Federal Triangle.

More than half a million annual visitors learn why crime doesn't pay by touring the headquarters of the FBI. The attraction is especially popular with kids. To beat the crowds, arrive for the one-hour **tour** before 8:45am or write to a senator or congressperson for a scheduled reservation as far in advance as possible (details in chapter 1).

The tour begins with a short videotape presentation about the priorities of the bureau: organized crime, white-collar crime, terrorism, foreign counterintelligence, illicit drugs, and violent crimes. En route, you'll learn about this organization's history (it was established in 1908) and its activities over the years. There are photos of the 10 most wanted fugitives; 444 of them (including seven women) have made the list since its inception in 1950, and 417 have been captured (130 apprehended through direct citizen cooperation).

Other exhibits deal with white-collar crime, organized crime, terrorism, drugs, and agent training. On display are more than 5,000 weapons, most confiscated from criminals like Al Capone and Bonnie and Clyde; they're used for reference purposes.

You'll also visit the DNA lab, the Firearms Unit (where it's determined whether a bullet was fired from a given weapon), the Material Analysis Unit (where from a tiny piece of paint the FBI can determine the approximate make and model of a car), the unit where hairs and fibers are examined, and a Forfeiture and Seizure Exhibit—a display of jewelry, furs, and other proceeds from illegal narcotics operations. The tour ends with a bang, when an agent gives a sharpshooting demonstration. He also talks about the FBI's firearms policy and gun safety.

John F. Kennedy Center for the Performing Arts. New Hampshire Ave. NW (at Rock Creek Pkwy.). ☎ **800/444-1324** for information or tickets, or

202/416-8341. Free admission. Daily 10am–midnight. Metro: Foggy Bottom (there's a free shuttle service from the station). Bus: 80 or 81 from Metro Center.

Opened in 1971, the Kennedy Center is both our national performing arts center and a memorial to John F. Kennedy. Set on 17 acres overlooking the Potomac, the striking $73 million facility, designed by noted architect Edward Durell Stone, houses an opera house, a concert hall, two stage theaters, a theater lab, and a film theater. The best way to see the Kennedy Center, including areas you can't visit on your own, is to take a free 50-minute guided **tour,** given daily between 10am and 1pm. Once again, you can beat the crowds by writing in advance to a senator or congressperson for tickets for a 9:30 or 9:45am VIP tour (details in chapter 1).

If you'd like to attend performances during your visit, call the toll-free number above and request the current issue of *Kennedy Center News Magazine,* a free publication that describes all Kennedy Center happenings and prices.

After the tour, walk around the building's terrace for a panoramic 360° view of Washington and plan a meal in one of the Kennedy Center restaurants (details in "At Sightseeing Attractions" in chapter 4). See chapter 8 for specifics on theater, concert, and film offerings. There is limited parking below the Kennedy Center.

✪ **Washington National Cathedral.** Massachusetts and Wisconsin aves. NW (entrance on Wisconsin Ave.). ☎ **202/537-6200.** Suggested donation $2 for adults, $1 for children under 12. May 1 to Labor Day Mon–Fri 10am–9pm, Sat 10am–4:30pm, Sun 7:30am–4:30pm; the rest of the year Mon–Sat 10am–4:30pm, Sun 7:30am–4:30pm. Metro: Tenleytown; then about a 20-minute walk. Bus: Any N bus up Massachusetts Avenue from Dupont Circle or any 30 series bus along Wisconsin Avenue.

Pierre L'Enfant's 1791 plan for the capital city included "a great church for national purposes," but, possibly because of early America's fear of mingling church and state, more than a century elapsed before the foundation for Washington National Cathedral was laid. Its actual name is the Cathedral Church of St. Peter and St. Paul. Though it's Episcopal in denomination, it has no local congregation and seeks to serve the entire nation as a house of prayer for all people. It has been the setting for every kind of religious observance from Jewish to Serbian Orthodox.

A church of this magnitude (it's the sixth-largest cathedral in the world!) took a long time to build. Its principal (but not original) architect, Philip Hubert Frohman, worked on the project from 1921 until his death in 1972. The foundation stone was laid in 1907 using the mallet with which George Washington set the Capitol cornerstone. It was completed with the placement of the final stone atop a pinnacle on the west front towers on September 29, 1990, 83 years to the day since it was begun.

English Gothic in style (with several distinctly 20th-century innovations, such as a stained-glass window commemorating the flight of *Apollo 11* and containing a piece of moon rock), the cathedral is built in the shape of a cross, complete with flying buttresses and gargoyles. Its 57-acre landscaped grounds have two lovely gardens; four schools, including the College of Preachers; an herb garden; a greenhouse; and a shop called The Herb Cottage.

The best way to explore the cathedral and see its abundance of art, architectural carvings, and statuary is to take a 45-minute **tour.** They leave continually from the west end of the nave, Monday to Saturday 10am to 3:15pm and Sunday 12:30 to 2:45pm.

Allow additional time to tour the grounds or "close," and to visit the Observation Gallery where 70 windows provide panoramic views. Tuesday and Wednesday afternoon tours are followed by a high tea in the Observation Gallery; reservations are required and a fee is charged. And you can, of course, attend **services** at the cathedral (Monday to Saturday at 7:30am, noon, 2:30pm, and 4pm; Sunday at 8, 9, and 11am and 4 and 6:30pm). September to June there's a folk guitar mass on Sunday at 10am.

✪ **Bureau of Engraving & Printing.** 14th and C sts. SW. ☎ **202/ 874-3188** or 202/874-2330. Free admission. Mon–Fri Apr 1–Sept 30 9am–1:50pm; Jun 1–Aug 31 additional evening tours 4–7:30pm; Oct l–Mar 31 9am–2pm. Closed Dec 25–Jan 1 and federal holidays. Metro: Smithsonian (Independence Avenue exit).

This is where they make the paper money. A staff of 2,600 works around the clock churning it out at the rate of about 22.5 million notes a day. But although the money is the big draw, it's not the whole story. The bureau prints many other products, including 25 billion postage stamps per year, presidential portraits, and White House invitations.

As many as 5,000 people line up each day to get a peek at all that moola, so early arrival, especially during the peak tourist season, is essential (unless you have secured VIP tickets from your senator or congressperson; details in chapter 1). From April 1 through September 30 (when you must obtain a ticket that specifies a tour time), the ticket booth on Raoul Wallenberg Place (formerly 15th Street) opens at 7:45am. Be there! The rest of the year no ticket is needed;

you just have to line up on 14th Street. *Note:* June 1 through August 31, there are evening tours from 4 to 7:30pm as well. Tickets are required; the booth opens at 3:30pm.

The 40-minute **guided tour** begins with a short introductory film. Then you'll see, through large windows, the processes that go into the making of paper money: the inking, stacking of bills, cutting, and examination for defects. Most printing here is done from engraved steel plates in a process known as "intaglio," the hardest to counterfeit because the slightest alteration will cause a noticeable change in the portrait in use. Additional exhibits include bills no longer in use, counterfeit money, and a $100,000 bill designed for official transactions (since 1969, the largest denomination printed for the general public is $100).

✪ **The Vietnam Veterans Memorial.** Just across from the Lincoln Memorial (east of Henry Bacon Dr. between 21st and 22nd sts. NW). ☎ **202/ 634-1568.** Free admission. Rangers on duty 8am–midnight daily. Ranger-led programs are given throughout the day June through Labor Day. Metro: Foggy Bottom.

To my mind, the most poignant sight in Washington is the Vietnam Veterans Memorial: two long, black granite walls inscribed with the names of the men and women who gave their lives, or remain missing, in the longest war in our nation's history. Even if no one close to you died in Vietnam, it's emotionally wrenching to watch visitors grimly studying the directories at either end to find out where their husbands, sons, and loved ones are listed. The slow walk along the 492-foot wall of names—close to 60,000 people, many of whom died very young—is a powerful evocation of the tragedy of all wars. And whatever your views on the war, it's also affecting to see how much the monument means to Vietnam vets who visit it.

The memorial was conceived by Vietnam veteran Jan Scruggs and built by the Vietnam Veterans Memorial Fund, a nonprofit organization that raised $7 million for the project. The VVMF was granted a two-acre site in tranquil Constitution Gardens to erect a memorial that would make no political statement about the war and would harmonize with neighboring memorials.

Yale senior Maya Ying Lin's design was chosen in a national competition open to all citizens over 18 years of age. It consists of two walls in a quiet, protected park setting, angled at 125° to point to the Washington Monument and the Lincoln Memorial. The wall's mirrorlike surface reflects surrounding trees, lawn, and monuments.

The names are inscribed in chronological order, documenting an epoch in American history as a series of individual sacrifices from the date of the first casualty in 1959 to the date of the last death in 1975.

The wall was erected in 1982. In 1984, a life-size sculpture of three Vietnam soldiers by Frederick Hart was installed at the entrance plaza. Another sculpture, the Vietnam Veterans Women's Memorial, depicting three servicewomen tending a wounded soldier was installed on Veterans Day 1993. Limited parking is available along Constitution Avenue.

✪ **United States Holocaust Memorial Museum.** 100 Raoul Wallenberg Place (formerly 15th St. SW; near Independence Ave., just off the Mall). ☎ **202/488-0400.** Free admission. Daily 10am–5:30pm. Closed Yom Kippur and Dec 25. Metro: Smithsonian.

Washington's multitude of museums celebrate the knowledge, the glory, and the creative achievements of human civilization. This museum reminds us of what can happen when civilization goes awry. It serves the dual purpose of commemorating the dead and educating the living to the dangers of prejudice and fanaticism and the fragility of freedom.

Even the building housing the museum is designed to reflect the bleakness of the Nazi era—to disorient the visitor with false perspectives and eerily somber spaces. An outer wall is reminiscent of an extermination camp's exterior brickwork, and towers evoke the guard towers of Auschwitz.

Upon entering, you will be issued an identity card of an actual victim of the Holocaust. By 1945, 66% of those whose lives are documented on these cards were dead. The tour begins on the fourth floor, where the events of 1933 to 1939 are portrayed. Exhibits focus on the rise of Nazism—book burnings, the Nuremberg Laws, and the terror of "Kristallnacht" in 1938, when hundreds of Jewish synagogues and businesses were destroyed. A winding path takes you to a border crossing where the near impossibility of escape is dramatized. No countries will admit you; you're forced to return to the horror.

On the third floor (documenting the years 1940 to 1944), constricting walls symbolize the narrowing choices of people caught up in the Nazi machine. You'll board a Polish freight car of the type used to transport Jews from the Warsaw ghetto to Treblinka and hear recordings of survivors telling what life in the camps was like. A reconstructed Auschwitz barracks, the yellow stars Jews were forced to wear, instruments of genocide, and a gas-chamber door are among thousands of artifacts bearing silent witness to this grim era.

On the second floor, the focus turns to a more heartening story: how non-Jews throughout Europe, by exercising individual action and responsibility, saved Jews at great personal risk. The saga continues with exhibits on the liberation of the camps, life in DP camps, emigration to Israel and America, and the Nuremberg trials. The tour ends in the hexagonal Hall of Remembrance, a place to meditate on what you've experienced and light a candle for the victims.

Dozens of educational interactive videos further enhance understanding, as do films, lectures, cultural events, and temporary exhibits. The displays are designed so you can shield children (or yourself) from the most graphic material. This museum is not like any other you've ever visited. It's a deeply affecting encounter with evil—an opportunity to learn the lessons of history and the role of individual responsibility in protecting freedom and preserving human rights.

Allow at least four or five hours to see the exhibits. I would not recommend bringing children under 12 to this museum; even for older children, however, it's advisable to prepare them for what they'll see.

Touring Tips: Because so many people want to visit the museum, tickets specifying a visit time (in 15-minute intervals) are required. Reserve them via Protix (☎ 800/400-9373). There's a small service charge. You can also get them at the museum beginning at 10am daily (lines form earlier). If for some reason you can't obtain tickets, there are sections of the museum you can see without them.

✪ **Union Station.** 50 Massachusetts Ave. NE. ☎ **202/371-9441.** Free admission. Daily 24 hours. Shops, Mon–Sat 10am–9pm, Sun noon–6pm. Metro: Union Station.

In Washington, D.C., the very train station where you arrive is itself a noteworthy sightseeing attraction. Union Station, a monument to the great age of rail travel built between 1903 and 1907, was painstakingly restored in the 1980s to its original grandeur at a cost of $160 million. The station was designed by noted architect Daniel H. Burnham, an enthusiast of French beaux arts neoclassicism and a member of the McMillan Commission, an illustrious task force assembled in 1900 to beautify the Mall and make the city an appropriately imposing world capital.

When it opened in 1907, this was the largest train station in the world. Its Ionic-colonnaded exterior is of white granite, and 100 eagles are portrayed in the facade. Out front are a replica of the Liberty Bell and a monumental statue of Columbus. The station's interior, entered through graceful 50-foot Constantinian arches, is finished with extravagant materials: acres of white marble flooring with red "Champlain dots," bronze grilles, elaborate coffered ceilings (embellished with a half million dollars' worth of 22-karat gold leaf!), and rich Honduran mahogany. Off the Main Hall is the East Hall, one of the most beautiful areas of the station, with scagliola marble walls and columns, a gorgeous hand-stenciled skylight ceiling, and stunning murals of classical scenes inspired by ancient Pompeian art. Today it's the station's plushest shopping venue.

After the 1960s, with the decline of rail travel, the station fell on hard times. Rain damage caused parts of the roof to cave in, and the entire building—with floors buckling, rats running about, and mushrooms sprouting in damp rooms—was sealed in 1981. That same year, Congress enacted legislation to preserve and faithfully restore this national treasure.

Today, Union Station is once again a vibrant entity, a transportation/dining/shopping/entertainment center patronized by locals and visitors alike. About 100 retail shops on three levels offer a wide array of merchandise. The skylit Main Concourse, extending the entire length of the station, has become the primary shopping area as well as a ticketing and baggage facility. And a nine-screen cinema complex and beautiful food court have been installed on the lower level. For information on Union Station restaurants and shops, see chapter 7 and "At Sightseeing Attractions" in chapter 4.

✪ **Ford's Theatre & Lincoln Museum.** 511 10th St. NW (between E and F sts.). ☎ **202/426-6924.** Free admission. Daily 9am–5pm. Closed Dec 25. Metro: Metro Center.

On April 14, 1865, President Lincoln was in the audience of Ford's Theatre; everyone was laughing at a funny line from Tom Taylor's celebrated comedy, *Our American Cousin,* when actor John Wilkes Booth grabbed center stage by shooting the president. After Lincoln's assassination, the theater was closed by order of Secretary of War Edwin M. Stanton. For many years afterward it was used as an office by the War Department. In 1893, 22 clerks were killed when three floors of the building collapsed. It remained in disuse until the 1960s, when it was remodeled and restored to its appearance on the night of the tragedy.

Except when rehearsals or matinees are in progress (call before you go), visitors can see the theater and trace Booth's movements on that fateful night. Free 15-minute talks on the history of the theater and the story of the assassination are given throughout the day (call for exact times). Be sure to visit the **Lincoln Museum** in the basement, where exhibits—including the Derringer pistol used by Booth and a diary in which he outlines his rationalization for the deed—focus on events surrounding Lincoln's assassination and the trial of the conspirators.

The House Where Lincoln Died (The Petersen House). 516 10th St. NW. ☎ **202/426-6924.** Free admission. Daily 9am–5pm. Closed Dec 25. Metro: Metro Center.

After the shooting at Ford's Theater, Lincoln was carried across the street to the home of William Petersen, a tailor. Now furnished with period pieces, it looks much as it did on that fateful April night. You'll see the front parlor where an anguished Mary Todd Lincoln spent the night with her son, Robert.

Twelve years after Lincoln's death, the house was sold to Louis Schade, who published a newspaper called the *Washington Sentinel* in its basement for many years. In 1896, the government bought the house for $30,000, and it is now maintained by the National Park Service.

5　More Attractions

✪ **Phillips Collection.** 1600 21st St. NW (at Q St.). ☎ **202/387-2151.** Admission Sat–Sun, $6.50 adults, $3.25 seniors and students, free for children under 18; contribution suggested Tues–Fri. Tues–Sat 10am–5pm, Sun noon–7pm (noon–5pm Jun–Aug, Thurs nights till 8:30pm). Closed Mon, Jan 1, July 4, Thanksgiving Day, and Dec 25. Metro: Dupont Circle (Q St. exit).

Conceived as "a museum of modern art and its sources," this intimate establishment, occupying an elegant 1890s Georgian Revival mansion and a later wing, houses the exquisite collection of Duncan and Marjorie Phillips, avid collectors and proselytizers of modernism. Carpeted rooms, with leaded- and stained-glass windows, oak paneling, plush chairs and sofas, and frequently, fireplaces create a comfortable, homelike setting for viewing art. Today the collection includes more than 2,500 works. Goya, van Gogh, and Cézanne are among the "sources" or forerunners of modernism represented. Modern notables include Rothko, Kandinsky, Matisse, Klee, Degas, Picasso, and others. It's a collection no art lover should miss.

Free **tours** are given on Wednesday and Saturday at 2pm, and a full schedule of events includes gallery talks, lectures, and free concerts in the ornate music room (every Sunday at 5pm, September to May; early arrival is advised at these popular performances). Thursdays the museum stays open until 8:30pm for **Artful Evenings** with music, gallery talks, and a cash bar; admission is $5.

Corcoran Gallery of Art. 17th St. NW (between E St. and New York Ave.). ☎ **202/638-3211** or 202/638-1439. Free admission. Wed and Fri–Mon 10am–5pm, Thurs 10am–9pm. Closed Tues, Jan 1, and Dec 25. Metro: Farragut West or Farragut North.

The first art museum in Washington (and one of the first in the nation), the Corcoran Gallery was housed from 1874 to 1896 in the redbrick and brownstone building that is now the Renwick. The collection outgrew its quarters and was transferred in 1897 to its present beaux arts building, designed by Ernest Flagg.

The collection itself, shown in rotating exhibits, focuses chiefly on American art. A prominent Washington banker, William Wilson Corcoran was among the first wealthy American collectors to realize the importance of encouraging and supporting this country's artists. The collection comprehensively spans American art from 18th-century portraiture to the 19th-century works of Remington, Sargent, and Homer to 20th-century moderns like Nevelson, Warhol, and Rothko.

The Corcoran is not, however, an exclusively American art museum. On the first floor is the collection from the estate of Sen. William Andrews Clark, an eclectic grouping of Dutch and Flemish masters, European painters, French impressionists, Barbizon landscapes, Delft porcelains, a Louis XVI salon doré transported in toto from Paris, and more. Other non-American aspects of the museum's collection include a room of exquisite Corot landscapes, another of medieval Renaissance tapestries, and numerous Daumier lithographs donated by Dr. Armand Hammer.

Free 30-minute **tours** are given at 12:30pm (and on Thursday also at 7:30pm). Pick up a schedule of events—temporary exhibits, gallery talks, concerts, art auctions, and more. There's a charming restaurant on the premises (details in "At Sightseeing Attractions" in chapter 4).

National Museum of Women in the Arts. 1250 New York Ave. NW (at 13th St.). ☎ **202/783-5000.** Suggested contribution, $3 adults, $2 children. Mon–Sat 10am–5pm, Sun noon–5pm. Closed Jan 1, Thanksgiving Day, and Dec 25. Metro: Metro Center.

Celebrating "the contribution of women to the history of art," this relatively new museum (opened 1987) is Washington's 72nd but a national first. Founders Wilhelmina and Wallace Holladay, who donated the core of the permanent collection—more than 200 works by women spanning the 16th through the 20th century—became interested in women's art in the 1960s. After discovering that no women were included in H. W. Janson's *History of Art,* a standard text (this, by the way, did not change until 1986!), the Holladays began collecting art by women, and the concept of a women's art museum (to begin correcting the inequities of under-representation) soon evolved.

Since its opening, the collection has grown to more than 2,000 works by artists including Rosa Bonheur, Frida Kahlo, Helen Frankenthaler, Barbara Hepworth, Georgia O'Keeffe, Camille Claudel, Lila Cabot Perry, Mary Cassatt, Elaine de Kooning, and Käthe Kollwitz, along with many other lesser known but notable artists from earlier centuries.

The museum is housed in a magnificent Renaissance Revival landmark building designed in 1907 as a Masonic temple by noted architect Waddy Wood. The charming and sunny Mezzanine Cafe serves light lunches Monday through Saturday—soups, salads, and sandwiches.

United States Botanic Garden. 100 Maryland Ave. (at the east end of the Mall). ☎ **202/225-8333.** Free admission. Daily 9am–5pm. Metro: Federal Center SW.

Originally conceived by Washington, Jefferson, and Madison, and opened in 1820, the Botanic Garden is a series of connected glass-and-stone buildings and greenhouses filled with pots of brightly colored flowers, rock beds of ferns, Spanish moss, palms, and shrubs. Tropical, subtropical, and desert plants highlight the collection. The Conservatory, inspired by 17th-century French orangeries, is entered via a room with two reflecting pool fountains under a skylight. Poinsettias bloom at Christmas, chrysanthemums in fall; spring is heralded by lilies, tulips, hyacinths, and daffodils; and a large collection of orchids is on display year-round. The Summer Terrace, with umbrella tables amid plants and flower beds overlooking the Capitol's reflecting pool, is a lovely spot for a picnic lunch. The complex also includes adjacent Bartholdi Park, about the size of a city block, with a stunning cast-iron classical fountain created by Frédéric Auguste Bartholdi, designer of the Statue of Liberty. For information on special shows, tours, lectures, and classes, call the above number.

✪ **Dumbarton Oaks.** 1703 32nd St. NW (entrance to the collections on 32nd St., between R and S sts.; garden entrance at 31st and R sts.). ☎ **202/**

339-6401. Garden, $3 adults, $2 children under 12 and senior citizens; collections, free. Garden (weather permitting), Nov–Mar, daily 2–5pm; Apr–Oct, daily 2–6pm. Collections, Tues–Sun 2–5pm. Gardens are closed federal holidays and Dec 24.

This 16-acre estate is a research center for studies in Byzantine and pre-Columbian art and history, as well as landscape architecture. Its yards, which wind gently down to Rock Creek Ravine, are magical, modeled after European gardens. The pre-Columbian museum, designed by Philip Johnson, is a small gem, and the Byzantine collection is a rich one.

The unusual collection originated with Robert Woods Bliss and his wife, Mildred. In 1940, they turned over the estate, their extensive Byzantine collection, a library of works on Byzantine civilization, and 16 acres (including 10 acres of exquisite formal gardens) to Mr. Bliss's alma mater, Harvard, and provided endowment funds for continuing research in Byzantine studies. In the early 1960s, they also donated their pre-Columbian collection and financed the building of a wing to house it, as well as a second wing for Mrs. Bliss's collection of rare books on landscape gardening.

The historic music room, furnished in French, Italian, and Spanish antiques, was the setting for the 1944 Dumbarton Oaks Conversations about the United Nations. Don't miss the formal gardens, which include an Orangery, a Rose Garden (final resting place of the Blisses amid 1,000 rose bushes), wisteria-covered arbors, herbaceous borders, groves of cherry trees, and magnolias. You can picnic nearby in Montrose Park.

National Geographic Society's Explorers Hall. 17th and M sts. NW. ☎ **202/857-7588.** Free admission. Mon–Sat 9am–5pm, Sun 10am–5pm. Closed Dec 25. Metro: Farragut North (Connecticut Ave. and L St. exit) or Farragut West.

The National Geographic Society was founded in 1888 for "the increase and diffusion of geographic knowledge." At Explorers Hall, dozens of fascinating displays, most of them using interactive videos, put that knowledge literally at your fingertips. In Geographica, on the north side of the hall, you can touch a tornado, find out what it's like inside the earth, explore the vast Martian landscape, and study the origin of humankind. Many of the video exhibits have overtones of environmental awareness.

Also on display are a scale model of Jacques Cousteau's diving saucer in which he descended to 25,000 feet; the flag and dog sled, among other equipment, of Adm. Robert E. Peary, the first man to reach the North Pole; an *Aepyornis maximus* egg, from Madagascar's extinct 1,000-pound flightless "elephant bird"; and the world's largest freestanding globe.

Within walking distance of the White House, this is a great place to take the kids, but they should be at least 9 or 10 years old. Younger children will probably not understand most of the exhibits.

The Folger Shakespeare Library. 201 E. Capitol St. SE. ☎ **202/544-7077.** Free admission. Mon–Sat 10am–4pm. Closed federal holidays. Metro: Capitol South.

"Shakespeare taught us that the little world of the heart is vaster, deeper, and richer than the spaces of astronomy," wrote Ralph Waldo Emerson in 1864. A decade later, Amherst student Henry Clay Folger was profoundly affected upon hearing a lecture by Emerson similarly extolling the bard. Folger purchased an inexpensive set of Shakespeare's plays and went on to amass the world's largest collection of his printed works, today housed in the Folger Shakespeare Library.

The building itself has a marble facade decorated with nine bas-relief scenes from Shakespeare's plays; it's a striking example of art deco classicism. A statue of Puck stands in the west garden, and quotations from the Bard and from contemporaries such as Ben Jonson adorn the exterior walls. An Elizabethan garden on the east side of the building is planted with flowers and herbs of the period, many of them mentioned in the plays.

The facility, which houses some 250,000 books, 100,000 of which are rare, is an important research center not only for Shakespearean scholars, but for those studying any aspect of the English and continental Renaissance. And the oak-paneled Great Hall has an intricate plaster ceiling decorated with Shakespeare's coat of arms, fleurs-de-lis, and other motifs. On display are rotating exhibits from the permanent collection: books, paintings, playbills, Renaissance musical instruments, and more.

At the end of the Great Hall is a theater designed to suggest an Elizabethan theater where plays, concerts, readings, and Shakespeare-related events take place (see chapter 8 for details).

Free walk-in **tours** are given at 11am.

United States Navy Memorial. 701 Pennsylvania Ave. NW. ☎ **800/ 723-3557** or 202/628-3557. Free admission. Mon–Sat 9:30am–5pm, Sun noon–5pm. Closed Thanksgiving, New Year's Day, and Dec. 25. Metro: Archives/Navy Memorial.

Authorized by Congress in 1980 to honor the men and women of the U.S. Navy, this memorial is comprised of a 100-foot-diameter circular plaza bearing a granite world map flanked by fountains and waterfalls salted with waters from the seven seas. A statue of *The Lone Sailor* watching over the map represents all who have served in the navy. And two sculpture walls adorned with bronze bas-reliefs commemorate navy history and related maritime services.

The building adjoining the memorial houses a naval heritage center in which museum highlights include interactive video kiosks proffering a wealth of information about navy ships, aircraft, and history; the Navy Memorial Log Room, a computerized record of past and present navy personnel; the Presidents Room, honoring six U.S. presidents who served in the navy and two who were secretary of the navy. Guided **tours** are available from the front desk, subject to staff availability. The plaza is the scene of many free band concerts in spring and summer; call for details.

The Korean War Veterans Memorial. Just across from the Lincoln Memorial (east of French Drive, between 21st and 23rd sts. NW). ☎ **202/634-1568.** Free admission. Rangers on duty 8am–midnight daily. Metro: Foggy Bottom.

This privately funded new memorial, focusing on an American flag, honors those who served in Korea, a three-year conflict (1950–53) that produced almost as many casualties as Vietnam. It consists of a circular "Pool of Remembrance" in a grove of trees and a triangular "Field of Service." The latter is highlighted by statues of 19 infantrymen, with several emerging from the woods creating the impression there are legions to follow. In addition, a 164-foot-long black granite wall depicts the array of combat and combat support troops that served in Korea (nurses, chaplains, airmen, gunners, mechanics, cooks, and others); a raised granite curb lists the 22 nations that contributed to the UN's effort there; and a commemorative area honors KIAs, MIAs, and POWs. Limited parking is available along Ohio Drive.

6 Outside the District

Arlington National Cemetery. Just across the Memorial Bridge from the base of the Lincoln Memorial. ☎ **703/607-8052.** Free admission. Apr–Sept 8am–7pm, until 5pm the rest of the year. Metro: Arlington National Cemetery. If you come by car, parking is $1.25 an hour for the first three hours, $2 an hour thereafter. The cemetery is also accessible via Tourmobile.

Upon arrival, head over to the **Visitor Center,** where you can view exhibits, pick up a detailed map, use the restrooms (there are

Arlington National Cemetery

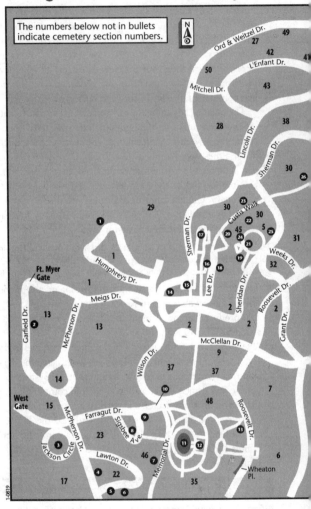

The numbers below not in bullets indicate cemetery section numbers.

N

Ord & Weitzel Dr.
L'Enfant Dr.
Mitchell Dr.
Lincoln Dr.
Sherman Dr.
Custis Walk
Weeks Dr.
Humphreys Dr.
Ft. Myer Gate
Lee Dr.
Sheridan Dr.
Roosevelt Dr.
Grant Dr.
Meigs Dr.
Garfield Dr.
McPherson Dr.
Wilson Dr.
McClellan Dr.
West Gate
Farragut Dr.
Sigsbee Ave.
Jackson Circle
Lawton Dr.
Memorial Dr.
Roosevelt Dr.
Wheaton Pl.

122

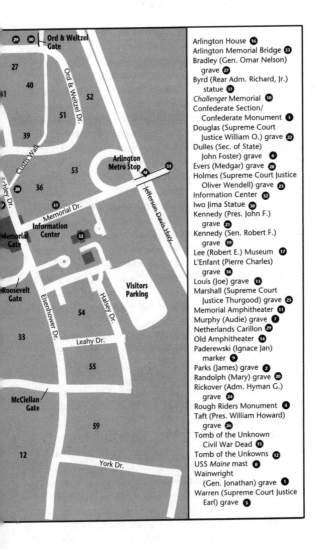

Arlington House **16**
Arlington Memorial Bridge **33**
Bradley (Gen. Omar Nelson) grave **27**
Byrd (Rear Adm. Richard, Jr.) statue **31**
Challenger Memorial **10**
Confederate Section/ Confederate Monument **3**
Douglas (Supreme Court Justice William O.) grave **22**
Dulles (Sec. of State John Foster) grave **6**
Evers (Medgar) grave **28**
Holmes (Supreme Court Justice Oliver Wendell) grave **23**
Information Center **32**
Iwo Jima Statue **30**
Kennedy (Pres. John F.) grave **21**
Kennedy (Sen. Robert F.) grave **19**
Lee (Robert E.) Museum **17**
L'Enfant (Pierre Charles) grave **18**
Louis (Joe) grave **13**
Marshall (Supreme Court Justice Thurgood) grave **25**
Memorial Amphitheater **11**
Murphy (Audie) grave **7**
Netherlands Carillon **29**
Old Amphitheater **14**
Paderewski (Ignace Jan) marker **9**
Parks (James) grave **2**
Randolph (Mary) grave **20**
Rickover (Adm. Hyman G.) grave **24**
Rough Riders Monument **4**
Taft (Pres. William Howard) grave **26**
Tomb of the Unknown Civil War Dead **15**
Tomb of the Unkowns **12**
USS *Maine* mast **8**
Wainwright (Gen. Jonathan) grave **1**
Warren (Supreme Court Justice Earl) grave **5**

123

no others until you get to Arlington House), and purchase a Tourmobile ticket allowing you to stop at all major sights and then reboard whenever you like. Service is continuous, and the narrated commentary is informative. (See "Getting Around" in chapter 2 for details.) However, if you've got lots of stamina, consider doing the tour on foot. Riding the Tourmobile with crowds of tourists (usually in a holiday mood) makes me feel like I'm at Universal Studios. Walking provides a more contemplative experience. You could compromise by walking some of the distance and then riding some. And speaking of that holiday mood, the cemetery staff asked me to remind you that this is still an active cemetery where tourists should observe the proper decorum.

This famous national shrine occupies approximately 612 acres on the high hills overlooking the capital from the west side of the Memorial Bridge. It honors many national heroes and more than 240,000 war dead, veterans, and dependents. Many graves of the famous at Arlington bear nothing more than simple markers. Five-star Gen. John J. Pershing's is one of those. Secretary of State John Foster Dulles is buried here. So are Pres. William Howard Taft and Supreme Court Justice Thurgood Marshall. Cemetery highlights include:

The **Tomb of the Unknowns,** containing the unidentified remains of service members from both world wars, the Korean War, and the Vietnam War. It's an unembellished massive white-marble block, moving in its simplicity. Inscribed are the words: "Here rests in honored glory an American Soldier known but to God." Changing of the guard is performed every half hour April to September and every hour on the hour October to March.

Arlington House (☎ **703/557-0613**) was for 30 years (1831–61) the residence of Robert E. Lee. Lee married the greatgrand-daughter of Martha Washington, Mary Anna Randolph Custis, who inherited the estate upon the death of her father. It was at Arlington House that Lee, having received the news of Virginia's secession from the Union, decided to resign his commission in the U.S. Army. During the Civil War the estate was taken over by Union forces, and troops were buried there. A year before the defeat of the Confederate forces at Gettysburg, the estate was bought by the U.S. government. A fine example of Greek Revival architecture combined with many features of the grand plantation houses of the early 1800s, it has been administered by the National Park Service since 1933.

Guided tours of the house are given continuously throughout the day by park rangers in pre–Civil War costume. About 30% of the furnishings are original. Slave quarters and a small museum adjoin. Admission is free. It's open daily 9:30am to 4:30pm October to March, until 6pm April to September; closed January 1 and December 25.

Pierre Charles L'Enfant's grave was placed near Arlington House at a spot that is believed to offer the best view of Washington, the city he designed.

Below Arlington House is the **gravesite of John Fitzgerald Kennedy.** Simplicity is the key to grandeur here, too. John Carl Warnecke designed a low crescent wall embracing a marble terrace, inscribed with memorable words of the 35th U.S. president, including his famous utterance, "And so my fellow Americans, ask not what your country can do for you, ask what you can do for your country." Jacqueline Kennedy Onassis rests next to her husband, and Sen. Robert Kennedy is buried close by. The Kennedy graves attract streams of visitors. Arrive as close to 8am as possible to experience the mood of quiet contemplation the site evokes when it's not mobbed with tourists. Looking north, there's a spectacular view of Washington.

About 1¹/₂ miles from the Kennedy graves, the **Marine Corps Memorial,** the famous statue of the marines raising the flag on Iwo Jima, stands near the north (or Orde-Weitzel Gate) entrance to the cemetery as a tribute to Marines who died in all wars. In summer there are military parades on the grounds on Tuesday evenings at 7pm.

Close to the Iwo Jima statue is the **Netherlands Carillon,** a gift from the people of the Netherlands, with 50 bells. Every spring thousands of tulip bulbs are planted on the surrounding grounds. Carillon concerts take place from 2 to 4pm on Saturday during April, May, and September; from 6 to 8pm on Saturday from June to August. (Sometimes the hours change; call 703/285-2598 before you go.) Visitors are permitted to enter the tower to watch the carillonneur perform and enjoy panoramic views of Washington.

7 Parks & Gardens

Like most cities, Washington has manicured pockets of green amid its high-rise office buildings and superhighways. Unlike most cities, it's also extensively endowed with vast natural areas all centrally located within the District: thousands of parkland acres, two rivers, a tree-lined canalside trail, an untamed wilderness area, and a few thousand cherry trees.

ROCK CREEK PARK

A 1,750-acre valley within the District of Columbia, extending 12 miles from the Potomac River to the Maryland border (another 2,700 acres), ✪ **Rock Creek Park** is one of the biggest and finest city parks in the nation.

The park's offerings include the Carter Barron Amphitheater (see chapter 8), playgrounds, picnic areas, an extensive system of beautiful wooded hiking trails, tennis courts, and a golf course.

For full information on the wide range of park programs and activities, visit the **Rock Creek Nature Center,** 5200 Glover Rd. NW (☎ **202/426-6829**), Wednesday to Sunday 9am to 5pm; or **Park Headquarters,** 3545 Williamsburg Rd. NW (☎ **202/282-1063**), Monday to Friday 7:45am to 4:15pm. The Nature Center itself is the scene of numerous activities, including weekend planetarium shows for kids (minimum age four) and adults, nature films, crafts demonstrations, live animal demonstrations, and guided nature walks, plus a daily mix of lectures, films, and other events.

There's convenient **free parking** throughout the park. To get to the Nature Center by public transport, take the Metro to Friendship Heights and transfer to an E2 or E3 bus to Military Road and Oregon Avenue/Glover Road.

POTOMAC PARK

West and East Potomac Parks, their 720 riverside acres divided by the Tidal Basin, are most famous for their spring display of **cherry blossoms** and all the hoopla that goes with it.

West Potomac Park has 1,300 trees bordering the Tidal Basin. It's the focal point of many of the week-long celebrations. The trees bloom for a little less than two weeks beginning somewhere between March 20 and April 17; April 5 is the average date. See the calendar of events in chapter 1 for further details.

East Potomac Park also has **picnic grounds; 24 tennis courts,** including five indoors and three lit for night play (☎ 202/554-5962); one 18-hole and two 9-hole **golf courses** (☎ 202/863-9007); a large **swimming pool** (☎ 202/727-6523); and **biking** and **hiking** paths by the water. West Potomac Park encompasses Constitution Gardens; the Vietnam, Korean, Lincoln, and Jefferson Memorials; a small island where ducks live; and the Reflecting Pool.

CHESAPEAKE & OHIO CANAL NATIONAL HISTORICAL PARK (C&O CANAL)

Note: Due to extensive flooding early in 1996, the towpath was in disrepair; it is hoped that by the time of your visit, it will have been restored.

One of the great joys of living in Washington is the ✪ **C&O Canal** and its unspoiled 184¹/₂-mile towpath. One leaves urban cares and stresses behind while hiking, strolling, jogging, cycling, or boating in this lush, natural setting of ancient oaks and red maples, giant sycamores, willows, and wildflowers. But it wasn't always just a leisure spot for city people. It was built in the 1800s, when water routes were considered vital to transportation. Even before it was completed, however, the B&O Railroad, which was constructed at about the same time and along the same route, had begun to render it obsolete. Today, perhaps, it serves an even more important purpose as a cherished urban refuge.

Canal Activities   Headquarters for canal activities is the **Office of the Superintendent,** C&O Canal National Historical Park, P.O. Box 4, Sharpsburg, MD 21782 (☎ **301/739-4200**). Another good source of information is the National Park Service office at **Great Falls Tavern Visitor Center,** 11710 MacArthur Blvd., Potomac, MD 20854 (☎ **301/299-3613**). At this 1831 tavern, you can see museum exhibits and a film about the canal; there's also a bookstore on the premises. And April to November, Wednesday to Sunday, the **Georgetown Information Center,** 1057 Thomas Jefferson St. NW (☎ **202/653-5844**), can also provide maps and information. Call ahead for hours at all the above.

Stop at **Fletcher's Boat House,** described in "Active Sports," below (☎ **202/244-0461**), to rent **bikes** or **boats** or purchase bait and tackle (or a license) for **fishing.** A snack bar and picnic area are on the premises. It's also accessible by car.

Also enjoyable is the **mule-drawn 19th-century canal boat trip** led by Park Service rangers in period dress. They regale passengers with canal legend and lore and sing period songs. These boats depart Wednesday through Sunday from mid-April to early November; call **202/653-5844** or 301/299-3613 for departure times. Tickets are available at the Georgetown Information Center or the Great Falls Tavern (address and phone for both above). The fare is $5 for adults, $3.50 for children under 12 and seniors over 62.

UNITED STATES NATIONAL ARBORETUM

A research and educational center focusing on a vast variety of land-scape plants, the ✪ **U.S. National Arboretum,** 3501 New York Ave. NE (☎ **202/245-2726**), is a must-see for the horticulturally inclined. Its 9$^1/_2$ miles of paved roads meander through 444 hilly acres of azaleas (the most extensive plantings in the nation), magno-lias, hollies, dwarf confers, and boxwoods. The highlight for me is the **National Bonsai and Penjing Museum,** which includes a Bicentennial gift from Japan of 53 beautiful miniature trees, some of them more than three centuries old. The **Herb Garden,** another highlight, includes an historic rose garden with 100 old-fashioned fragrant varieties. And a magnificent sight is the arboretum's **acropolis,** 22 of the original U.S. Capitol columns designed by Ben-jamin Latrobe in a setting created by the noted English landscape artist Russell Page.

Magnolias and early bulbs bloom in late March or early April; rhododendrons, daffodils, and flowering cherry trees in mid-April; azaleas and peonies in May; lilies and crape myrtles in summer. In autumn, the arboretum is ablaze in reds and oranges as the leaves change color.

The arboretum is open daily 8am to 5pm, the bonsai collection 10am to 3:30pm. Everything is closed December 25. Take bus B2 from the Stadium Armory Metro station to Bladensburg Road and R Street NE. Or hop in a taxi; it's only a few dollars. If you drive, **parking** is free (you can drive through if you wish). Frequent tours, lectures, and workshops (including bonsai classes) are offered, and a comprehensive guidebook is available in the gift shop.

THEODORE ROOSEVELT ISLAND

A serene 88-acre wilderness preserve, Theodore Roosevelt Island is a memorial to our 26th president, in recognition of his contributions to conservation. It's an island preserve of swamp, marsh, and upland forest that's a haven for rabbits, chipmunks, great owls, fox, musk-rat, turtles, and groundhogs. It's a complex ecosystem in which cat-tails, arrow arum, and pickerelweed growing in the marshes create a hospitable habitat for abundant bird life. And willow, ash, and maple trees rooted on the mudflats create the swamp environment favored by the raccoon in its search for crayfish. You can observe these flora and fauna in their natural environs on 2$^1/_2$ miles of foot trails. In the northern center of the island, overlooking an oval terrace encircled by a water-filled moat, stands a 17-foot bronze statue of Roosevelt.

To get to the island, take the George Washington Memorial Parkway exit north from the Theodore Roosevelt Bridge. The **parking** area is accessible only from the northbound lane; from there, a pedestrian bridge connects the island with the Virginia shore. You can also rent a canoe at Thompson's Boat Center (see "Boating" in "Active Sports," below) and paddle over, or walk across the pedestrian bridge at Rosslyn Circle, two blocks from the **Rosslyn Metro** station. **Picnicking** is permitted on the grounds near the memorial.

For further information, contact the District Ranger, Theodore Roosevelt Island, George Washington Memorial Parkway, c/o Turkey Run Park, McLean, VA 22101 (☎ **703/285-2598**).

8 Especially for Kids

Check for special children's events at museum information desks when you enter; better yet, call the day before you go to find out what's available. Also keep in mind the Friday "Weekend" section of the *Washington Post* lists numerous activities (mostly free) for kids: special museum events, children's theater, storytelling programs, puppet shows, video-game competitions, and so forth. In addition to the major monuments, here's a rundown of the biggest kid-pleasers in town (for details, see the full entries earlier in this chapter):

National Air and Space Museum. Spectacular IMAX films (don't miss), planetarium shows, missiles, rockets, and a walk-through orbital workshop.

National Museum of Natural History. A Discovery Room just for youngsters, an insect zoo, shrunken heads, and dinosaurs.

National Museum of American History. The Foucault Pendulum, locomotives, Archie Bunker's chair, and an old-fashioned ice-cream parlor.

Federal Bureau of Investigation. Gangster memorabilia, crime-solving methods, espionage devices, and a sharpshooting demonstration.

Bureau of Engraving and Printing. Kids enjoy looking at immense piles of money as much as you do.

National Zoological Park. Kids always love a zoo, and this is an especially nice one.

Ford's Theatre and Lincoln Museum and the **House Where Lincoln Died.** Booth's gun and diary, the clothes Lincoln was wearing the night he was assassinated, and other such grisly artifacts. Kids adore the whole business.

National Geographic Society's Explorers Hall. A moon rock, the egg of an extinct "elephant bird" (if it hatched it would weigh 1,000 pounds), numerous interactive videos. The magazine comes alive.

9   Organized Tours

BY BUS

Even if you have just a few days to spend in Washington, I think you can do better on your own. However, a guided motorcoach tour can provide a good city overview.

The **Gray Line** (☎ 202/289-1995) offers a variety of tours, among them: "Washington After Dark" (three hours), focusing on night-lit national monuments and federal buildings; the "Washington, D.C., All-Day Combination Tour," which includes major Washington sights plus Arlington National Cemetery, Mount Vernon, and Alexandria; and the full-day "Interiors of Public Buildings," visiting Ford's Theatre, the Jefferson Memorial, the Museum of American History, the Capitol, the Supreme Court, the National Air and Space Museum, and the National Archives. Some tours use British double-decker buses. There are also trips as far afield as Colonial Williamsburg, Harper's Ferry, Gettysburg, and Charlottesville. Tours depart from Gray Line's Union Station terminal, with pickups at most major hotels. Headsets and tour tapes in foreign languages are available for certain afternoon tours.

A local company, **All About Town,** 519 6th St. NW (☎ 202/393-3696), offers a similar range of tours. Pickup is offered at major hotels. Call for details or, once again, inquire at your hotel desk.

Consider, too, **Tourmobile** and **Old Town Trolley** tours (see "Getting Around" in chapter 2 for details).

BY BOAT

Since Washington is a river city, why not see it by boat? **Spirit of Washington Cruises,** Pier 4 at 6th and Water streets SW (☎ 202/554-8000), offers a variety of such trips, both within the district and as far afield as Mount Vernon, from early March to December. Lunch and dinner cruises include a 20-minute high-energy musical revue. Call for departure times and prices, and make reservations in advance.

BY BOAT ON WHEELS

A company called **DC Ducks** (☎ **202/966-3825**) features unique land and water tours of Washington aboard the red, white, and blue DUKW, an amphibious army vehicle (boat with wheels) from World War II that accommodates 30 passengers. Ninety-minute guided tours aboard the open-air canopied craft include a land portion taking in major sights—the Capitol, Lincoln Memorial, Washington Monument, the White House, and Smithsonian museums—and a 30-minute Potomac cruise. Tickets can be purchased and the vehicle boarded just outside the main entrance to Union Station. There are departures daily during tour season (April to November); call for hours. Tickets cost $20 for adults, $10 for children 5 to 12, under five free.

10 Active Sports

BICYCLING Both **Fletcher's Boat House** and **Thompson's Boat Center** (see "Boating," below, for addresses) rent bikes, as does **Big Wheel Bikes,** 1034 33rd St. NW, right near the C&O Canal just below M Street (☎ **202/337-0254**). There's another Big Wheel shop on Capitol Hill at 315 7th St. SE (☎ **202/543-1600**); call for hours. Photo ID and a major credit card are required to rent bicycles.

The *Washington Post* Friday "Weekend" section lists cycling trips. See also Rock Creek Park, the C&O Canal, and the Potomac Parks in "Parks and Gardens," earlier in this chapter, for details on their biking facilities.

BOATING **Thompson's Boat Center,** 2900 Virginia Ave. at Rock Creek Parkway NW (☎ **202/333-4861** or 202/333-9543), rents canoes, kayaks, and rowing shells (recreational and racing). They also offer sculling and sweep-rowing lessons. Photo ID and a $20 deposit are required for rentals..

Late March to mid-September, you can rent paddleboats on the north end of the Tidal Basin off Independence Avenue (☎ **202/ 479-2426**). Hours are 10am to about an hour before sunset daily.

Fletcher's Boat House, Reservoir and Canal roads (☎ **202/ 244-0461**), is right on the C&O Canal, about a 3.2-mile wonderfully scenic walk from Georgetown. It's been owned by the same family since 1850! Open March to mid-November, Fletcher's rents canoes and rowboats and sells fishing licenses, bait, and tackle. ID is required (a driver's license or major credit card). A snack bar and restrooms here are welcome after that hike. And there are picnic tables (with barbecue grills) overlooking the Potomac. You don't have to walk to Fletcher's; it's accessible by car (west on M Street to Canal Road) and has plenty of free parking.

CAMPING   There are numerous camping areas along the C&O Canal, starting at Swain's Lock, 16 miles from Georgetown. Contact the **Office of the Superintendent,** C&O Canal National Historical Park, P.O. Box 4, Sharpsburg, MD 21782 (☎ **301/ 739-4200**), for more information.

FISHING   The Potomac River around Washington provides an abundant variety of fish, some 40 species, all perfectly safe to eat. Good fishing is possible from late February to November, but mid-March to June (spawning season) is peak. Perch and catfish are the most common catch, but during bass season a haul of 20 to 40 is not unusual. The Washington Channel offers good bass and carp fishing year-round.

A **fishing license** is required. You can obtain one at various locations around the city, among them **Fletcher's Boat House** (☎ **202/244-0461;** details above). Cost for nonresidents is $7.50 for a year, $3 for a 14-day permit. Residents pay $5.

GOLF   Within the District itself East Potomac Park and Rock Creek Park have the only public courses. The 18-hole **Rock Creek Golf Course** and clubhouse, at 16th and Rittenhouse streets NW (☎ **202/882-7332**), are open to the public daily year-round from dawn to dusk. You will find a snack bar and lockers on the premises, and you can rent clubs and carts. A fee is charged. **East Potomac Park** has one 18-hole, par-72 and two 9-hole courses. For details, call **202/554-7660.**

HIKING   Check the *Washington Post* Friday "Weekend" section for listings of hiking clubs; almost all are open to the public for a small fee. Be sure to inquire about the difficulty of any hike you plan to join.

There are numerous hiking paths. The **C&O Canal** offers 184½ miles alone; it would be hard to find a more scenic setting than the 9½ miles of road at the **arboretum** (see "Parks and Gardens," earlier in this chapter); **Theodore Roosevelt Island** has more than 88 wilderness acres to explore, including a 2½-mile nature trail (short but rugged); and in **Rock Creek Park** there are 15 miles of hiking tails for which maps are available at the Visitor Information Center or Park Headquarters.

HORSEBACK RIDING   The **Rock Creek Park Horse Center,** near the Nature Center on Glover Road NW (☎ **202/362-0117**), offers rental horses for trail rides and riding instruction; there are 14 miles of woodland bridle paths to explore. Call for ride times. No riding experience is required.

ICE-SKATING   My favorite place for winter skating is on the **C&O Canal,** its banks dotted with cozy fires at which one can warm frozen extremities. Call **301/299-3613** for information on ice conditions. Guest Services operates the **National Sculpture Garden Ice Rink** on the Mall at 7th Street and Constitution Avenue NW (☎ 202/371-5341), the **Pershing Park** outdoor rink at 14th Street and Pennsylvania Avenue NW (☎ 202/737-6938), and a huge hockey-size indoor facility, the **Fort Dupont Ice Arena,** at 3779 Ely Place SE, at Minnesota Avenue in Fort Dupont Park (☎ 202/581-0199). All three offer skate rentals. Call for hours and admission prices.

   Note: The Pershing Park rink will be closed for repairs much of this year; call ahead.

JOGGING   A **parcourse jogging path,** a gift from Perrier, opened in Rock Creek Park in 1978. Its 1¹/₂-mile oval route, beginning near the intersection of Cathedral Avenue and Rock Creek Parkway, includes 18 calisthenics stations with instructions on prescribed exercises. There's another Perrier parcourse, with only four stations, at 16th and Kennedy streets NW. Other popular jogging areas are the **C&O Canal** and the **Mall.**

SWIMMING   There are 45 swimming pools in the District run by the **D.C. Department of Recreation Aquatic Program** (☎ 202/576-6436). Call for hours and details on locations.

TENNIS   There are 144 outdoor courts in the District (60 of them lit for night play) at 45 locations. Court use is on a first-come, first-served basis. For a list of locations, call or write the **D.C. Department of Recreation,** 3149 16th St. NW, Washington, DC 20010 (☎ 202/673-7646). Most courts are open year-round, weather permitting. In addition, there are courts in **Rock Creek** and **East Potomac Parks** (see "Parks and Gardens," earlier in this chapter, for details).

11   Spectator Sports

For tickets to most events, call **800/551-SEAT** or 202/432-SEAT.

FOOTBALL   The **Washington Redskins** play their home games at the 55,000-seat RFK Stadium, East Capitol Street between 19th and 20th streets SE (☎ 202/547-9077 or 202/546-3337). Tickets are virtually impossible to obtain; if you really must go, your best bet is to call a local ticket broker and be prepared to pay a king's ransom. (Check the *Washington Post* classified section under "Tickets" to find brokers.)

The **Baltimore Ravens** (formerly the Cleveland Browns until Art Modell moved the team and broke the city's heart) will play their home season in Baltimore's Memorial Stadium until a new facility is built for them. For information, call **410/547-5696.**

BASEBALL   Lovely 48,000-seat **Camden Yards,** 333 W. Camden St. (between Howard and Conway streets), Baltimore (☎ 410/685-9800), is home to the American League's **Baltimore Orioles.** Unlike recent ultramodern sports stadiums and ugly domes, Camden Yards is a real old-fashioned ballpark, which incorporates features of its urban environment, such as the old B&O Railroad yards. A renovated brick warehouse serves as a striking visual backdrop beyond the right-field fence.

Tickets (which range from $3 to $25) were once impossible to get; now it's possible but still tough, so call **800/551-SEAT** or 410/481-SEAT well in advance of your visit if you want to catch a game. There are usually scalpers outside the stadium before a game; use your judgment if try this option. And there's a D.C. ticket office as well, at 914 17th St. NW (☎ 202/296-2473). From Union Station in Washington, take a MARC train to Baltimore, which lets you off right at the ballpark. If you're driving, take I-95 north to Exit 53.

BASKETBALL   The **Washington Bullets** and the **Georgetown Hoyas** play home games at the USAir Arena, Exit 15A or 17A off the Capital Beltway in Landover, Maryland (☎ 301/350-3400); usually they also play a few games each season in the Baltimore Arena, 201 W. Baltimore St., a few blocks from the Inner Harbor in Baltimore (☎ 410/347-2020). The Bullets will be moving to the MCI Center, a $170 million, 20,000-seat sports and entertainment complex at 7th and F streets NW, when construction is complete.

HOCKEY   Home ice for the **Washington Capitals** is the USAir Arena (see above for address and phone number), though they will eventually move to the MCI Center. The **Baltimore Bandits,** a farm team for the Mighty Ducks, play about 40 games between late September and early June in the Baltimore Arena, 201 W. Baltimore St., a few blocks from the Inner Harbor in Baltimore (☎ **410/ 347-2020**).

Washington Scandals: A Walking Tour

Start: Watergate Hotel (Metro: Foggy Bottom).
Finish: The Supreme Court.
Time: Approximately three hours.
Best Times: Anytime.

Ask Americans if they think their elected leaders are by and large a strait-laced, high-minded bunch and you'll get a collective roll of the eyes. The reason, of course, is that scandalous news never stops pouring out of the nation's capital. Politics and dirty deeds seem to be inseparable; Washington lore is rich with stories of politicians arriving here burning with lofty ideals and ambition only to fall prey to one or another of the grubby demons of human nature. And the sins of the government are thrown into spectacular relief by the klieg lights of the capital's scandal press, which makes its living feeding the public's appetite for news from the gutter.

As Mark Twain put it, Washington houses the only "distinctly native American criminal class." In the spirit of that great American curmudgeon, this tour wades through 200-odd years of avarice, lust, and plain idiocy as cause for amusement and fodder for a healthy skepticism. The framers of our Constitution were indeed wise when they labored to build a government that would keep any individual from accruing too much power—as you'll now be reminded, power is often too great a burden for human frailties to bear.

From the Foggy Bottom Metro, make a U-turn to your right after exiting the Metro station; walk through a small park to New Hampshire Avenue. Follow it the equivalent of one block, to Virginia Avenue. You'll see the curving facade of the:

1. **Watergate Hotel/Apartment/Office Complex,** 2650 Virginia Ave. Just after 1am on June 17, 1972, on the sixth floor of the Watergate, a security guard found a taped-over lock on an office door of the Democratic Party's national headquarters. Suspecting foul play, he called the police, who arrived at the scene to find five well-dressed men huddled under the furniture, all wearing

Walking Tour—Washington Scandals

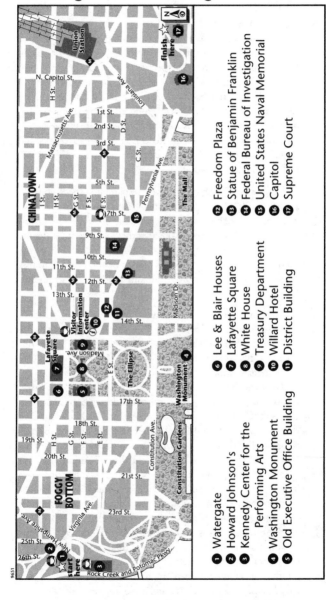

1. Watergate
2. Howard Johnson's
3. Kennedy Center for the Performing Arts
4. Washington Monument
5. Old Executive Office Building
6. Lee & Blair Houses
7. Lafayette Square
8. White House
9. Treasury Department
10. Willard Hotel
11. District Building
12. Freedom Plaza
13. Statue of Benjamin Franklin
14. Federal Bureau of Investigation
15. United States Naval Memorial
16. Capitol
17. Supreme Court

rubber gloves and in possession of high-tech spy gear and 32 sequentially numbered $100 bills.

Thus began the Watergate scandal, perhaps the darkest shadow ever cast over the federal government. By the time the details of the "dirty tricks" perpetrated by the Committee to Re-elect the President ("CREEP") emerged, 25 members of Pres. Richard Nixon's staff had received jail terms at the hands of Judge "Maximum John" Sirica; Nixon himself, facing sure impeachment for reasons of perjury, obstruction of justice, misuse of federal funds, and politicization of federal agencies, had resigned (on August 9, 1974); and an outraged "throw-the-bums-out" attitude had settled over the nation.

🍵 **TAKE A BREAK**   The lovely restaurant at the **Watergate Hotel** (☎ 202/298-4455) might be an apt place for you to have breakfast or lunch as you begin the scandals tour. The distinguished new chef formerly worked at the Four Seasons's premier restaurant; while dining, you can enjoy splendid views of the Potomac River and Theodore Roosevelt Island. Another nearby option might be one of the restaurants at the **Kennedy Center** (see chapter 4 for details).

Directly across Virginia Avenue is the:

2. **Howard Johnson's Hotel** where G. Gordon Liddy hung out to do his share of the dirty work on the Democrats. The former FBI agent and the counsel to CREEP was paid $235,000 in cash for his Watergate work.

Now take Virginia Avenue to the traffic light at 25th Street and turn right, following the curve of the sidewalk around to the:

3. **Kennedy Center for the Performing Arts.** Walk inside and to the back of the Grand Foyer, where a large bust of John F. Kennedy (by Robert Berks) faces the Opera House. We now know that JFK, he of the high-minded idealism and inspirational vision of the presidency as a new "Camelot," was less than pure both in his practice of politics and in his personal life. His administration engaged in more than the usual amount of skullduggery, from the enlistment of the Chicago mob's help during the 1960 elections to secret assassination plots. "Operation Mongoose," the most notorious of the latter, targeted Cuba's Fidel Castro; various plans (in which the Mafia may also have played a role) to take out the Cuban leader turned on improbable devices such as poisoned pens, LSD-laced cigars, and exploding seashells.

And then there were the women: Jack Kennedy, like most of the men in his family, was a compulsive philanderer. He and wife, Jackie, may have looked the perfect couple, but their marriage was termed "an understanding" at best by a family friend. He may have slowed down after a fashion upon becoming president. He reportedly called a friend one day and said, "There are two naked girls in the room but I'm sitting here reading the *Wall Street Journal*. Does that mean I'm getting old?" Jackie took it all with resigned hauteur; upon finding a pair of panties in the White House bed, she turned to her husband and said, "Here, find out who these belong to—they're not my size." He carried on well-documented affairs with such notables as Jayne Mansfield, Kim Novak, Angie Dickinson, and Marilyn Monroe, who, according to columnist Earl Wilson, is supposed to have said after a night with Jack, "Well, I think I made his back feel better." (Monroe was later passed on to brother Bobby Kennedy; much as Jack did, Bobby would eventually unceremoniously dump her. Peter Brown and Patte Barham's *Marilyn: The Last Take* (Dutton, 1992) suggests that Monroe's death in 1962 was not a suicide but murder. Fed up with her treatment at the hands of the Kennedys, Monroe had begun to act on threats to go public about her relationships with them. The coroner in the case has said that the Nembutal that killed her could not have been a simple overdose of pills; it was likely administered by injection in a spot unlikely to be discovered during autopsy. Brown and Barham suggest that Bobby Kennedy had something to do with it.)

Another blow to the Kennedy mystique came in 1988 when Judith Campbell Exner, stricken with terminal cancer, decided to clear her conscience. She revealed that during her $2^1/_2$-year affair with JFK, she functioned as courier between the president and the mob, delivering packages and arranging meetings between Kennedy and Chicago Mafia godfather Sam Giancana.

From the rooftop terrace of the Kennedy Center, you can see several recognizable Washington landmarks, among them the:

4. **Washington Monument.** Today, even George Washington would not find himself above reproach. Although he came into plenty of money when he married Martha Dandridge Custis (she owned 17,000 acres of land and a Williamsburg town house), the general disdained the modest salaries other revolutionary generals earned and accorded himself an expense account of $449,261.50—an emperor's ransom in those days—over his eight

G. Gordon Liddy & the Watergate Follies

The strength of our democracy is in public consensus and the constitutional safeguards that protect the integrity of that consensus. In the early 1970s, Richard Nixon's administration was willing to bypass any number of those safeguards in the name of gaining four more years. As columnist William White wrote, "We know that politics is extremely rough, but most people in it do, at some point, recognize a line, admittedly indefinable, but a line beyond which you just don't go."

G. Gordon Liddy was general counsel to the Committee to Re-elect the President (CREEP) at a time when the Nixon campaign was muscling major corporations for illegal contributions. It was also a time when the unfortunates on Nixon's infamous "enemies list" (ostensible political opponents who ranged from George McGovern to David Brinkley to Tony Randall) were treated as threats to national security and subjected to wiretapping, burglaries, and tax audits. Liddy was only slightly atypical in his belief that the American "fatherland" was smothering in permissive flab; in his eyes all was fair in the war for the soul of the country. He was fond of proving his own self-discipline by holding his hand over an open flame. And when CREEP director Jeb Magruder muttered something about "getting rid" of some "enemy" in Liddy's presence, the good soldier grimly announced to a subordinate "I have been ordered to kill [the 'enemy']" (he was persuaded that wasn't what Magruder had in mind).

Liddy's first proposal to Presidential Counsel John Dean and Attorney General John Mitchell for doing in the Democrats was a wild million-dollar plan that involved kidnapping radical leaders as well as launching a floating whorehouse off Miami Beach in hopes of luring prominent Democrats into compromising positions. When Mitchell told him to come back with something more "realistic," the plan to break into and bug the Democratic National Committee's offices in the Watergate Hotel was born. After two botched attempts and one successful entry (on May 27, 1972), Mitchell ordered Liddy to go back for better information. Liddy's team broke in again on June 17, and the rest is history.

A portrait of the burglary, CREEP's other activities, and the remarkable G. Gordon Liddy began to emerge during the Watergate congressional hearings. John Dean testified that an aggrieved Liddy told him after the disastrous break-in that he would never talk and "If anyone wished to shoot him on the street he was ready." An incredulous public was astounded that Liddy's harebrained schemes even reached the president's ears. That this was indeed the case became fully apparent only when Nixon was finally prevailed upon, in August 1974, to release the taped White House conversations between himself and his chief of staff, Bob Haldeman, from June 23, 1972. As George F. Will put it, the tapes were "more of a smoking howitzer than a smoking gun." Here's a portion:

Nixon: Well, who's the ass————that did [authorize the break-in]? Is it Liddy? Is that the fellow? He must be a little nuts.

Haldeman: He is.

Nixon: I mean he just isn't well screwed on, is he? Is that the problem?

Haldeman: No, but he was under pressure, apparently, to get more information, and as he got more pressure, he pushed the people harder to move harder————.

Nixon: Pressure from Mitchell?

Haldeman: Apparently.

Nixon: All right, fine, I understand it all. We won't second-guess Mitchell and the rest.

Nixon then went on to agree with Haldeman on a cover-up scheme to tell the FBI to "lay off" its investigation of the break-in because any further breaks in the investigation "would be very unfortunate . . . for the country." As the contents of the tapes broke, it was clear that the President himself was complicit in all the "dirty tricks" perpetrated by his staff, complicit in the myriad ways his administration stepped over (one might even say obliterated) that "indefinable line." He resigned from office four days later.

years' service. And he reportedly showed the worst possible taste in mistresses, most notably Mary Gibbons, who pumped Washington about his military plans during their trysts and then passed the information on to William Tryon, the royal governor of New York. Tryon capitalized on it by raiding American seaport towns and destroying much-needed supplies.

Return to Virginia Avenue. Turn right onto it (follow the pointing arm of the Benito Juarez statue). At 23rd Street, turn right and walk to H Street. Turn right and follow it through the campus of George Washington University, including the university yard, between 20th and 21st streets. Continue in the same direction on H Street. Make a left on 19th Street and a right on Pennsylvania Avenue. Just across 17th Street, you will notice the multicolumned:

5. Old Executive Office Building. When the Iran-Contra scandal began to break in November 1986, it was as deeply disturbing as any revelation from Washington since Watergate. The Reagan administration, in its zeal to topple the socialist Sandinista government in Nicaragua, had illegally sold arms to Ayatollah Khomeini's Iran to fund a ragtag army of "freedom fighters" in Nicaragua known as the "Contras." There were many parallels between the two scandals: Both revealed glimpses of a secret government accountable only to the president (and that in a very hazy way), financed with ill-gotten public funds, and used to carry out policies against the express wishes of the Congress. Watergate had its "plumbers" and the "dirty-tricks" committee; Iran-Contra had CIA director William Casey speaking approvingly to Oliver North of a permanent, "off the shelf, self-sustaining, stand-alone entity that could perform certain activities on behalf of the United States." In the sanctimonious North, Iran-Contra had its very own G. Gordon Liddy. North was the chief architect of the Iran-Contra policy, which political analyst Frances Fitzgerald called "as stupid as any since the Trojans took in that gigantic wooden horse." But during the congressional hearings into the matter in 1987, North somehow became a hero to many by virtue of his G.I. Joe persona and such flag-waving statements as this one: "I am proud to work for that commander-in-chief. And if the commander-in-chief tells this lieutenant colonel to go stand in the corner and sit on his head, I will do so."

But history did not quite repeat itself. In the bowels of this enormous gray building, North and his pretty blond secretary,

Fawn Hall, showed that the misfortunes endured by Nixon and his staff had not been in vain: Determined not to leave a smoking gun on the order of Nixon's White House tapes, they shredded evidence of the affair. Through their efforts and the stubborn resistance of Reagan and his officials to congressional questions about the imbroglio ("I can't recall" became a refrain throughout the hearings), most of the miscreants got off with a slap on the wrist or scot-free. Hall—who concisely captured the spirit of Iran-Contra when she told Congress, "Sometimes you have to go above the written law"—later tried to cash in on her involvement in the affair, signing with the William Morris talent agency. In 1994 she turned up again, on her way into a rehab center for treatment of cocaine addiction. Oliver North has made the most of his notoriety, publishing a book in 1991 and making a strong run for the U.S. senate in Virginia in 1994. Ronald Reagan's "Teflon" reputation was finally tarnished by Iran-Contra; either he lied in steadfastly denying involvement in the cloak-and-dagger theatrics of his subordinates, or he was troublingly out of touch with the policies perpetrated in his name. If it's the latter, perhaps when he said, "Every night I go to bed knowing that there are things that I am not aware of," he was justifiably paranoid.

Across Pennsylvania Avenue from the Old Executive Office Building (just past the Renwick Gallery), the brick house with the dormer windows is:

6. Lee House (built 1824), which, with the adjacent **Blair House** (built 1858), has served as the president's official guest house since 1943. Blair House was once the home of Montgomery Blair, the attorney of Dred Scott, a slave who wanted to be declared a free man because he had lived for a time with his master in a free territory. His case made its way to the Supreme Court in 1857, at which point it became a focal point in the struggle over slavery in the new territories between abolitionist and proslavery forces. With the nation looking to the court to solve a problem Congress could not, Chief Justice Roger B. Taney (a Southerner) delivered the infamous majority opinion that a Negro had no rights that "a white man was bound to respect"; therefore, Scott's case had no merit. Abolitionists were outraged, and the nation moved within a hair's breadth of civil war.

In this house, Robert E. Lee was offered the command of the Union Army. Though he supported the Union, his greater loyalty was to his home state of Virginia. He turned the offer down, creating a furor in the federal capital.

Continuing along Pennsylvania Avenue, you'll cross Jackson Place and come to:

7. Lafayette Square. This small public park, its Pennsylvania Avenue side flanked by heroic statues of Rochambeau and Lafayette, has been the site of several dark incidents. In 1859 Daniel Sickles, a congressman from New York, discovered that his friend Philip Barton Key (whose father was Francis Scott Key, author of "The Star-Spangled Banner") had been carrying on an affair with his wife, Teresa. When Key next signaled Teresa from Lafayette Square outside the Sickleses' window, the infuriated Sickles rushed outside and shot Key dead. The murder sparked the sort of sensational tabloid coverage that is commonplace today. When the case came to trial, Sickles's lawyer made successful use of a "temporary insanity" defense, and his client was acquitted. Afterward, however, Sickles was anything but repentant: "Of course I intended to kill him," he told friends. "He deserved it."

In 1917 women's suffragists demonstrated in Lafayette Square and were arrested, charged with "obstructing traffic." Among them was Alice Paul, founder of the National Woman's Party in 1913 and author of the Equal Rights Amendment in 1923. Paul and the other women were jailed in the abandoned Occoquan Workhouse, where they had to sleep on the floor and were given worm-filled food. When they chose to go on a hunger strike, they were force-fed with tubes stuck up their nostrils and down their throats. Women's right to vote would not be ratified until 1920.

Lafayette Square continues to be a focal point for protests by individuals and groups that find the actions, or inaction, of the government scandalous in one way or another. Many consider it scandalous as well that the park is filled with homeless people, especially since it lies directly across the street from the:

8. White House. Many who've held the highest office in the land rose to the top precisely because they were ruthless and unprincipled, so it should come as no surprise that the White House's history is stained with scandal. John F. Kennedy was not the only president to enjoy illicit passion within these walls. Warren G. Harding, president from 1921 until his death in 1923, was reported to have enjoyed the favors of mistress Nan Britton in a closet near the Oval Office; the family dog once sniffed them out there. (Britton, 30 years Harding's junior, had a daughter she alleged was conceived with Harding on the couch of his office when he was a senator. After his death, she tried unsuccessfully to get a portion of his estate for her child and in 1927 published a bestseller called *The President's Daughter*. It was dedicated to "all unwed mothers, and to their innocent children whose fathers usually are not known to the world.") Before he became president, Harding carried on a 15-year affair with Carrie Fulton Phillips, a German sympathizer and the wife of an old friend. The Hardings and the Phillipses socialized and even took trips together. When Harding ran for the presidency, the Secret Service paid off the couple and continued to supply them with "hush money" until Harding's death.

Harding had much more serious trouble in his choice of friends than with women. During his short term, a long list of his close associates, most of them part of what was called the "Ohio gang," made fast money brokering shady deals in smoke-filled rooms. Though he publicly lauded Prohibition, he was an eager participant in all-night White House poker games with his cronies, at which a full complement of illegal alcohol was available. Washington insider Alice Roosevelt Longworth, daughter of Teddy Roosevelt, considered him a "slob" who imbued the White House "with the air of a loose speakeasy." The most infamous scandal attributed to his venal associates was Teapot Dome, in which two cabinet secretaries earned enormous kickbacks from private oilmen in exchange for turning over two huge government oil reserves to them for peanuts. Not long before he died, Harding said, "I can take care of my enemies all right. But my friends, my God-damn friends . . . they're the ones who keep me walking the floor nights." It's no wonder he keeled over from a heart attack.

Franklin Delano Roosevelt allegedly had lovers in the White House: lifetime love Lucy Mercer and his secretary Missy Lehand. Lucy Mercer was with FDR when he died in Warm Springs, Georgia, but she discreetly departed before Eleanor arrived.

Through the years, certain White House wives have been known for their eccentricities in personality or spending. Mary Todd Lincoln, who was often ill-tempered and mentally unstable, got so carried away while redecorating the White House that she overran by $6,700 a hefty appropriation of $20,000. When he got wind of his wife's profligate spending, Honest Abe was incensed: "[The overrun] can never have my approval," he fumed. "I'll pay it out of my own pocket first—it would stink in the nostrils of the American people to have it said the President of the United States had approved a bill overrunning an appropriation of $20,000 for *flub dubs,* for this damned old house, when the soldiers cannot have blankets!"

Jackie Kennedy, who observed upon her arrival at the White House that "it looked as though furnished from discount stores," fought off rumors of her husband's womanizing with lavish spending on furnishings and her own wardrobe. Nancy Reagan, on the other hand, merely "borrowed" the designer clothes she wore.

Perhaps the most reviled of all presidential wives was Edith Bolling Wilson (a great descendant of Pocahontas), who, for all intents and purposes, ran the White House for a year and a half after Woodrow Wilson suffered a severe stroke in 1919. He was left partially paralyzed and was often bedridden, but the severity of his condition was kept secret from the American people. Edith screened all his memos and callers, essentially determining matters of state herself. Unlike Mary Todd Lincoln and Jackie Kennedy, Edith Wilson was a frugal first lady; during World War I, she put sheep to graze on the White House lawn rather than pay someone to mow it.

Although her books were written from the viewpoint of Millie (the family dog), George Bush's housewifely spouse, Barbara, was popular with the public. Chief of Staff John Sununu, the "fat little pirate" (so-called by a Bush staffer) who was Bush's right-hand man through the 1988 campaign and the early years of his presidency, was not. The bumptious, relentlessly abrasive former governor of New Hampshire ruffled feathers all over Washington. When it was revealed that he had a penchant for using government jets and limos for pleasure trips, his downfall was swift and unceremonious. He resigned in December 1991; when the news was announced, a senior White House official greeted a reporter's call by singing, "Ding, dong, the witch is dead. . . . "

Next to the White House, on Pennsylvania Avenue between East Executive Avenue and 15th Street, stands the:

9. Treasury Department, fronted by an Ionic colonnade under a pediment. The nation's first secretary of the treasury, the brilliant, tempestuous Alexander Hamilton, saw his presidential ambitions wrecked on the shoals of his affair with a married woman named Maria Reynolds. Reynolds's unscrupulous husband, James, didn't mind the affair at all; he began leaning on Hamilton for small sums to keep his mouth shut. Hamilton continued seeing Maria and paying off her husband for some years, until Mr. Reynolds, finding himself in hot water with the law, asked Hamilton to pull some strings for him. When Hamilton refused, Reynolds made good on his threat to publish the sordid details of the affair. Hamilton responded by publishing his own version of events. In a humiliating public confession on the level of televangelist Jimmy Swaggart's, he described his affair as "an amorous connection, detected . . . by the husband, imposing on me the necessity of a pecuniary composition with him, and leaving me afterwards under a duress for fear of disclosure. . . . There is nothing worse in the affair than an irregular and indelicate amour. . . . I have paid pretty severely for the folly and can never recollect it without disgust and self condemnation." As news of Hamilton's pamphlet spread, the statesman became the laughingstock of his Federalist party; all hopes of higher office were lost to him. He was killed in a duel with Aaron Burr on July 11, 1804—not over love, but politics.

☕ **TAKE A BREAK** You'll pass the **Old Ebbitt Grill,** 675 15th Street NW, at G Street (☎ 202/347-4801), a landmark Washington restaurant, on your left en route to your next stop, the Willard. It has stood at two other nearby locations: One was two doors down from Rhodes Tavern, where it is said British generals toasted each other as they watched Washington burn during the War of 1812. Though its interior is ultraelegant—with beveled mirrors, gaslight sconces, etched-glass panels, and Persian rugs strewn on beautiful oak and marble floors—its prices are moderate. The menu changes daily; lunch entrées might range from burgers to pasta dishes to a fried oyster sandwich or crabcake platter. Lunch is served Monday through Friday from 11am to 5pm and Saturday from 11:30am to 4pm; Sunday brunch is 9:30am to 4pm.

At the Treasury Department, turn right onto 15th Street and follow it to Pennsylvania Avenue. Cross 15th Street. Coming up on your left is the stately:

10. Willard Hotel at 1401 Pennsylvania Avenue NW. The Willard has been center stage for Washington's hardball politics and seamy deals for more than 100 years. In fact, it was in the lobby of the original Willard Hotel (razed in 1901 to make way for the present structure) that the term *lobbyist* was coined. Ulysses S. Grant, who partook of many a cigar and brandy at the Willard, was often pestered here by people seeking to influence government business; hence he began to refer to them as "lobbyists." Apparently his associates peddled their influence freely—by the end of Grant's administration, his vice president, Navy Department, Department of the Interior, and Diplomatic Service were all under the cloud of scandal. During and after the Civil War, government was almost completely beholden to business; robber barons would come to places like the Willard and buy votes from politicians for a few glasses of good whiskey, supplemented by satchels of cash. The wheelers and dealers got rich in the process; as labor organizer Mother Jones put it, "You steal a pair of shoes, you go to jail. You steal a railroad, and you go to the U.S. Senate."

When muckraking journalists began to publish exposés of government corruption in mass-market magazines in the first decade of the 20th century, things began to change. But the arrogance of industrialists who were used to getting their way is clear in the response of banker J. P. Morgan to a reform effort by Pres. Theodore Roosevelt: "If we've done anything wrong," he said to the president, "send your man to see my man, and they will fix it up."

Take a minute to admire the Willard's sumptuously restored interior. Then, exit the hotel, cross 14th Street, and cross the avenue to the rather ornate building at the corner of 14th and Pennsylvania Avenue South, the:

11. **District Building,** headquarters of the mayor of Washington. He's baaaaaack! On January 2, 1995, "Mayor-for-Life" Marion Barry was sworn in for a fourth term, marking one of the most improbable comebacks in American political history.

Marion Barry was busted by FBI agents after being videotaped taking two long hits from a crack pipe at the capital's Vista Hotel on January 18, 1990. The arrest ended a year's worth of ugly rumor and speculation that Barry—who presided over the nation's capital as it was consumed by an epidemic of drug use and violence, becoming the "murder capital" of the country—was himself a user. Testimony presented at Barry's trial on 11 drug charges and three perjury counts showed the mayor to be the very picture of depravity; in columnist George Hackett's words, he was "a fidgety drug addict, eager to snort cocaine or smoke crack any time, almost any place."

Charles Lewis, a former city employee convicted of drug dealing in 1989, told of the numerous times he and Barry had used drugs together, the favors the mayor granted to his drug pal (with Barry's help, Lewis rose from his modest city job to broker a personnel-management deal between the District and the Virgin Islands), and of the women Barry consorted with on his frequent drugs-and-sex junkets. One of these was a former model named Rasheeda Moore, who testified at the trial that she and Barry had used drugs together "at least 100 times." It was Moore who baited the trap the FBI set for him at the Vista. A sordid, enduring image from the videotape of the arrest is the slump-shouldered handcuffed Barry being led away, cursing Moore.

Barry surrendered his job and eventually served a six-month sentence in a federal prison in Petersburg, Virginia, where he reportedly enjoyed the attentions of a prostitute in the prison's visiting room. Thirty to 50 other inmates and guests were in the room, including one Floyd Robertson, who said "It was blatant. . . . There's no way on God's green earth anybody with . . . common sense would be able to not know what was going on in that corner." The incident surprised no one who saw Barry appear on the Sally Jessy Raphaël show to talk about his sexual addiction. Of his compulsive womanizing, Barry said, "It was all part of the addiction. This disease is cunning, baffling, powerful. It destroys your judgment."

Incredibly, the people of Washington, D.C.—despite his well-documented lapses in judgment, despite the fact that 14 members of his administration had been found guilty of fiscal wrongdoing—decided in November 1994 to return Marion Barry to his office in this building.

Opposite the District Building, on Pennsylvania Avenue, walk through:

12. Freedom Plaza. On the upper terrace of the plaza is part of Pierre Charles L'Enfant's original plan for the federal capital, rendered in black and white stone and bookended by a fountain at one end and an equestrian statue of General Pulaski at the other. L'Enfant laid out the city with sweeping diagonal boulevards, open plazas, and circles, but his impetuous behavior and penchant for ignoring orders, overspending his budgets, and disregarding landowners with prior claims led George Washington to relieve him of his duties after only a year. One of his coworkers, Benjamin Banneker, a freed slave who worked as a surveyor, made a copy of L'Enfant's blueprints from memory, and the city envisioned by the Frenchman was ultimately built, without just remuneration for its creator. L'Enfant became obsessed with making ever more fantastic claims against the government (he asked for $95,000; the federal government offered $35,000), and lived the rest of his life on the charity of friends. He died penniless in Maryland.

Proceed along Pennsylvania Avenue to 12th Street. On your right, in front of the Old Post Office, is a:

13. Statue of Benjamin Franklin, which pays homage to this Renaissance man of America's early years. Over the course of his life he was many things—printer, writer, scientist, patriot, and diplomat—but with his wit, urbanity, and joy in the pleasures of life, he was also a notorious rake. Although he wrote an essay called "Eight Reasons Older Women Are Preferable to Younger Women" later in his life, he had an illegitimate son with a younger woman and had the nerve to ask his (older) wife to raise the child. She did, and the biological mother moved into their home and worked as a maid. Franklin never tried to hide the affair or the child (perhaps that's why nothing much was made of it in the pages of history), and the boy, William, grew up to become governor of New Jersey.

Note: Though it's not an official refreshment stop, there is a food court inside the Old Post Office. Whether you stop in for a bite or not, its stunning Romanesque interior merits a look.

The building festooned with flags at Pennsylvania Avenue and 10th Street is the headquarters of the:

14. Federal Bureau of Investigation (FBI), which aggressively fills the block. The building takes its name from the Bureau's first director, J. Edgar Hoover. Hoover built the new agency into a law enforcement empire and became enormously powerful in the process, running his fief with scant interference through the tenures of eight presidents (1924–72). By the time he died in 1972, Hoover was feared and hated by millions for his agency's habit of bending civil liberties laws, especially when gathering information on suspected "subversives"—nonconformists of any stripe.

After Hoover's death, rumors of misuse of FBI funds and other abuses of office began to percolate, but the final blow to Hoover's status as an American icon came with the publication of Anthony Summers's *Official and Confidential* (1993). The book's revelations about Hoover's homosexuality, transvestism, and 42-year-long relationship with Clyde Tolson (Hoover's right hand at the FBI) were notable on the one hand because, as columnist Frank Rich noted, "For connoisseurs of hypocrisy, it is hard to beat the spectacle of our No. 1 G-man—the puritanical, blackmailing spy on the sex lives of Martin Luther King and the Kennedys, the malicious persecutor of 'sex deviates'—getting all dolled up in . . . cunning little cocktail ensembles." But much more serious is Summers's finding that mobster Meyer Lansky and others in organized crime allegedly obtained pictures of Hoover and Tolson having sex and used them to blackmail Hoover into protecting them from major prosecutions.

Continue along Pennsylvania Avenue. On your left, between 8th and 9th Streets, is the:

15. United States Naval Memorial, depicting a lone sailor surveying the world's bodies of water. Around the outside of the monument achievements in naval history are represented. The navy has found the 1990s rough going. A 22-year-old radioman named Allen Schindler was harassed "24 hours a day" by shipmates aboard the U.S.S. *Belleau Wood* after they found out he was gay; in October 1992, he was beaten to death by fellow sailor Terry Helvey. There have been several other instances of gay-bashing involving sailors in recent years. In December 1993, three young and promising officers stationed in Coronado, California, became entangled in an amorous triangle that ended in a double murder and suicide. But the most far-reaching scandal to touch the navy in many years is the deplorable behavior of naval aviators at their 1991 Tailhook Association convention in Las Vegas. In a scene that would have made *Animal House*'s parties look like polite wine-and-cheese affairs, a mob of drunken pilots assaulted and sexually molested 26 women, many of them naval officers, in the hallways of the Las Vegas Hilton. Many senior navy officials were in the hotel at the time, and, as one outraged victim said, "Not one of them said, 'Stop!'"

☕ **TAKE A BREAK** A great choice in this area is **Jaleo,** a Spanish regional/tapas restaurant at 480 7th St. NW, at E Street (☎ 202/628-7949). Housed in the Civil War–era Lansburgh Building, Jaleo is exuberantly colorful, with a casual-chic interior focusing on a large mural of a flamenco dancer based on John Singer Sargeant's painting, *Jaleo.* Background music appropriately ranges from the Gipsy Kings to Spanish guitar. A meal here consists of a variety of small dishes priced at $1.95 to $7.50—perhaps patatas bravas (crisp-fried chunks of red potato topped with a piquant chili sauce and aioli), marinated steamed mussels served on a bed of haricots verts, and eggplant flan with red pepper sauce. Jaleo is open for lunch Monday through Saturday from 11:30am to 2:30pm, with a limited tapas menu from 2:30 to 5:30pm; dinner is served nightly from 5:30pm.

Farther east, Pennsylvania Avenue runs directly into the:

16. Capitol. You're looking at its west, or back, side, the only part of the facade that remains from the original building, the cornerstone of which was laid by George Washington himself. Capitol architect Benjamin Latrobe died prematurely in an accident here; he was killed when construction superintendent John Lenthall removed a support arch that Latrobe deemed necessary, causing part of the building to collapse on top of the unfortunate Latrobe.

The House of Representatives (to the right of the dome) and the Senate (to the left) have produced their share of scoundrels. The Democrats, it's said, get in trouble with sex and the Republicans with money, but there have been some crossovers.

Where to begin? Perhaps the most unsavory senator of all (and it had nothing to do with sex or money, but with fear) was Republican Sen. Joseph P. McCarthy (Wisconsin, 1947–57), who conducted a heavy-handed witch hunt of Communists and alleged Communists, resorting to "guilt by association" and scare tactics.

When it comes to drinking and womanizing, the person who most readily comes to mind is Massachusetts Sen. Ted Kennedy, whose life could be characterized as one long scandal—from Chappaquiddick and the tragic drowning of Mary Jo Kopeckne to the Palm Beach "incident" in which his nephew William Kennedy Smith was accused (and acquitted) of raping a woman at the family vacation compound on Easter weekend in 1991 (Ted Kennedy was at the estate at the time).

Gary Hart, Democratic senator from Colorado, was within reach of his party's presidential nomination in 1987 when he was caught by two pesky reporters from the *Miami Herald* leaving through the back door of his town house with shapely Donna Rice. A furor ensued over the former divinity professor's ethics; when reports uncovered evidence of yet more adulterous liaisons, he was forced to abandon his presidential ambitions for the dubious consolation of becoming the butt of David Letterman's jokes. ("Top 10 List of Gary Hart Pick-Up Lines: 'Can a

Kennedy-esque guy buy you a drink?' 'Have you ever seen a front-runner naked?'" etc.)

On October 7, 1974, Wilbur Mills, Arkansas congressman and chairman of the House Ways and Means Committee, was stopped by police at Washington's cherry-tree–lined Tidal Basin at 2am for speeding and driving without the headlights on. His date for the evening, professional stripper Fanne Foxe, also known as the "Argentine firecracker," panicked and plunged into the Basin, taking Mills's career straight into the drink with her.

South Carolina Congressman John Jenrette was already under investigation for selling underwater land in Florida when his name became linked to Abscam. He and a few of his associates were caught selling congressional favors to men they thought were Arab sheiks but were really FBI agents. In the tape that was made of a deal in action, Jenrette admitted, "I've got larceny in my heart." The equally pleasant crook and congressman Michael Meyer simply said, "Bullshit walks, money talks." To top off the whole mess, Jenrette and his wife Rita were spotted having sex one night on the steps of the Capitol's west side. Jenrette was later arrested for shoplifting shoes and ties, and the now ex-Mrs. Jenrette wrote a tell-all tome called *My Capitol Secrets,* then exposed herself even more fully to the public in *Playboy* magazine.

Barney Frank, Democratic congressman from Massachusetts, made the headlines in 1990 when it was disclosed that his boyfriend was running a male prostitution ring out of Frank's Capitol Hill town house.

And in the fall of 1991, taxpayers were horrified to learn that 252 members of the House of Representatives and 51 former members had overdrafts (many into the thousands of dollars) with the House Bank.

Walk around the Capitol and make your way to the imposing:

17. Supreme Court. In 1963 and 1964, the Warren Commission, led by Chief Justice Earl Warren (who served from 1953 to 1969), investigated the assassination of John F. Kennedy and determined that gunman Lee Harvey Oswald acted alone, a conclusion that few believe today. This could be the major cover-up of the century.

On October 15, 1991, Clarence Thomas, who had been chairman of the Equal Employment Opportunity Commission under Pres. Ronald Reagan, became the 106th Supreme Court justice, but not without great controversy. At his confirmation hearing, a former aide, Anita Hill, leveled charges of sexual harassment against Thomas, who labeled it "high-tech lynching." Thomas and Hill came to the hearings with sparkling reputations for character and integrity: Hill calmly delivered her specific, graphic testimony, and Thomas responded with agonized denials. In the end, the only truths revealed were that either Hill or Thomas was a monumental liar, and that these two people had been swept up by the relentless undertows of partisan politics and the media's scandal machine. Thomas was confirmed by the Senate by a two-vote margin.

Some say Hill's action made it easier for other women to come forward in sexual harassment situations. Case in point: In November 1992, 10 women pressed charges of sexual harassment against Oregon Sen. Bob Packwood, who managed to keep the allegations quiet until after his reelection.

Stay tuned for upcoming scandals.

From here, you can get the Metro at either Capitol South or Union Station.

Shopping

*T*he city's most delightful shopping area is historic Georgetown, with hundreds of boutiques, antique shops, and a neo-Victorian mall that provides excellent browsing. You'll also enjoy some exotic shopping in Adams-Morgan. I've briefly touched on a few interesting shops in the District as well as the major malls and department stores. But for comprehensive coverage of D.C.'s shopping scene, consult the complete *Frommer's Washington, D.C.*

1 Shopping A to Z

ANTIQUES

Georgetown Antiques Center. 2918 M St. NW.

This building houses two shops: the **Cherub Antiques Gallery** (☎ 202/337-2224), specializing in art nouveau and art deco, art glass, perfume bottles, Liberty arts and crafts, and Louis Icart etchings; and **Michael Getz Antiques** (☎ 202/338-3811) offering American, English, and continental silver, porcelain lamps, and fireplace accessories.

ART REPRODUCTIONS, PRINTS & ENGRAVINGS

All of the art museums detailed in chapter 5 have noteworthy shops. There are marvelous high-quality items at all the Smithsonian museum shops as well—unique toys, craft items, posters, art reproductions, and so forth.

Spectrum Gallery. 1132 29th St. NW (just below M Street). ☎ 202/333-0954.

A cooperative venture (since 1968) in which 32 professional Washington area artists, including painters, potters, sculptors, photographers, collagists, and printmakers, share in shaping gallery policy, maintenance, and operation. The art is reasonably priced.

Washington, D.C., Shopping

Appalachian Spring **4**
Barnes & Noble **11**
Betsey Johnson **7**
Borders Books
  & Music **16**
Britches **6**
Central Liquor **25**
Christ Child
  Opportunity Shop **3**
Fashion Center at
  Pentagon City **9**
Georgetown Antiques
  Center **11**
Government Printing
  Office Bookstore **26**
Hecht's **22**
Indian Craft Shop **19**
Kramerbooks &
  Afterwords **15**

Lambda Rising **13**
Mazza Gallerie **1**
Melody Record Shop **14**
Olsson's Books
  & Records **5**
Pavilion at the
  Old Post Office **23**
Penn Camera Exchange **24**
Saks Jandel **1**
Secondhand Rose **2**
Shops at Georgetown
  Park **8**
Shops at National Place **21**
Sidney Kramer Books **18**
Spectrum Gallery **12**
Sunny's Surplus **20**
Tower Records **17**
Union Station **27**
Yes! Bookshop **10**

157

BOOKS

Barnes & Noble. 3040 M St. NW. ☎ **202/965-9880.**

This vast, three-story Georgetown bookstore, part of a national chain, has an upstairs cafe, as well as extensive collections of travel books, children's literature, and software.

Borders Books & Music. At the corner of 18th and L sts. NW. ☎ **202/466-4999** for books, 202/466-6999 for music. Metro: Farragut North.

This fabulous 37,000-square-foot two-level bookstore-cum-cultural center sells hardcover books at 10% off and discounts hardcover best-sellers and staff selections 30%. It also sells CDs, video- and audiotapes, and a wide selection of periodicals and out-of-state newspapers. The store also boasts a pleasant cafe.

Government Printing Office Bookstore. 710 N. Capitol St. NW (between G and H sts.). ☎ **202/512-0132.** Metro: Union Station.

The Government Printing Office (GPO), founded in 1861, is now the world's largest printer, with close to 16,000 titles (books and pamphlets) in print. Every conceivable area is covered, from *Starting and Managing a Small Business on Your Own* to the *Everglades Wildguide.* The GPO bookstore also sells books of photographs, sets of actual photographs, CD-ROMs and diskettes, prints, lithographs, and posters. There's another bookstore at 1510 H St. NW (☎ **202/653-5075**).

Kramerbooks & Afterwords. 1517 Connecticut Ave. NW (between Q St. and Dupont Circle). ☎ **202/387-1400.** Metro: Dupont Circle.

This San Francisco–style bookstore combines with a popular restaurant (see chapter 4 for details), so you can buy a book and read it over lunch. Employees here display their current favorites on the counter and discuss literature with customers. It's also one of the few places anywhere you can buy a book at 7:30am—or at midnight for that matter.

Lambda Rising. 1625 Connecticut Ave. NW (between Q and R sts.). ☎ **202/462-6969.** Metro: Dupont Circle.

Washington's gay and lesbian bookstore, Lambda Rising carries books, magazines, T-shirts, music videos, games, and gift items. The store also serves as a gay information center.

Olsson's Books & Records. 1239 Wisconsin Ave. NW (between M and N sts.). ☎ **202/338-6712** for recordings, 202/338-9544 for books.

This independent quality bookstore chain has about 60,000 to 70,000 books on its shelves covering almost every subject area. You'll find a good selection of magazines, CDs, cassettes, and remaindered books as well. Additional locations include 1200 F St. at Metro Center (☎ 202/347-3686 for books); 418 7th St. NW (☎ 202/638-7610 for books); and 1307 19th St. NW, just off Dupont Circle (☎ 202/785-1133 for books).

Sidney Kramer Books. 1825 I St. NW., in International Square ☎ **202/ 293-2685.** Metro: Farragut West.

This bookstore specializes "in the business of Washington": politics, economics, defense, world history, military history, area studies, and business management. The people-watching is almost as good as the browsing. Kramer also offers comprehensive travel, fiction, and children's book sections. Call for a free catalog.

Yes! Bookshop. 1035 31st St. NW. ☎ **202/338-7874,** or 800/YES-1516 for a free catalog.

A wealth of literature on personal growth and New Age subjects can be found at this unique store, along with books on health, natural medicine, men's and women's studies, Jungian psychology, and Native American traditions. Yes! also sells CDs, cassettes, and instructional videotapes.

CRAFTS

Appalachian Spring. 1415 Wisconsin Ave. NW (at P Street). ☎ **202/ 337-5780.**

A store that brings country crafts to citified Georgetown. They sell pottery, jewelry, newly-made quilts in traditional and contemporary patterns, stuffed animals, candles, hand-blown glassware, glorious weavings, and simple country toys. Everything in the store is made by hand in the United States. There's another branch in Union Station.

Indian Craft Shop. Department of the Interior, 18th and C sts. NW. ☎ **202/208-4056.** Metro: Farragut West.

This shop's wares are of a very high quality, and the price range is wide: I found many lovely small Navajo weavings for $16 to $18 (larger rugs can go up to $3,000) and attractive pieces of jewelry, including Navajo, Zuni, and Hopi, in varied price ranges. The store also offers a large choice of Eskimo walrus ivory carvings and an outstanding selection of pottery. *Note:* You need a photo ID to enter the building.

DEPARTMENT STORES

In addition to the below-listed, Washington boasts branches of prestigious New York and West Coast stores. **Lord and Taylor** is at

5255 Western Ave. NW (☎ 202/362-9600) and **Neiman-Marcus** is located in Mazza Gallerie on upper Wisconsin Avenue (☎ 202/966-9700). Other department stores are mentioned under "Malls/Shopping Complexes," below.

Hecht's. 12th and G sts. NW. ☎ **202/628-6661.** Metro: Metro Center.

Hecht's stores have been in Washington for a century. But this much newer branch (built in 1985) is anything but fusty. It's a full-service department store, featuring brand names in clothing for the whole family and contemporary and traditional home furnishings. There are 16 Hecht's stores in the D.C. area; check the phone book for additional locations.

FASHION

Betsey Johnson. 1319 Wisconsin Ave. NW. ☎ **202/338-4090.**

New York's flamboyant flower-child designer has a Georgetown shop. She personally decorated the bubble gum pink walls. Her sexy, offbeat play-dress-up styles are great party and club clothes for the young and the still-skinny.

Britches of Georgetown. 1247 Wisconsin Ave. NW. ☎ **202/338-3330.**

A store much patronized by well-dressed Washington men, Britches sells moderate to expensive dress apparel, both its own label and designer wear like Hugo Boss, Southwick, and Nick Hilton. Also check out its casual/sportswear division, **Britches Great Outdoors,** at 1225 Wisconsin Ave. NW (☎ **202/333-3666**).

Saks Jandel. 5510 Wisconsin Ave. NW. ☎ **301/652-2250.** Metro: Friendship Heights.

Attracting an international clientele, Saks Jandel features major European and American designers: Chanel, Valentino, Christian Dior, Yves St. Laurent Rive Gauche, Isaac Mizrahi (they did a promo for his fabulous movie *Unzipped*), John Galliano, Prada, and many others. A section called The Right Stuff caters to a young/young-at-heart crowd (designers include Moschino, Ozbek, and Alberta Ferretti).

MALLS/SHOPPING COMPLEXES

The Fashion Centre at Pentagon City. 1100 S. Hayes St. (at Army-Navy Dr. and I-395). ☎ **703/415-2400.** Metro: Pentagon City.

This Arlington, Virginia, mall has nothing to do with America's defense establishment. It's a plush four-level shopping complex, anchored by Macy's and Nordstrom, with more than 160 shops, restaurants, and services adjoining a Ritz-Carlton hotel. Dining choices include several restaurants plus 13 food-court eateries. There are six movie theaters, the Metro stops right in the mall, and parking is provided for 4,500 cars.

Mazza Gallerie. 5300 Wisconsin Ave. NW (between Western Ave. and Jenifer St.). ☎ **202/686-9515.** Metro: Friendship Heights.

Billing itself as "Washington's answer to Rodeo Drive," this *très chic,* four-level mall has more than 40 high-end boutiques under a skylit atrium. There are excellent on-premises restaurants, a triplex movie theater, and an American Express travel agency/currency exchange. The mall is located at the D.C./Maryland border; there's two-hour free indoor parking as well as paid valet parking.

The Pavilion at the Old Post Office. 1100 Pennsylvania Ave. NW. ☎ **202/289-4224.** Metro: Federal Triangle.

Opened in 1983 in one of the capital's oldest federal buildings—an actual 1899 government postal department—the Pavilion is the tallest structure in the city, after the Washington Monument. Its 10 floors soar 196 feet to a skylight ceiling and are crowned by a 315-foot clock tower. The atrium is lined with balconied corridors reminiscent of an Italian palazzo, while the exterior stonework, turrets, and massive arches were inspired by the Romanesque cathedrals of 12th-century France. Today the building houses boutiques and restaurants, and its hub is a performing-arts stage, the scene of daily lunchtime, afternoon, and early evening free entertainment. The shops and restaurants are undergoing a total renovation at this writing.

The Shops at Georgetown Park. 3222 M St. NW (at Wisconsin Avenue). ☎ **202/298-5577.**

This four-story complex of about 100 shops combines a sedate Federal exterior with a flamboyant Victorian interior, all fountains and ornate chandeliers. It's a bastion of the nation's most exclusive specialty stores; also on the premises are several restaurants as well as a Food Court. Georgetown Park maintains a full-service Concierge Center that offers gift wrapping, worldwide shipping, gift certificates, and sightseeing information.

The Shops at National Place. Entrance on F St. NW (between 13th and 14th sts.) or via the J. W. Marriott at 1331 Pennsylvania Ave. NW. ☎ **202/783-9090.** Metro: Metro Center.

A Rouse Company project (like Baltimore's Harborplace and New York's South Street Seaport), this four-tiered, 125,000-square-foot retail complex houses close to 100 stores and eateries in the renovated National Press Building. With its terra-cotta floors, balconies, columns, and fountains, it's a most attractive setting for serious shopping. All the mall regulars are here.

Union Station. 50 Massachusetts Ave. NE. ☎ **202/371-9441.** Metro: Union Station.

Union Station, with about 100 high-quality shops, has become one of Washington's most frequented retail complexes. The setting is magnificent, there are lots of great eateries (details in chapter 4), and the stores here offer a wide array of unique and high-quality merchandise. The plushest emporia are in the **East Hall,** with wares displayed in handsome brass-trimmed mahogany kiosks amid tall palm trees, or in alcoves flanked by scagliola marble columns. Women's clothing boutiques predominate on the **Concourse Mezzanine Level,** and there are also shops located in the **West Hall** and the **Main Floor Level** of the Concourse.

PHOTOGRAPHIC EQUIPMENT

Penn Camera Exchange. 915 E St. NW. ☎ **800/347-5770** or 202/347-5777. Metro: Metro Center.

Penn offers big discounts on all major brand-name equipment such as Olympus, Canon, Minolta, Pentax, Vivitar, and Nikon. The store has been owned and operated by the camera-buff Zweig family since 1953; their staff is quite knowledgeable, their inventory wide-ranging. Most of the merchandise is new and comes with a U.S. warranty, but you'll also find good buys on used equipment here.

RECORDS/CDS/AUDIOCASSETTES/VIDEOCASSETTES

Under "Books," above, see **Borders Books and Music** and **Olsson's Books and Records.**

Melody Record Shop. 1623 Connecticut Ave. NW. ☎ **202/232-4002.** Metro: Dupont Circle (Q Street exit).

CDs, cassettes, and tapes are discounted 10% to 20% here, new releases 20% to 40%. There's a wide variety of rock, classical, jazz, pop, show, and folk music, as well as a vast number of international selections. This is also a good place to shop for discounted electronic equipment.

Tower Records. 2000 Pennsylvania Ave. NW (at the corner of 21st and I sts.). ☎ **202/331-2400.** Metro: Foggy Bottom.

Without a doubt, this 23,000-square-foot store houses the largest selection of cassettes and CDs in town. There are large departments for jazz, rock, soul, classical, world, and any other type of music you might favor, plus a vast inventory of videocassettes (for sale and rental) and CD-ROMs. Another section focuses on books about music and alternative culture. Tower also functions as a **TicketMaster** outlet.

RESALE & THRIFT SHOPS

Christ Child Opportunity Shop. 1427 Wisconsin Ave. NW. ☎ **202/ 333-6635.**

Proceeds from merchandise bought here go to children's charities. Among the donated first-floor items, I saw a wicker trunk for $5 and the usual thrift shop jumble of jewelry, clothes, shoes, and hats. Upstairs, higher quality merchandise is left on consignment; it's more expensive, but if you know antiques, you might find bargains in silver, china, quilts, and other items. Good browsing.

Secondhand Rose. 1516 Wisconsin Ave. NW (between P and Q sts.). ☎ **202/337-3378.**

This upscale second-floor consignment shop specializes in designer creations by Chanel, Armani, Donna Karan, Calvin Klein, Ralph Lauren, and others, sold at about a third of the original price. Everything is in style, in season, and in excellent condition. It's also a great place to shop for furs, designer shoes and bags, and costume jewelry.

VINTAGE CLOTHING

Sunny's Surplus. 1416 H St. NW. ☎ **202/347-2774.** Metro: McPherson Square.

If you like the *M*A*S*H* look, this is the place. They carry a full line of military surplus (mostly new, some used), including jeans, T-shirts, work shoes and clothing, insulated underwear, heavy thermal socks, rainwear and winter garments, pea coats, camouflage fatigues, army blankets, camping accessories, even World War I Snoopy helmets. Other branches are at 912 F St. NW (☎ 202/737-2032) and 3342 M St. NW (☎ 202/333-8550).

WINES & LIQUORS

Central Liquor. 726 9th St. NW (between G and H sts.) ☎ **202/737-2800.** Metro: Gallery Place.

Central Liquor abounds in bottled booze—more than 35,000 items on display, including thousands of wines ranging from Gallo to Château Mouton Rothschild. Not just wines, but liquors, cordials, and other alcoholic potables are all discounted 10% to 25%, with special sales on loss leaders.

Washington, D.C., After Dark

*W*ashington offers a wealth of nighttime activities. In addition to the listings below, check the Friday "Weekend" section of the *Washington Post* for information on activities around town. *City Paper,* available free at restaurants and bookstores, is another good source. For more comprehensive coverage of Washington's nightlife, consult the complete *Frommer's Washington, D.C.*

TICKETS

TICKETplace, located in George Washington University's Lisner Auditorium, 1730 21st St. NW (at H Street) (☎ **202/TICKETS**), is a service of the Cultural Alliance of Greater Washington. On the day of performance only (except Sunday and Monday, see below), you can buy half-price tickets (for cash only) to performances at most major Washington area theaters and concert halls. The facility also serves as a **TicketMaster** outlet. TICKETplace is open Tuesday to Friday noon to 6pm and Saturday 11am to 5pm; half-price tickets to Sunday and Monday shows are sold on Saturday. Closest Metro: Foggy Bottom.

Full-price tickets for most performances in town can also be bought through **TicketMaster** (☎ **202/432-SEAT**) at **Hecht's Department Store,** 12th and G streets NW. You can purchase tickets to Washington theatrical, musical, and other events before you leave home by calling **800/551-SEAT.** Another similar ticket outlet is **Protix** (☎ **800/955-5566** or 703/218-6500).

1 Theater

Almost anything on Broadway has either been previewed in D.C. or will eventually come here. Washington also has several nationally acclaimed repertory companies, as well as a theater specializing in Shakespearean productions.

Arena Stage. 6th St. and Maine Ave. SW. ☎ **202/488-3300.** Tickets $23–$42; discounts available for students, people with disabilities, groups, and senior citizens. A limited number of half-price tickets, called HOTTIX, are available 90 minutes before most performances (call for details). Metro: Waterfront.

Founded by the brilliant Zelda Fichandler, the Arena Stage, now in its fifth decade, is the home of one of the oldest acting ensembles in the nation. Several works nurtured here have moved to Broadway, and many graduates have gone on to commercial stardom, among them Ned Beatty and James Earl Jones. Arena's subscription-season productions are presented on two stages: the **Fichandler** (a theater-in-the-round) and the smaller, fan-shaped **Kreeger.** In addition, the Arena houses the **Old Vat,** a space used for new play readings and special productions.

Ford's Theatre. 511 10th St. NW (between E and F sts.). ☎ **202/347-4833** for listings; 800/955-5566 or 703/218-6500 to charge tickets. Tickets $24–$36; discounts available for families, also for senior citizens at matinee performances and any time on the "day of" for evening shows; both seniors and students with ID can get "rush" tickets an hour before performances if tickets are available. Metro: Metro Center or Gallery Place.

This is the actual theater where, on the evening of April 14, 1865, actor John Wilkes Booth shot President Lincoln. The assassination marked the end of what had been John T. Ford's very popular theater; it remained closed for more than a century. In 1968, Ford's reopened, completely restored to its 1865 appearance, based on photographs, sketches, newspaper articles, and samples of wallpaper and curtain material from museum collections. Ford's season is more or less year-round (it's closed for awhile in the summer). Several of its productions have gone on to Broadway and off-Broadway.

National Theatre. 1321 Pennsylvania Ave. NW. ☎ **202/628-6161.** Tickets $25–$65; discounts available for students, senior citizens, military personnel, and people with disabilities. Metro: Metro Center.

The luxurious, Federal-style National Theatre, elegantly renovated in 1983, is the oldest continuously operating theater in Washington (since 1835) and the third-oldest in the nation. It's exciting just to see this stage on which such notables as John Barrymore and Helen Hayes performed. The National is the closest thing Washington has to a Broadway-style playhouse. It also offers free Saturday-morning children's theater, summer films, and Monday-night showcases of local groups and performers. Call 202/783-3370 for details.

Shakespeare Theatre. 450 7th St. NW (between D and E sts.). ☎ **202/393-2700.** Tickets $13–$49.50, $10 for standing-room tickets sold two hours before sold-out performances; discounts available for students and senior citizens. Metro: Archives or Gallery Place.

This internationally renowned classical ensemble company, which for two decades performed at The Folger Shakespeare Library, moved to these larger quarters in 1992. It offers three Shakespearean productions plus another classical work each September-to-June season. Furthermore, the company offers admission-free summer Shakespearean productions at the Carter Barron Amphitheatre in Rock Creek Park (call **202/628-5770** for details), usually for two to three weeks in June; tickets are available the day of performance only on a first-come, first-served basis.

Source Theatre Company. 1835 14th St. NW (between S and T sts.). ☎ **202/462-1073** for information; 800/955-5566 or 703/218-6500 to charge tickets. Tickets $20–$25, OFF HOURS shows $15, Washington Theatre Festival shows $8–$15.

Washington's major producer of new plays, the Source also mounts works of such established playwrights as David Mamet and Arthur Miller. The theater is also used for an OFF HOURS series of productions geared to a contemporary urban audience. Annual events here include the Washington Theatre Festival each July, a four-week showcase of new plays.

Studio Theatre. 1333 P St. NW. ☎ **202/332-3300.** Tickets $18.50–$29.50, Secondstage shows $14. Discounts available for students and senior citizens. Metro: Dupont Circle or McPherson Square.

The Studio has consistently produced interesting contemporary plays and garnered numerous awards. Many plays come here from off-Broadway. The Studio also houses **Secondstage,** a 50-seat space on the third floor where emerging artists, directors, and actors can showcase their work. The season runs year-round.

Woolly Mammoth Theatre Company. 1401 Church St. NW (between P and Q sts.). ☎ **202/393-3939.** Tickets $17–$27. They offer a range of ticket discounts, including reduced prices for seniors and students, two-for-the-price-of-one admissions, and pay-what-you-can nights; inquire at the box office. Free parking across the street. Metro: Dupont Circle, about five blocks away. You might prefer to take a cab from there, since the neighborhood is often rather deserted at night; on request, staff members will call a cab for you after the show.

Established in 1980, the Woolly Mammoth offers four productions each year-long season, specializing, according to a publicist, in "new, offbeat, and quirky plays." This company has garnered 14 Helen Hayes Awards, among other accolades, and is consistently reviewed by *The New York Times.*

2 Other Performing Arts

The following listings are a potpourri of places offering a mixed bag of theater, opera, classical music, headliners, jazz, rock, dance, and comedy. Here you'll find some of the top entertainment choices in the District.

MULTICULTURAL FACILITIES

The Folger Shakespeare Library. 201 E. Capitol St. SE. ☎ **202/ 544-7077.** Metro: Capitol South.

The **Folger Consort,** an early music ensemble, performs medieval, Renaissance, and baroque music, troubadour songs, madrigals, and court ensembles; between October and May, they give 30 concerts over the course of seven weekends. Tickets are $15 to $27.

The Folger also presents a full October-to-June season each year of **theatrical programs** relating to Shakespeare and other literary greats. In addition, an **evening lecture series** and **poetry and fiction readings** feature writers, artists, actors, and performers; call for information and ticket prices.

John F. Kennedy Center for the Performing Arts. At the southern end of New Hampshire Ave. NW and Rock Creek Pkwy. ☎ **800/444-1324** or 202/ 467-4600. Discounts of 50% are offered (for most attractions) to students, seniors 65 and over, people with permanent disabilities, and enlisted military personnel with a valid ID. Metro: Foggy Bottom (though it's a fairly short walk, there's a free shuttle between the station and the Kennedy Center, departing every 15 minutes from 7pm to midnight). Bus: 80 or 81 from Metro Center.

Our national performing arts center, the hub of Washington's cultural and entertainment scene, is actually made up of five different theaters: the **Opera House,** a plush 2,300-seat theater designed for ballet, modern dance, musical comedy, and opera; the **Concert Hall,** home of The National Symphony Orchestra; the **Terrace Theater,** a 500-seat venue where small chamber works, choral recitals, musicals, cabarets, and modern-dance performances are presented; the **Eisenhower Theater,** which presents wide range of dramatic productions; and the **Theater Lab,** which by day is a children's theater, and by night becomes a cabaret. Also affiliated with the Kennedy Center is the **AFI** (American Film Institute), a 224-seat theater that features classic and foreign films, works of independent filmmakers, and themed festivals. You can find out what is scheduled during your stay (and charge tickets) before leaving home by calling the above toll-free number. Half-price tickets are available for full-time students, senior citizens, enlisted person-nel, and people with disabilities (call 202/416-8340 for details).

Warner Theatre. 1299 Pennsylvania Ave. NW (entrance on 13th St., between E and F sts.). ☎ **800/551-SEAT** to charge tickets; 202/783-4000 or 202/432-SEAT. Play tickets $32.50–$60. Metro: Metro Center.

Opened in 1924 as the Earle Theatre (a movie/vaudeville palace) and restored to its original appearance in 1992, this stunning neoclassical-style theater features a gold-leafed grand lobby and auditorium. The Warner offers year-round entertainment, alternating dance performances and Broadway/off-Broadway shows with headliner entertainment.

Wolf Trap Farm Park for the Performing Arts. 1551 Trap Rd., Vienna, Va. ☎ **703/255-1868,** Protix 703/218-6500 to charge tickets. Summer Festival $18–$45 seats, $10–$20 lawn; Barn tickets average $10–$18.

The country's only national park devoted to the performing arts, Wolf Trap, just 30 minutes by car from downtown D.C., offers a star-studded **Summer Festival Season** from late May to mid-September. Performances take place in the 7,000-seat **Filene Center,** about half of which is under the open sky. You can also buy cheaper lawn seats on the hill. If you do, arrive early (the lawn opens 90 minutes before the performance), and bring a blanket and a pic-nic dinner. Year-round, jazz, pop, country, folk, bluegrass, and chamber musicians perform in the pre-Revolutionary, 350-seat **Barns of Wolf Trap** at 1635 Trap Rd., also the summer home of the Wolf Trap Opera Company. Call 703/938-2404 for informa-tion and directions.

MOSTLY HEADLINERS

Baltimore Arena. 201 W. Baltimore St., Baltimore, Md. ☎ **800/551-SEAT** or 410/481-SEAT for tickets; 410/347-2020.

This 13,500-seat arena, a few blocks from Baltimore's Inner Har-bor, is home to several local sports teams. Big-name concerts and family entertainment shows also play here. To get here by car, take I-95 north to I-395 (stay in the left lane) to the Inner Harbor exit and follow Howard Street to the Arena. You can also take a MARC train from Union Station.

Constitution Hall. 18th and D sts. NW. ☎ **202/638-2661** or 202/628-4780; 202/432-SEAT or 800/551-SEAT to charge tickets. Tickets $15–$50. Metro: Farragut West.

This beautiful 3,746-seat Federal-style auditorium is the national headquarters for the Daughters of the American Revolution.

Merriweather Post Pavilion. 10475 Little Patuxent Pkwy. (just off Rte. 29 in Columbia, MD). ☎ **410/730-2424** for information; 410/481-6500, 703/218-6500, or 800/955-5566 to charge tickets. Tickets $17–$50 pavilion, $15–$23 lawn.

During the summer there's celebrity entertainment almost nightly at the Merriweather Post Pavilion, about 40 minutes by car from downtown D.C. There's reserved seating in the open-air pavilion (overhead protection provided in case of rain) and general-admission seating on the lawn (no refunds for rain). If you choose the lawn seating, bring blankets and picnic fare.

The Patriot Center. George Mason University, 4400 University Dr., Fairfax, VA. ☎ **703/993-3000;** 703/573-SEAT to charge tickets.

This 10,000-seat facility hosts major headliners. To get here by car, take the Wilson Bridge to Braddock Road West, and continue about 8 miles to University Drive.

Robert F. Kennedy Memorial Stadium/D.C. Armory. 2400 E. Capitol St. SE. ☎ **202/547-9077;** 800/551-SEAT or 202/432-SEAT to charge tickets. Metro: Stadium-Armory.

It takes a superstar to pack this 55,000-plus-seat facility.

USAir Arena. Exit 15A or 17A off the Capital Beltway in Landover, Md. ☎ **800/551-SEAT** to charge tickets or 301/350-3400.

This 19,000-seat arena hosts a variety of concerts and headliner entertainment, in between sporting events.

3 The Club & Music Scene

Two especially hot nightlife districts are **Adams-Morgan** and the area around **U and 14th streets NW,** the latter a newly developing district and, even now, a pretty dangerous part of town. In fact, both of these neighborhoods can be a little dubious. When you're clubbing, stick to the major thoroughfares and stay off deserted side streets.

COMEDY CLUBS & CABARET

In addition to the below-listed, be sure to catch Gross National Product (see box below). Big-name comedians also perform around town at such places as **Constitution Hall.**

The Improv. 1140 Connecticut Ave. NW (between L and M sts.). ☎ **202/ 296-7008.** Cover $10 Sun–Thurs, $12 Fri–Sat, plus a two-drink minimum (waived if you dine). Metro: Farragut North.

The Improv features top performers on the national comedy club circuit as well as comic plays and one-person shows. Show times are

---

Today's Headlines, Tomorrow's Punchlines

Washington's hilarious political-comedy troupe, **Gross National Product,** does first-rate impersonations of all the capital's major players, from a Clinton look-alike who is a virtual clone to a definitively Doleful Bob. With clever acts and brilliant improvisation, they've been spoofing government since 1980 in shows like *BushCapades, Clintoons, A Newt World Order,* and, most recently, *GNP on the Dole.* Be sure to catch a GNP show while you're in town. It's an archetypal Washington experience. They generally play either the Bayou in Georgetown or the Old Vat theater at Arena Stage. Best bet: Call GNP directly at 202/783-7212 for show information and reservations.

8:30pm Sunday to Thursday, 8:30 and 10:30pm Friday and Saturday. You must be 18 to get in.

Marquee Cabaret. In the OMNI Shoreham Hotel, 2500 Calvert St. NW (at Connecticut Ave.). ☎ **202/234-0700.** Cover $7–$21 depending on the entertainment. Metro: Woodley Park–Zoo.

A hotel with a long history of providing great entertainment, the Shoreham today features talented ensembles in its plush art deco nightclub. Political satirist Mark Russell played the room for 20 years.

DANCE CLUBS

See also Tracks below under "Gay Clubs." Its format varies, and some nights the clientele there is predominantly straight.

Black Cat. 1831 14th St. NW (between S and T sts). ☎ **202/667-7960.** Cover $5–$10 for concerts; no cover in the Red Room. Metro: U Street-Cardozo.

This comfortable, low-key Gen-X grunge bar has a large, funky, red-walled living-roomy lounge with booths and tables, a red-leather sofa, pinball machines, a pool table, and a jukebox. There's live music in the adjoining room, essentially a large dance floor with stages at either end. Entertainment includes alternative rock, jazz performers, and occasional poetry readings.

Capitol Ballroom. Half and K sts. SE. ☎ **202/554-1500.** Cover Fri–Sat $7 before 11pm, $9 after 11pm; other nights $5–$25, depending on the performer. Metro: Waterfront.

Occupying a cavernous boiler-company warehouse, the Capitol Ballroom is generally a Gen-X mecca. It's also D.C.'s largest club, accommodating upward of 1,500 people a night. Friday night Buzz Parties here feature six DJs playing techno, house, and jungle music. Saturday nights are similar, though the music mix is alternative/ industrial, progressive, and techno. The rest of the week is given over to live concerts.

Coco Loco. 810 7th St. NW (between H and I sts.). ☎ **202/289-2626.** Cover $5–$10. Valet parking $4. Metro: Gallery Place.

This is one of D.C.'s liveliest clubs. Thursday through Saturday nights, come for a late tapas or mixed-grill dinner (see chapter 4 for details) and stay for international music and dancing, with occasional live bands. Friday and Saturday nights, the entertainment includes a sexy 11pm floor show featuring Brazilian exhibition dancers who begin performing in feathered and sequined Rio Rita costumes and strip down to a bare minimum.

Deja Vu. 2119 M St. NW. ☎ **202/452-1966.** Cover Fri–Sat $3, no cover or drink minimum Sun–Thurs. Metro: Dupont Circle or Foggy Bottom.

This 10-room Victorian extravaganza, with a dance floor, eight bars, and two restaurants on the premises, has been popular for many years with a young professional crowd. A DJ plays Top 40 tunes and other dance music. You can dine here (reservations advised) at Blackie's House of Beef (steaks, prime rib) or Lulu's New Orleans Café (creole/Cajun and seafood entrées) with both indoor and outdoor seating.

Kilimanjaro. 1724 California St. NW (between 18th St. and Florida Ave.). ☎ **202/328-3838** or 202/328-3839. Cover $5–$8; there's always a two-drink minimum.

This popular reggae/calypso/African music club is fittingly exotic— dimly lit, with candles aglow in red-glass holders and zebra skins adorning the walls. There are two separate dance areas; on weekends, sometimes a different band plays in each. Music alternates between DJs and live performances. You can dine here on such menu items as *nyama ya mbuzi*, East African–style charcoal-grilled goat. Best way to get here is by taxi.

9:30 Club. 815 V St. NW. ☎ **202/393-0930.** Cover $5–$30, depending on the performer. Metro: U Street-Cardozo.

Like so many of its genre housed in a vast converted warehouse, this major live-music venue hosts frequent record company parties and features a wide range of top performers. It's only open when there's a show on (call ahead), and, obviously, the crowd varies with the performer. There are four bars, two on the main dance-floor level, one in the upstairs VIP room, and another in the distressed-looking cellar.

River Club. 3223 K St. NW. ☎ **202/333-8118.** Cover $10 (if you're not dining). Valet parking is available.

Isn't it romantic? This elegant art deco Georgetown nightspot evokes the sophisticated dine-and-dance clubs that flourished in the 1920s and 1930s, bringing unprecedented champagne-and-caviar glamour to the Washington nightlife scene. The clientele is glittery and gorgeous (wear your best), and there are often limos waiting out front. You can hang out at the large bar up front or have dinner at the tables surrounding the circular dance floor.

Spy Club. 805 15th St. NW (between H and I sts., in Zei Alley). ☎ **202/289-1779.** Cover $8–$10. Metro: McPherson Square.

The Spy Club has two dance areas (each featuring a different DJ); the main room is punctuated by "Gothic" columns and the smaller is the Latin-themed Cubana Room. Thursday is college night; DJs provide an alternative mix. Friday and Saturday feature cutting-edge mixes of high-energy house, techno, and European music, and the crowd is chic Gen-X. The dress code prohibits sneakers or T-shirts.

State of the Union. 1357 U St. NW. ☎ **202/588-8810.** Generally no cover. Metro: U Street-Cardozo.

This funky-with-style distressed-ornate club has a hammer and sickle carved into the entrance hall, a bust of Lenin over the bar, and a big painting of Rasputin on a back wall. The hip crowd is mid-20s to about 35, interracial, and international. The music is very avant-garde. You might also happen upon a poetry reading. There's an interesting selection of beers, not to mention homemade vodka.

GAY CLUBS

Dupont Circle is the gay hub of Washington, D.C., with at least 10 gay bars within easy walking distance of each other. At the three listed below, you'll find natives happy to tell you about (or take you to) the others.

The Circle Bar & Tavern. 1629 Connecticut Ave. NW (between Q and R sts.). ☎ **202/462-5775.** No cover. Metro: Dupont Circle.

This slick-looking three-story club is the largest gay bar in the Dupont Circle area. It attracts a racially mixed gay and lesbian crowd (about 80% male). The Underground level, which has a dance floor, is the setting for many weekend events. The main floor has two bars, a great jukebox stocked with rock classics, and a pool table. The upstairs Terrace centers on a big rectangular bar adorned with flowers. When the weather is fine, the big open-air terrace is a delight.

J.R.'s. 1517 17th St. NW (between Q and Church sts.). ☎ **202/328-0090.** No cover. Metro: Dupont Circle.

More intimate than the above, this casual all-male Dupont Circle club draws a crowd that is friendly, upscale, and very attractive. The interior—not that you'll be able to see much of it because J.R.'s is always sardine-packed wall to wall—has a high, pressed-tin ceiling and exposed brick walls hung with neon beer signs.

Tracks. 1111 1st St. SE. ☎ **202/488-3320.** Cover $5–$10. Metro: Navy Yard.

This vast high-energy club is my favorite place to dance in D.C. Its chic-rather-than-funky interior houses a main dance floor centered on a mirrored ball, another with a zigzag display of video monitors. DJs provide the music, and the crowd is appealingly unhinged. Other pluses: an outdoor volleyball court, a pool table, video games, and a snack bar.

ROCK & JAZZ

The Bayou. 3135 K St. NW (under the Whitehurst Freeway, near Wisconsin Ave.). ☎ **202/333-2897.** Cover $5–$25.

This lively nightclub, located on the Georgetown waterfront, features a mixed bag of live musical entertainment, mostly progressive, reggae, and alternative sounds. Performers are up-and-coming national groups, with occasional big names playing the club for old time's sake. In addition, there are occasional comedy group shows such as political satirists Gross National Product (see box above). Except for shows appealing to all age groups, no one under 18 is admitted.

Blues Alley. 1073 Wisconsin Ave. NW (in an alley below M St.). ☎ **202/ 337-4141.** Cover $13–$40, plus $7 food or drink minimum.

Blues Alley, in Georgetown, has been Washington's top jazz club since 1965. There are usually two shows nightly at 8 and 10pm; some performers also do midnight shows on weekends. Reservations are essential (call after noon); since seating is on a first-come, first-served basis, it's best to arrive no later than 7pm and have dinner. Sometimes well-known visiting musicians get up and jam with performers.

Utopia. 1418 U St. NW. ☎ **202/483-7669.** No cover. Metro: U Street-Cardozo.

Unlike many music bars that offer snack fare, the arty New York/ Soho–style Utopia is serious about its restaurant operation. There's a moderately priced international menu, an interesting wine list and a large selection of beers and single-malt scotches. The bold, colorful paintings in the front room are by Moroccan owner Jamal Sahri. The music is a mixture of live blues, jazz, and a well-stocked jukebox.

4 The Bar Scene

The Big Hunt. 1345 Connecticut Ave. NW (between N St. and Dupont Circle). ☎ 202/785-2333. Metro: Dupont Circle.

This casual and comfy Dupont Circle hangout for the twenty- to thirtysomething crowd has a kind of *Raiders*/explorer/jungle theme. Pine walls in one downstairs room are adorned with exotic travel posters and animal skins. Another area has leopard-skin–patterned booths under canvas tenting. The candlelit basement is relatively low-key if you're in search of a spot for quiet conversation. A menu offers typical bar food; more to the point is a beer list with close to 30 varieties on tap, most of them microbrews.

Champions. 1206 Wisconsin Ave. NW (just north of M St.). ☎ 202/ 965-4005.

This Georgetown spot is D.C.'s premier hangout for athletes and sports groupies. The heaviest singles action takes place at the first-floor bar; the upstairs bar is more laid back. The attractive interior is chockablock with autographed sports photos, posters, and artifacts. Many TV monitors air nonstop sporting events. Champions is always packed, and they don't take reservations, so arrive early.

Clyde's. 3236 M St. NW. ☎ 202/333-9180.

A Georgetown institution for more than three decades, this New York–style pub, consisting of several cozy bars and dining rooms, is mobbed every evening with an upscale crowd of young professionals, college students, political types, and old-line Washingtonians (see chapter 4 for food offerings). Drinks include a choice of 10 draft beers and 7 microbrews.

Fox & Hounds. 1533 17th St. NW (between Q and Church sts.). ☎ 202/ 232-6307. Metro: Dupont Circle.

A very friendly neighborhood bar that also offers good singles action. Genial owner George Mallios describes it as "*Cheers* for the twentysomething set." Spring through fall, the large patio fronting 17th Street is packed nightly. Customers love the wide variety of coffee-liqueur drinks, premium wines by the glass, imported beers, and microbrews.

Old Ebbitt Grill. 675 15th St. NW (between F and G sts.). ☎ **202/ 347-4801.** Metro: McPherson Square or Metro Center.

The Old Ebbitt (described in detail in chapter 4) offers a lot of glamour in its sumptuous gaslit Victorian bars and dining areas. The latter are where Washington's power-lunch elite meets to eat. The former include a great oyster bar, The Old Bar, and Grant's Bar (complete with a classic gilt-framed bar nude). Drink choices include draft and microbrew beers.

Ozio. 1835 K St. NW. ☎ **202/822-6000.** Metro: Farragut North or Farragut West.

This subterranean cigar-and-martini club has Persian rugs strewn on concrete floors, and comfortable seating in plush armchairs and sofas. The lighting is nightclubby, and the music mellow. Exotic-looking cigar men come by during the evening with humidors; if you're a novice, they'll guide you through the rituals. Perfect vodka and gin martinis and other sophisticated libations (including a choice of 20 single-malt scotches) enhance the experience.

Sequoia. 3000 K St. NW (at Washington Harbour). ☎ **202/944-4200.** No cover. Paid parking available at the Harbour.

Especially on weekend nights when the weather is balmy, this is Washington's hottest alfresco singles scene. Even if you don't meet anyone, Sequoia's awninged terrace bar overlooking the Potomac is a gorgeous place to spend an evening.

5 More Entertainment

FREE SHOWS

In D.C. some of the best things at night are free—or so cheap they might as well be free.

MILITARY BAND CONCERTS

The U.S. Army Band, "Pershing's Own" (☎ 703/696-3399), has performances at 8pm every Friday on the east steps of the Capitol and every Tuesday at the Sylvan Theatre on the grounds of the Washington Monument, as well as other scheduled concerts. Arrive early to get a good seat, and bring a picnic dinner and blanket to outdoor shows.

The U.S. Navy Band (☎ 202/433-2525 for a 24-hour recording, or 202/433-6090), performs a similar variety of music, alternately at 8pm Monday nights on the east steps of the Capitol and at 8pm Tuesday nights at the U.S. Navy Memorial, 701 Pennsylvania Ave. NW. Call for other scheduled concerts.

The U.S. Marine Band, "The President's Own" (☎ 202/433-4011 for a 24-hour recording, or 202/433-5809), alternates performances June to August on the east steps of the Capitol on Wednesday at 8pm and at the Sylvan Theatre on Sunday at 8pm. It offers additional free concerts throughout the year; call for details.

Finally, there's the U.S. Air Force Band, "America's International Musical Ambassadors" (☎ 202/767-5658 for a 24-hour recording, or 202/767-4310). June through August, various units (jazz, show groups, country, orchestral) can be seen on the east steps of the Capitol on Tuesday at 8pm and at the Sylvan Theatre on Friday at the same time.

HEADLINERS: MOSTLY JAZZ

Anheuser-Busch, together with local radio stations, sponsors two fabulous outdoor summer concert series in conjunction with the National Park Service.

Big names in jazz, pop, rock, Latin, and avant-garde music perform in the 4,200-seat Carter Barron Amphitheatre, Colorado Avenue and 16th Street NW, in Rock Creek Park (☎ 202/426-6837 or 202/619-7222) from mid-June to the end of August on Friday and Saturday nights at 8pm. Tickets are relatively inexpensive, about $16. Seating is on a first-come, first-served basis, so arrive early and get in line.

Under the same sponsorship is a series of jazz concerts on the lawn in the Fort Dupont Summer Theatre, Minnesota Avenue SE at Randle Circle, in Fort Dupont Park (☎ 202/426-7723 or 202/619-7222), every Friday or Saturday at 8:30pm from sometime in July to the end of August. Bring a blanket and a picnic dinner; arrive early (by 6pm) to get a good spot on the lawn. No tickets required; admission is free.

OTHER OUTDOOR CONCERTS

Concerts at the Capitol, an American Festival, is sponsored jointly by the National Park Service and Congress. It's a series of free summer concerts with the National Symphony Orchestra that take place at 8pm on the west side of the Capitol on Memorial Day, July 4, and Labor Day. Seating is on the lawn, so bring a picnic. For further information call 202/619-7222.

Concerts on the Canal, sponsored by the Mobil Corporation, are free afternoon concerts at the Foundry Mall right on the C&O Canal between 30th and Thomas Jefferson streets NW, just below M Street (☎ 703/866-7150). They take place every other Sunday afternoon (4 to 6:30pm) from early June through August.

Accommodations, 29–55. *See also*
  Accommodations Index
    Adams-Morgan, 51–53
    best bets, 31–32
    Capitol Hill/Mall, 54–55
    for children, 39
    discounts on, 29–30
    downtown, 32–38
    Dupont Circle, 45–51
    Foggy Bottom, 40–44
    Georgetown, 40–44
    North Washington, 51–53
    reservations, 30
    near the White House, 38–40
Adams-Morgan, 20, 169
    accommodations, 51–53
    restaurants, 77–79
Addresses, locating, 16–17
African Art, National Museum
    of, 102–3
After dark, 164–77
Air Force Band, U.S., 176
Airports, 11, 12–13
Air & Space Museum, National,
    98–99, 129
Air travel, 11–13
Albert Einstein Planetarium, 99
American Express, 27
American Film Institute (AFI),
    167
Amtrak, 10, 13–14
Anacostia Museum, 106
Annual events, festivals and fairs,
    3–8
Antiques, 4, 155
Arena Stage, 164–65
Arlington House, 124–25
Arlington National Cemetery,
    121–25
    by Tourmobile, 25–26
Army Band, U.S., 6, 175
Arthur M. Sackler Gallery, 102

Art museums
    Arthur M. Sackler Gallery, 102
    Corcoran Gallery of Art, 117
    Dumbarton Oaks, 118–19
    Freer Gallery of Art, 104
    Hirshhorn Museum &
      Sculpture Garden, 101–2
    National Gallery of Art,
      108–9
    National Museum of African
      Art, 102–3
    National Museum of
      American Art, 99–100
    National Museum of Women
      in the Arts, 117–18
    National Portrait Gallery,
      100
    Phillips Collection, 116–17
    Renwick Gallery of the
      National Museum of
      American Art, 101
Art reproductions, shopping for,
    155
Arts and crafts, shopping for, 159
Arts & Industries Building, 105

Baltimore Arena (Maryland),
    134, 135, 168
Baltimore Bandits, 135
Baltimore Orioles, 134
Baltimore Ravens, 134
Baltimore-Washington
    International Airport, 11,
    12–13
Banneker, Benjamin, 149–50
Barry, Marion, 148–49
Bars, 174–75
Baseball, 134
Basketball, 134
Bed & breakfasts, 30–31, 37–38,
    50–51, 53
Bicycling, 126, 127, 131
Blair House, 143

Blue Room (White House), 86
Boat cruises, 130–31
Boating, 127, 129, 131–32
Bookstores, 158–59
Boston, air shuttle to/from, 12
Bureau of Engraving & Printing, 111–12, 129
    VIP tours, 3, 111
Buses, 22
    for senior citizen travelers, 10
    to/from airports, 12–13
    tours, 130. *See also* Tourmobile
    to Washington, D.C., 14
Bush, Barbara, 146

Cabaret, 169–70
Calendar of events, 3–8
Camden Yards (Baltimore, Maryland), 134
Cameras and film, 162
Camping, 132
Canal boat trips, 127
C&O Canal, 5, 127, 132
Capitol Hill, 17
    accommodations, 54–55
    restaurants, 60–65
Capitol Reservations, 30
Capitol, the, 87–88, 152–53
    for disabled travelers, 9
    restaurants, 80
    touring tips, 88
    VIP tours, 2, 88
Cars and driving, 14, 23
Carter Barron Amphitheater (Rock Creek Park), 126, 166, 176
Casey, William, 142–43
Castle, the (Smithsonian Information Center), 3, 15, 28, 96
Cathedral Church of St. Peter and St. Paul, 110–11
Cherry Blossom Events, 4, 126
Chesapeake & Ohio National Historical Park, 5, 127, 132
Children
    accommodations, 39
    restaurants, 58, 71
    sightseeing, 129–30

Chinese New Year Celebration, 3–4
Classical music, 167
    free concerts, 6, 175–77
Cleveland, Grover, 86
Climate, 3
Clothing, shopping for, 159–62, 163
Comedy clubs, 169–70
Concerts, free, 6, 175–77
Congressional tours, VIP, 1–3
Congresspersons, 27
Constitution, at National Archives, 107
Constitution Hall, 168, 169
Corcoran Gallery of Art, 117
    restaurants, 80
Cost of everyday items, 2
Crafts, shopping for, 159

Dance clubs, 170–72
DC Ducks, 131
Declaration of Independence, at National Archives, 107
Department stores, 159–60
Dial-a-Museum, 28, 96
Dial-a-Park, 28
Disabled travelers, 8–9
Discovery Theater (Arts & Industries Building), 105
District Building, 148–49
Doctors, 27
Downtown, 17
    accommodations, 32–38
    restaurants, 60–65
Drugstores, 27
Dulles International Airport, 11, 12–13
Dumbarton Oaks, 118–19
Dupont Circle, 20, 172
    accommodations, 45–51
    restaurants, 72–77

East Building (National Gallery of Art), 108
East Room (White House), 86
Emergencies, 27
Engravings, shopping for, 155
Enid A. Haupt Garden, 103

Entertainment, 164–77
Exner, Judith Campbell, 139

Fashion, shopping for, 159–62, 163
Fashion Centre at Pentagon City, 160–61
Fast facts, 27–28
Federal Bureau of Investigation, 109, 129, 150–51
    VIP tours, 2
Festivals, 3–8
Fichandler, Zelda, 165
Fishing, 127, 132
Fletcher's Boat House (C&O Canal), 127, 131–32
Foggy Bottom, 17, 20
    accommodations, 40–44
    restaurants, 67–72
Folger Consort, 167
Folger Shakespeare Library, 120, 167
Football, 134
Ford's Theatre, 115–16, 130, 165
Fort Dupont Ice Arena, 133
Fort Dupont Summer Theatre, 176
Fourth of July, 6
Frank, Barney, 153
Franklin, Benjamin, statue of, 150
Franklin Delano Roosevelt Memorial, 95
Frederick Douglass National Historic Site Tour, 26
Free concerts, 6, 175–77
Freedom Plaza, 149–50
Free lectures, 90, 167
Freer Gallery of Art, 104

Gardens
    Dumbarton Oaks, 118–19
    Enid A. Haupt Garden, 103
    Folger Shakespeare Library, 120
    tours of, 5, 7

    United States Botanic Garden, 118
    United States National Arboretum, 128
Gay men travelers, 10–11, 172–73. *See also* Lesbian travelers
Georgetown, 20
    accommodations, 40–44
    restaurants, 67–72
Georgetown Antiques Center, 155
Georgetown Garden Tour, 5
Georgetown Hoyas, 134
Golf, 126, 132
Gray Line, 130
Green Room (White House), 86
Greyhound, 10, 14
Gross National Product (Comedy Group), 170

Haldeman, Bob, 141
Hamilton, Alexander, 146–47
Harding, Warren G., 144–45
Hart, Gary, 152–53
Herb Garden (U.S. National Arboretum), 128
Hiking, 5, 126, 132–33
Hill, Anita, 154
Hirshhorn Museum & Sculpture Garden, 101–2
Historical and cultural museums
    Anacostia Museum, 106
    Arts & Industries Building, 105
    Lincoln Museum, 115–16, 130
    National Geographic Society's Explorers Hall, 119–20, 130
    National Museum of American History, 97, 129
    National Postal Museum, 104
    United States Holocaust Memorial Museum, 113–14
Historic houses
    Arlington House, 124–25
    Blair House, 143

House Where Lincoln Died
  (Peterson House), 116, 130
Lee House, 143–44
Hockey, 135
Holocaust Memorial Museum,
  United States, 113–14
Hoover, J. Edgar, 150–51
Horseback riding, 133
Hospitals, 27
House of Representatives, 1, 80,
  88, 152
House Where Lincoln Died
  (Petersen House), 116, 130
Howard Johnson's Hotel, 138

Ice-skating, 133
IMAX films, at National Air &
  Space Museum, 99, 129
Improv, The, 169–70
Independence Day, 6
Information sources, 1, 15–16,
  28. *See also* Telephone
  numbers, useful
Iran-Contra scandal, 142–43

James Madison Memorial
  Building (Library of Congress),
  107
Jazz, 173–74, 176
Jefferson, Thomas, 86, 94–95,
  107
Jefferson Memorial, 94–95
Jenrette, John, 153
Jogging, 133
John Adams Building (Library of
  Congress), 107
John F. Kennedy Center for the
  Performing Arts, 167–68
  Annual Kennedy Center
    Open House Arts Festival, 7
  restaurants, 80–81
  sightseeing, 109–10, 138–39
  VIP tours, 3, 110
Justice Douglas Reunion Hike, 5

Kennedy, John F., 138–39, 144
  gravesite of, in Arlington
    National Cemetery, 125

Kennedy, Ted, 152
Kennedy Center. *See* John F.
  Kennedy Center for the
  Performing Arts
Key, Francis Scott, 97, 144
Key, Philip Barton, 144
King, Martin Luther, Jr., 3
Korean War Veterans Memorial,
  121
Kramerbooks & Afterwords, 74,
  76, 158
K Street Restaurant Row, 65–67

Lafayette Square, 144
Lee, Robert E., 124–25, 143–44
Lee House, 143–44
L'Enfant, Pierre Charles, 16, 94,
  110, 125, 149–50
Lesbian travelers, 10–11, 172–
  73. *See also* Gay men travelers
Libraries and archives
  Folger Shakespeare Library,
    120
  Library of Congress, 106–7
  National Archives, 107–8
Library of Congress, 106–7
  restaurants, 81
Liddy, G. Gordon, 138, 140–41
Lincoln, Abraham, 100, 145–46
  Ford's Theatre, 115–16,
    130, 165
  House Where Lincoln Died
    (Peterson House), 116,
    130
  Lincoln Memorial, 91, 94
  Lincoln Museum, 115–16, 130
Lincoln, Mary Todd, 145
Liquor laws, 27
Liquor stores, 163

McCarthy, Joseph P., 152
Madison, Dolley, 86
Mall, the, 17
  accommodations, 54–55
Malls, shopping, 160–62
Marine Band, U.S., 176
Marine Corps Marathon, 7

Marine Corps Memorial (Arlington National Cemetery), 125

Marquee Cabaret, 170

Memorial Day, 5–6

Memorials and monuments
for disabled travelers, 9
Franklin Delano Roosevelt Memorial, 95
Jefferson Memorial, 94–95
Korean War Veterans Memorial, 121
Lincoln Memorial, 91, 94
United States Navy Memorial, 120–21, 151
Vietnam Veterans Memorial, 7, 112–13
Washington Monument, 90–91, 139, 142

Memorial Stadium (Baltimore, Maryland), 134

Merriweather Post Pavilion (Columbia, Maryland), 169

Metrorail, 21–22
for disabled travelers, 9
one-day passes, 26
to/from airport, 12

Mills, Wilbur, 153

Monroe, James, 86

Monuments. *See* Memorials and monuments

Mount Vernon, by Tourmobile, 25–26

Museums. *See also* Art museums; Historical and cultural museums; Natural history museums
Dial-a-Museum, 28, 96

Music
classical, 167
free concerts, 6, 175–77
jazz, 173–74, 176
rock, 173–74
shopping for, 162–63

National Air & Space Museum, 98–99, 129
restaurants, 81–82

National Arboretum, United States, 128

National Archives, 107–8

National Bonsai and Penjing Museum (U.S. National Arboretum), 128–29

National Gallery of Art, 108–9
restaurants, 82

National Geographic Society's Explorers Hall, 119–20, 130

National Museum of African Art, 102–3

National Museum of American Art, 99–100
Renwick Gallery of the, 101

National Museum of American History, 97, 129

National Museum of Natural History, 97–98, 129

National Museum of Women in the Arts, 117–18

National Portrait Gallery, 100

National Postal Museum, 104

National Sculpture Garden Ice Rink, 133

National Symphony Orchestra, 6, 176

National Theatre, 165

National Zoological Park, 105–6, 129
restaurants near, 82–83

Natural history museums
National Geographic Society's Explorers Hall, 119–20, 130
National Museum of Natural History, 97–98, 129

Navy Band, U.S., 175–76

Navy Memorial, United States, 120–21, 151

Neighborhoods, 17, 20. *See also* *specific neighborhoods*

Netherlands Carillon (Arlington National Cemetery), 125

New York, air shuttle to/from, 12

Nightlife, 164–77

Nixon, Richard, 136, 138, 140–41

North, Oliver, 142–43

Old Ebbitt Grill, 58, 64, 147, 175
Old Executive Office Building, 142–43
Old Town Trolley, 26
Onassis, Jacqueline Kennedy, 125, 139, 146
Opera House (Kennedy Center), 167

Parks
    Chesapeake & Ohio National Historical Park, 127, 132
    Dial-a-Park, 28
    Lafayette Square, 144
    Potomac Park, 126
    Rock Creek Park, 126, 133
    Theodore Roosevelt Island, 128–29, 132-33
Patriot Center (Fairfax, Virginia), 169
Paul, Alice, 144
Pavilion at the Old Post Office, 161
Performing arts, 164–69
Pershing Park, 133
Petersen House, 116, 130
Pharmacies, 27
Phillips Collection, 116–17
Photographic needs, 162
Planetarium, Albert Einstein, 99
Postal Museum, National, 104
Post office, 28
Potomac Park, 4, 126
Potomac River
    cruises, 130–31
    fishing, 132
Presidents. *See specific presidents*
Prints, shopping for, 155

Reagan, Nancy, 146
Reagan, Ronald, 142–43, 153
Recreational activities, 131–33
Red Room (White House), 86
Renwick Gallery of the National Museum of American Art, 101

Representatives, House of, 1, 80, 88, 152
Resale shops, 163
Restaurants, 56–84. *See also* **Restaurants Index**
    Adams-Morgan, 77–79
    best bets, 57–58
    for children, 58, 71
    by cuisine, 59–60
    downtown/Capitol Hill, 60–65
    Dupont Circle, 72–77
    Foggy Bottom, 67–72
    Georgetown, 67–72
    at sightseeing attractions, 80–84
    near the White House/ K Street Restaurant Row, 65–67
Robert F. Kennedy Memorial Stadium, 134, 169
Rock Creek Park, 126, 132, 133
Rock music, 173–74
Roosevelt, Franklin Delano, 86, 94, 145
    Franklin Delano Roosevelt Memorial, 95
Roosevelt, Theodore, 128, 148
Rotunda (the Capitol), 87–88

Sackler Gallery, 102
Safety, 28
St. Nicholas Festival, 7–8
Schindler, Allen, 151
Scott, Dred, 143
Senate, U.S., 1, 80, 88, 152–53
Senior citizen travelers, 9–10
Sequoia, 57, 70, 175
Shakespeare Theatre, 165–66
Shopping, 155–63
Sightseeing, 85–130, 136–54
    for disabled travelers, 9
    restaurants at attractions, 80–84
Single travelers, 10
Smithsonian Festival of American Folklife, 6

Smithsonian Institution, 95–106.
  See also specific museums
  for disabled travelers, 9
  Information Center (the
    "Castle"), 3, 15, 28, 96
Smithsonian Kite Festival, 4
Smithson, James, 95–96
Source Theatre Company, 166
Special events, 3–8
Spirit of Washington Cruises,
  130–31
Sports, 131–35
Stuart, Gilbert, 86, 100
Studio Theatre, 166
Subway, 21–22
  for disabled travelers, 9
  one-day passes, 26
  to/from airport, 12
Supreme Court, 88, 90, 153–54
Swimming pools, 126, 133
Sylvan Theatre, 6, 175

Taxis, 23–25
  to/from airport, 13
Telephone numbers, useful
  airlines, 11
  buses, 22
  car rentals, 23
  congresspersons, 27
  Dial-a-Museum, 28, 96
  Dial-a-Park, 28
  emergencies, 27
  Metrorail, 22
  reservations, 30
  Smithsonian Information
    Center, (the "Castle") 3, 15,
    28, 96
  special events, 3
  sporting events, 134
  taxis, 23
  tickets, 164
  visitor information, 1, 15, 28
  White House Visitor Center,
    15, 28
Tennis, 126, 133
Theater, 164–66

Theater Lab (Kennedy Center), 167
Theodore Roosevelt Island,
  128–29, 132–33
Thomas, Clarence, 153–54
Thomas Jefferson Building
  (Library of Congress), 107
Thompson's Boat Center, 129, 131
Thrift shops, 163
Tickets, 164
Tidal Basin, 4, 126
Tomb of the Unknowns
  (Arlington National Cemetery),
  5, 7, 124
Tourist information, 1, 15–16, 28
Tourmobile, 25–26
  for disabled travelers, 9
Tours. *See also* Old Town
  Trolley; Tourmobile
  by boat, 130–31
  by bus, 130
  VIP congressional, 1–3
Train travel, 10, 13–14
Transportation, 20–26
  for disabled travelers, 9
  to/from airports, 12–13
Travelers Aid Society, 15–16
Traveling
  to Washington, D.C., 11–14
Treasury Department, 146–47

Union Station, 13, 114–15
  restaurants, 71, 83–84
  shopping, 162
United States Botanic Garden, 118
United States Holocaust
  Memorial Museum, 113–14
United States National
  Arboretum, 128
United States Navy Memorial,
  120–21, 151
USAir Arena (Landover,
  Maryland), 134, 135, 169

Veterans Day, 7
Vietnam Veterans Memorial, 7,
  112–13
Vintage clothes, shopping for, 163

VIP congressional tours, 1–3
Visitor information, 1, 15–16, 28

Walking tour, of Washington
    scandals, 136–54
Warner Theatre, 168
Warren, Earl, 153
Washington, George, 86, 100,
    107, 149
    Washington Monument,
        90–91, 139, 142
Washington Bullets, 134
Washington Capitals, 135
Washington Monument, 90–91,
    139, 142
Washington National Airport,
    11, 12–13
Washington National Cathedral,
    110–11
    Open House, 6–7
Washington Redskins, 134
Washington scandals, walking
    tour of, 136–54
Watergate Hotel/Apartment/
    Office Complex, 41–42, 136,
    138
Watergate scandal, 136, 138,
    140–41
Weather, 3
West Building (National Gallery
    of Art), 108
Whistler, James McNeill, 104
White House, 86–87, 144–46
    accommodations near,
        38–40
    for disabled travelers, 9
    restaurants near, 65–67
    touring tips, 86–87
    VIP tours, 2, 86–87
    Visitor Center, 15, 28, 87
White House Candlelight Tours, 8
White House Easter Egg Roll, 4–5
White House Fall Garden Tours, 7
Willard Hotel, 32, 33, 36,
    147–48
Wilson, Edith Bolling, 146
Wines, shopping for, 163

Wolf Trap Farm Park for the
    Performing Arts (Vienna,
    Virginia), 168
Woolly Mammoth Theatre
    Company, 166

Zoo. *See* National Zoological Park

ACCOMMODATIONS
Canterbury Hotel, 46
Capitol Hill Suites, 54
Carlyle Suites, 49–50
Channel Inn, 32, 39, 54–55
Days Inn Downtown, 31, 36–37
Embassy Inn, 50
Four Seasons, 31, 32, 40–41
Georgetown Dutch Inn, 42
Georgetown Suites, 42–43
Hampshire Hotel, 48
Hay-Adams, 32, 38
Hostelling International—
    Washington, D.C., 37
Hotel Lombardy, 31, 43
Howard Johnson's Premier
    Hotel, 39, 44
Jefferson, The, 39–40
J.W. Marriott, 32–33
Kalorama Guest House, 53
Lincoln Suites Downtown, 40
Morrison Clark Inn, 32, 37–38
Normandy Inn, 48
Omni Shoreham, 32, 39, 51–52
Quality Hotel Downtown, 48–49
Reeds' Bed & Breakfast, 50–51
Renaissance Mayflower, 31, 45
Renaissance Washington, D.C.,
    Hotel, 33
Ritz-Carlton, 45–46
Savoy Suites Georgetown, 52–53
State Plaza Hotel, 44
Washington Courtyard by
    Marriott, 49
Washington Hilton & Towers,
    31, 39, 52
Watergate Hotel, 41–42
Willard Inter-Continental, 32,
    33, 36, 147–48

RESTAURANTS
1789, 68
Aditi, 69
America, 83–84
Asia Nora, 72–73
Bombay Palace, 66
B. Smith's, 83
Bukom Café, 79
Café des Artistes at
   the Corcoran, 80
Cafeteria (Library
   of Congress), 81
Cashion's Eat Place, 77–78
Chesapeake Bagel Bakery, 64
Cities, 77
Citronelle, 57–58, 67–68
City Lights of China, 74
Clyde's, 69–70, 174
Coco Loco, 57, 61, 64
Dirksen Senate Office Building
   South Buffet Room, 58, 71, 80
Encore Café, 80–81
Flight Line, 71, 81–82
Food Court (Union Station), 83
Gabriel, 73
Garden Cafe, 82
Garden Terrace, 58
Georgetown Bagelry, 70
Hors d'Oeuvrerie, 81
House of Representatives
   Restaurant, 80
Iron Gate Restaurant & Garden,
   57, 73
Jaleo, 151–52

Julia's, 79
Kramerbooks & Afterwords,
   74, 76
Legal Sea Foods, 58, 66
Le Lion d'Or, 65
Miss Saigon, 78
Mixtec, 79
Montpelier Room, 81
National Gallery Restaurants, 82
Nora, 72
Old Ebbitt Grill, 58, 64, 147,
   175
Patisserie Café Didier, 70–71
Peyote Cafe, 78–79
Pizzeria Paradiso, 57, 76
Prime Rib, 65–66
Raku, 76
Red Sage, 57, 60–61
Reeve's Restaurant & Bakery,
   64–65
Roof Terrace Restaurant, 58, 81
Sea Catch, 68–69
Seasons, 68
Sequoia, 57, 70, 175
Sholl's Cafeteria, 67, 71
Sichuan Pavilion, 66–67
Terrace Café, 82
Tombs, The, 71
Trio, 76–77
Uptown Bakers, 82–83
Vidalia, 57, 74
Willard Room, 57, 61
Wright Place, 82
Zed's, 72